The Self-Directed IRA Handbook:

An Authoritative Guide for Self-Directed Retirement Plan Investors and Their Advisors

Second Edition (2018)

www.sdirahandbook.com

www.directedira.com

Mat Sorensen, Attorney at Law

CEO, Directed IRA & Directed Trust Company

Except as permitted under the United States Copyright Act of 1976, Section 107 or 108, no part of this publication may be reproduced or distributed in any form or by any means, or stored in a database or retrieval system, without the prior written permission of the Publisher. Requests to the Publisher for permission should be addressed to Mat Sorensen, 3033 N Central Avenue, Suite 415, Phoenix, AZ 85012, or by e-mail to mat@kkoslawyers.com.

This publication is designed to provide accurate and authoritative information in regard to the subject matter covered. It is sold with the understanding that the publisher is not engaged in rendering legal, accounting or other professional service. If legal advice or other expert assistance is required, the services of a competent professional person should be sought.

From a Declaration of Principles Jointly Adopted by a Committee of the American Bar Association and a Committee of Publishers and Associations.

Any U.S. federal tax advice contained in this communication is not intended to be used and cannot be used, for the purpose of (i) avoiding penalties under the Internal Revenue Code or (ii) promoting, marketing or recommending to another party any transaction or tax-related matter[s].

TABLE OF CONTENTS

- Does UBIT Apply if my IRA Makes Numerous Loans with Different Borrowers?
- Frequently Asked Questions

ACKNOWLEDGMENTS

I would like to specifically thank my partner Mark J. Kohler, CPA and attorney. Mark introduced me to the subject of self-directed IRAs over twelve years ago, and continues to be a leading expert in the field. As a successful author of books on taxes and asset protection, Mark also shared valuable insights that helped me navigate the book writing process.

And last but not least, I would like to thank my clients, who have given me challenging questions, interesting research projects, and creative ideas regarding self-directed IRAs.

CHAPTER 1: What Is a Self-Directed IRA?

INTRODUCTION TO SELF-DIRECTED IRAs

A self-directed IRA is an IRA (Roth, Traditional, SEP, Inherited IRA, SIMPLE) where the custodian of the account allows the IRA to invest into any investment allowed by law. These investments typically include; real estate, promissory notes, precious metals, and private company stock.

KEY POINTS
■ *Among other things, a self-directed IRA can invest into real estate, private companies, promissory notes, or precious metals.*
■ *A self-directed IRA is administered by an IRA custodian who allows the IRA owner to invest into any investment allowed by law.*

The typical reaction I hear from investors is: "Why haven't I ever heard of self-directed IRAs before, and why can I only invest my current retirement plan into mutual funds or stocks?" The reason is that the large financial institutions that administer most U.S. retirement accounts don't find it administratively feasible to hold real estate or non-publicly traded assets in retirement plans. Additionally, most of these institutions are in the business of selling stocks, bonds, and mutual funds. This is their primary business and source of revenue, and many of them view real estate or non-publicly traded investments as a hassle. As a result, most investors aren't aware of alternative assets as an investment option.

Despite the major financial institutions' lack of interest in the self-directed retirement plan market, there are plenty of retirement plan custodians who specialize in catering to self-directed investments. These self-directed IRA custodians allow customers to invest their retirement accounts into real estate, private companies, hedge funds, note/trust deed lending, precious metals, and other "alternative" investments.

SELF-DIRECTED IRA INVESTMENT GAIN TAX TREATMENT

A self-directed IRA can invest in real estate or other alternative assets, and it will receive the same tax-deferred (Traditional) or tax-free (Roth) treatment that an IRA receives when you buy and sell stock or mutual funds in a retirement account. So, for example, when you buy and sell stock in your company 401(k) or a typical brokerage IRA, you don't pay capital gains tax on the gains from the sale of the stock. That is one of the key benefits of using retirement accounts to save and invest. Similarly, if you buy real estate or private stock and sell it for a gain from your self-directed IRA, you also don't pay capital gains tax on any gains from the sale.

The table below illustrates the identical tax favorable treatment between a self-directed IRA buying real estate or private company stock versus a standard IRA buying and selling publicly traded stock.

TABLE 1.1, IRA & SDIRA IDENTICAL TAX TREATMENT

	IRA	self-directed IRA
Investment	Publicly traded stock in IRA	Real estate or other alternative asset in a self-directed IRA
Purchase	1,000 shares at $50 a share = $50,000	Buy real estate for $50,000
Sale	$75,000	$75,000
Gain	= $25,000	= $25,000
Tax	No capital gains tax on $25,000 gain.	No capital gains tax on $25,000 gain.

A self-directed IRA can be any type of IRA. It can be a Roth IRA, a Traditional IRA, a SEP IRA, or even an inherited IRA. So, the first question you may be asking yourself is: "Can I self direct my retirement plan funds?"

CAN I SELF-DIRECT MY CURRENT RETIREMENT ACCOUNT FUNDS

Most retirement account owners have their funds in company 401(k) accounts, government or private pension plans, or in brokerage account IRAs. These retirement plans typically allow for investment options into publicly-traded stocks, bonds or mutual funds. Account owners are usually not allowed to invest their funds into real estate, non-publicly traded businesses, precious metals or other "alternative" investments.

According to federal law governing retirement plans, a retirement account can invest into any investment allowed by law, so long as the plan or the administrator of the account does not in some way restrict the account's investments. As a result, if you are unable to invest your retirement account into real estate or some other "alternative" investment, it is because your retirement plan administrator or the financial institution for your retirement account restricts your investments to specific types of investments. This is due to their business practices and not as a result of any legal restriction.

LEGAL TIP
❖ Your ability to self direct your current retirement plan funds depends on whether you are able to rollover or transfer these funds to a custodian who allows you to self direct your IRA.

Your ability to self direct your retirement account funds is typically dependent upon whether you are able to do a rollover or transfer of your current retirement account funds to a custodian who allows you to self direct your IRA. For example, if you have an existing IRA with a brokerage or bank, that IRA can always be transferred or rolled over to a custodian who allows you to self direct your account and who won't restrict your investments to mutual funds, stocks, and bonds. Also, if you have an old 401(k) account from a former employer, you are able to roll over those funds from your 401(k) account to a self-directed IRA custodian by doing a rollover.

PRACTICAL TIP
❖ If your retirement plan is with a current employer plan (e.g., 401(k)), then you likely won't be able to roll those funds out to a self-directed IRA custodian until you are at retirement age or until you leave that employer.

If you have a 401(k) or other type of company-sponsored retirement account with a current employer, then you are likely restricted from rolling over those funds to a self-directed IRA. The reason for this is that most employer retirement plans restrict their employees from moving funds outside of their plan. This is a restriction that is binding on the employee's account as long as the employee is employed by that employer.

If you are in this situation, then in order to roll out your funds you either have to leave employment with that employer or you need to see if the employer's plan (e.g. 401(k)) allows for what is called an "in-service withdrawal." An in-service withdrawal is a withdrawal whereby you can roll out a portion of your retirement plan funds for a specific use. Some of those uses are for things like disability or financial hardship but many plans also allow an employee to roll out a portion of the plan to an IRA of his or her choice as a rollover in-service withdrawal. Under law, the employee must be 59 ½, and you can only withdraw employee deferrals/contributions as employer contributions cannot be rolled out while still employed.

According to the IRS, 62% of 401(k) plans allow for in-service withdrawals that are not based on hardship. (IRS 2010 401(k) Questionnaire Results, www.irs.gov/retirement-plans.) If you have an existing 401(k) or other employer-sponsored plan and if you are 59 ½, it is likely that you will be able to do an in-service withdrawal from the employer plan, and that you will be able to roll/transfer funds over to a self-directed IRA. Be persistent to make sure that you get the right answer, as the typical easy answer is always "no." When in doubt, I'd recommend reading your employer's actual plan document to see if an in-service withdrawal would be allowed in your situation.

TRANSFERRING OR ROLLING OVER EXISTING RETIREMENT FUNDS TO A SELF-DIRECTED IRA

A retirement account may be moved to a different custodian by one of the following three methods.

1. <u>Trustee to Trustee Transfer</u>. A trustee to trustee transfer is a tax-free movement of your retirement funds from the current custodian directly to a self-directed IRA custodian. For example, a trustee to trustee transfer would occur when your brokerage IRA at your current custodian (e.g., Fidelity) is transferred directly to your IRA at a self-directed IRA custodian. No tax reporting or withholding occurs on a transfer.

2. <u>Direct Rollover</u>. A direct rollover is a trustee to trustee transfer from your 401(k), 403(b), or other employer account directly to your self-directed IRA custodian. The account owner does not touch the funds. A Form 1099-R is

issued, however, it will contain distribution code H in box 7 which indicates to the IRS and the account owner that a direct rollover occurred and that the 1099-R is not taxable.

3. <u>60-Day Rollover</u>. A 60-day rollover occurs when your funds are distributed to you from your current retirement account (IRA or employer plan) and re-deposited into a new retirement account, such as a self-directed IRA, within 60 calendar days. Failure to re-deposit the rollover funds into an IRA within 60 days will result in distribution of the account funds and any applicable taxes and early withdrawal penalties will apply. When conducting a 60-day rollover, your custodian reports the distribution to the IRS and may also withhold 20% for taxes. Additionally, you can only conduct one 60-day rollover per account per year. As a result, the preferred method of moving funds to a self-directed IRA is by a trustee to trustee transfer or as a direct rollover.

Regardless of the method used, the amounts transferred or rolled over (within 60 days) stay as tax favored retirement account funds and are *not* distributions subject to any tax or penalty. When moving existing IRA funds, the transfer and rollover process is simply the mechanism of changing the custodian of the account. When moving former employer plans funds (e.g. 401(k)) it is the process of changing the type of retirement account and the custodian of the account. In the end, transfer or rollover is the process of moving from a custodian who will *not* allow you to self direct your IRA to a custodian who *will* allow you to self direct your IRA.

The chart below summarizes common transfer/rollover situations and explains when you'd be able to transfer/rollover your current plan to a self-directed IRA.

TABLE 1.2, CAN I TRANSFER/ROLLOVER TO A SELF-DIRECTED IRA?

Situation	Transfer/Rollover
I have a 401(k) account with a former employer.	Yes, you can rollover to a self-directed IRA. *If it is a Traditional 401(k), it will be a self-directed IRA. *If it is a Roth 401(k), it will be a self-directed Roth IRA.
I have a 403(b) account with a former employer.	Yes, you can roll-over to a traditional self-directed IRA.
I have a Traditional IRA with a bank or brokerage.	Yes, you can transfer to a self-directed IRA.
I have a Roth IRA with a bank or brokerage.	Yes, you can transfer to a self-directed Roth IRA.
I inherited an IRA and keep the account with a brokerage or bank as an inherited IRA.	Yes, you can transfer to a self-directed inherited IRA.

TABLE 1.2, CAN I TRANSFER/ROLLOVER TO A SELF-DIRECTED IRA? (cont'd)

Situation	Transfer/Rollover
I don't have any retirement accounts but want to establish a new self-directed IRA.	Yes, you can establish a new self-directed Traditional or Roth IRA and can make new contributions according to the contribution limits and rules found in IRS Publication 590-A.
I have a 401(k) or other company plan with a current employer.	No, in most instances your current employer's plan will restrict you from rolling funds out of that plan. However, some plans do allow for an in-service withdrawal if you are at retirement age (55 or 59 ½).

Case Example 1.1: Jane has left her employer, ABC Corp. She is advised by ABC Corp. that she can roll her 401(k) plan over to her new employer's 401(k) or to an IRA account at an institution of her choice. Jane hears that she can invest her old 401(k) funds into real estate but is told by the bank where she'd like to establish an IRA that she can't buy real estate with an IRA. This is not because an IRA cannot own real estate. It is because the bank she is questioning will not allow *their* IRAs to hold real estate as an investment. Therefore, in order to purchase real estate, Jane needs to do a direct rollover of her 401(k) account to a custodian who allows her to self-direct her IRA.

FREQUENTLY ASKED QUESTIONS

Q. Can I self direct my current IRA at a brokerage firm?

A. Most likely, no, since most financial institutions which offer IRAs do not allow your IRA to invest in any investment allowed by law. Instead, they only allow your IRA to invest into investments which are easy for them to transact and administer, such as electronically traded stocks, bonds, and mutual funds.

Q. Can I self direct a Roth IRA or an SEP or SIMPLE IRA?

A. Yes. In addition to traditional IRAs, you can self direct all IRA accounts including Roth IRAs, SEP IRAs, and SIMPLE IRAs.

Q. Can I self direct my health savings account (HSA) or my 401(k) account for my self-employed business?

A. Yes, you can self direct 401(k) accounts for your own business, health savings accounts, and Coverdell education savings accounts.

Q. How are self-directed IRA custodians regulated?

A. In order to be an IRA custodian, the custodian must either be a bank, credit union, or regulated-trust company. All of these types of companies are licensed and regulated by the FDIC/OCC and/or by a State's Department of Financial Institutions.

CHAPTER 2: What Types of Investments Can a Self-Directed IRA Own?

SELF-DIRECTED IRA INVESTMENT OPTIONS

As previously discussed, a self-directed IRA can invest in real estate, private companies, precious metals, and numerous other non-traditional investments. The law only restricts a few specific types of investment assets. The most significant restrictions for self-directed IRAs are the prohibited transaction rules. These rules restrict not what investments your IRA may own but who your IRA may transact with. They are discussed at length in Chapters 4-7.

KEY POINTS
▪ *The only investment restrictions for IRAs are; collectible items, life insurance, S corporation stock, and investment transactions with parties that are prohibited to your IRA (e.g., IRA owner and certain family members).*
▪ *A self-directed IRA cannot transact with the IRA owner or certain family members as that results in a prohibited transaction.*

Under law, the only investments that are restricted in an IRA are the following:

Collectibles such as art, stamps, certain coins, alcoholic beverages, or antiques, IRC § 408(m);

Life insurance, IRC § 408(a)(3);

S-corporation stock, IRS Letter Ruling 199929029, April 27, 1999, IRC § 1361 (b)(1)(B); and

Any investment that constitutes a prohibited transaction pursuant to IRC § 4975 (e.g., purchase of any investment from a disqualified person such as the spouse of the retirement account owner). Prohibited transactions are covered at length in Chapters 4-7.

Since there are only a few restrictions on what a self-directed IRA may invest in, you are left with nearly limitless investment options. A self-directed IRA owner does not have to settle for the typical menu of mutual fund investments offered by standard IRA custodians.

Many retirement account owners have expressed frustration at being unable to invest their retirement accounts into something they know. For a large number of Americans, their retirement account is their largest source of investment dollars. Unfortunately, most account custodians limit investment options to publicly traded stocks or mutual funds, which the account owner may know little or nothing about.

> **PRACTICAL TIP**
>
> ❖ A self-directed IRA allows account owners to invest their retirement funds into assets they know.

Many investors feel like they are guessing at stock symbols or are reading incomprehensible mutual fund prospectuses when deciding where to invest their retirement account funds. Perhaps you work in the real estate industry, and you know of a good rental or investment property. Perhaps you want to invest in a new small business that looks promising and which you can get your self-directed IRA invested at the ground level. Or perhaps you're simply looking to diversify, or you're looking to hold more tangible assets like gold, silver, or other precious metals. A self-directed IRA can be an excellent tool and can be used for all types of investments. A self-directed IRA allows you to use your knowledge and expertise so that your IRA is invested into assets that you know and understand. A self-directed IRA also allows you to invest into whatever investment opportunities you may encounter, not just the ones that are publicly traded stocks, bonds, or mutual funds.

Over the years, I have assisted clients who have made the following investments with their self-directed IRAs.

TABLE 2.1, SELF-DIRECTED IRA INVESTMENT EXAMPLES

Single Family Rental Property	Multi Family Rental Property
Commercial Real Estate	Raw Land
Contractual Interest in Real Estate	Tenant In Common Interest In Real Estate
Water Rights	Mineral Rights, Oil and Gas
Real Estate Development	Tax Liens
LLC Membership Interest in the business of real estate, technology, manufacturing and other service businesses	Limited Partnership Interest ("LP") in the business of real estate, technology, manufacturing and other service businesses
Corporation, C corp, in technology, manufacturing and other service businesses	General Partnership Investment In Real Estate
Joint Venture Investment in Real Estate and numerous other industries	Real Estate Loan, Promissory Note and Deed of Trust/Mortgage
Restaurant partnership business.	Business Loan, Secured by Equipment/Assets of Business
Loan/Promissory Note Un-Secured	Purchase of Livestock

TABLE 2.1, SELF-DIRECTED IRA
INVESTMENT EXAMPLES (cont'd)

Gold, Silver, and other precious metals	IRA/LLC
Hedge Funds Investments	Private Placement Companies
Intellectual Property Patent Interest	Private Placement Memorandum Investments
Stock Options and Warrants	Non-Publicly Traded Company Ownership

When determining whether your self-directed IRA can make a particular investment the account owner should make the following analysis. First, is the investment something that a retirement account can own? For example, is the investment a collectible car, or a wine collection, or one of the other few items discussed earlier that are expressly disallowed?

After the initial determination is made, the second question to ask is whether the investment is with a disqualified person, as transactions with disqualified persons violate the prohibited transaction rules. The prohibited transaction rules are a set of rules found in IRC § 4975 and outline not *what* your self-directed IRA can invest in, but with *whom* your IRA may engage in a transaction. In essence, these rules prohibit your self-directed IRA from engaging in any transaction with yourself, some of your family members, and with certain business partners. The premise of these rules is that Congress did not want to allow tax-favored retirement accounts to make investments or transactions with persons who may collude with the IRA owner to make an unfair transaction that would improperly avoid taxes.

For example, if you currently own a duplex rental property in your personal name, you cannot sell the property you personally own to your self-directed IRA as this transaction violates the prohibited transaction rules. On the other hand, your self-directed IRA may purchase a duplex from someone who is not a family member or from a third party as they are not prohibited to your retirement account. The prohibited transaction rules will be discussed at length in later chapters. But for now, keep in mind that transactions or investments between your self-directed IRA and family members or certain business partners are often times restricted.

Lastly, because there are few restrictions placed on retirement plan investments, a self-directed IRA owner has tremendous investment options. Yet, just because your IRA can invest into a private company, precious metals, or into real estate doesn't mean that it should. self-directed IRA investors should still consider tax issues (see Chapter 15) and should always conduct adequate due diligence before investing their self-directed IRA (see Chapter 16).

FREQUENTLY ASKED QUESTIONS

Q. I have an existing business where I work and which I personally own 100%. Can I invest my IRA into that business?

A. No. This is a violation of the prohibited transaction rules. In general, your IRA investments need to be separate from your personal businesses. See Chapters 4-7 on prohibited transactions.

Q. Can my self-directed IRA buy a vacation rental property which I rent for 51 weeks and then use 1 week personally?

A. No. As discussed later, this personal use violates the prohibited transaction rules.

Q. Can my self-directed IRA loan a real estate investor money to purchase real estate?

A. Yes. The loan would typically be secured by the real estate but may also be un-secured. The principal and interest on the loan is paid back to the self-directed IRA.

Q. Can my self-directed IRA invest into a crowdfunding offering?

A. Yes. Crowdfunding investments are a new investment option authorized by the JOBS Act. These investments will allow individuals (including their IRAs) to invest in small company offerings that are not listed on public stock exchanges.

Q. Can my self-directed IRA invest in a start-up company whose LLC units or stock is not publicly registered?

A. Yes. There is no rule requiring the LLC or stock to be publicly traded. Beware of UBIT taxes which can sometimes apply in flow-through (e.g. LLC) operating companies. See Chapter 15, which extensively discusses UBIT tax.

Q. Can my self-directed IRA buy actual physical gold or other precious metals?

A. Yes. A self-directed IRA may own actual physical precious metals. The precious metals must meet certain purity requirements and may only be gold, silver, platinum, or palladium. See Chapter 12 for a more extensive discussion.

CHAPTER 3: How Does a Self-Directed IRA Invest?

A self-directed IRA investment must be held in the name of the IRA and must be executed by the self-directed IRA custodian. The IRA custodian acts only upon the written direction of the IRA owner.

KEY POINTS
▪ *IRAs, including self-directed IRAs, are trusts by law.*
▪ *A self-directed IRA can only be bound and can only act through the IRA custodian who is trustee of the IRA.*
▪ *The self-directed IRA owner directs the custodian who acts for the IRA.*

UNDERSTANDING WHAT A SELF-DIRECTED IRA IS

In order to understand how a self-directed IRA makes an investment it is helpful to break down what an IRA is under law. An IRA is created when an individual adopts an Individual Retirement Trust Account agreement with a company that is qualified to serve as trustee of an IRA. IRC § 408(a). This Individual Retirement Trust Account agreement is known as IRS Form 5305 and is used by all IRA custodians including standard investment custodians and self-directed custodians. There are different IRS approved trust account creation forms for Roth, Traditional, SEP, or SIMPLE IRA accounts. Under law, the IRA is actually a trust, and the IRA owner is the grantor beneficiary of the trust with the custodian meeting as the trustee of the trust.

Under the Individual Retirement Trust Agreement required by the IRS and pursuant to IRC § 408, an IRA will have the following characteristics:

1. The IRA investments must be held in the name of the IRA and not in the name of the IRA owner or beneficiary. For example, the IRA's investment will be held, titled, and vested as ABC Trust Company FBO John Smith Traditional IRA.
2. The Trustee of the IRA, as is common under trusts, has the authority to legally act for the IRA. The IRA owner gives instructions to the IRA custodian but cannot legally act for the IRA as the Trustee of the IRA solely holds this authority.
3. The Trustee of the IRA must be a federally chartered bank, federally chartered credit union, or state chartered financial institution which may include a state chartered bank, state chartered credit union, or state chartered trust company. IRC § 408(a)(2) and IRC § 408(n)(1).
4. An individual cannot serve as his or her own Trustee or custodian of the IRA since the law requires the Trustee of the IRA to be a financial institution or state chartered trust company. Most self-directed IRA custodians are state chartered trust companies subject to the regulation and oversight of a state banking commissioner.

Now that we have some of the legal characteristics of an IRA outlined, let's go over the steps in making a self-directed IRA investment.

STEPS IN MAKING A SELF-DIRECTED IRA INVESTMENT

Let's say that you want to purchase a rental property for $50,000 with your traditional IRA. Here are the steps you need to make to complete this investment.

STEP ONE: Establish an IRA with a self-directed IRA custodian. Again, this could be a Roth, Traditional, SEP, or SIMPLE. You can accomplish this by opening a new IRA account with a self-directed custodian and making a new contribution. You can also roll over or transfer over funds from an existing retirement account that you are unable to self direct (e.g., an existing IRA, prior employer 401(k) or 403(b), etc.).

STEP TWO: Prepare (or have an attorney or real estate broker/agent prepare) a real estate purchase contract for the property, listing the IRA as the buyer/purchaser. For example, if your IRA is with ABC Trust Company and your name is John Smith, then the buyer in the contract should read something like ABC Trust Company FBO John Smith Traditional IRA. Note: you should not complete the purchase contract in your personal name as you are not making the purchase personally. Your IRA is making the purchase. In most instances, the IRA custodian will ask the IRA owner to sign the contract as "read and approved" to ensure that the IRA owner has approved the terms of the document that the custodian will then be signing.

STEP THREE: Instruct the self-directed custodian of your IRA— in this example, ABC Trust Company—to complete the real estate purchase contract and to wire the funds that may be required as earnest money as part of the purchase. A self-directed IRA custodian will only execute documents and make investments for the IRA upon a written instruction from the IRA owner. This written instruction is typically known as a "buy-direction letter" or as a "direction of investment" in the industry. It is essentially a form whereby the IRA owner tells the custodian what documents to sign and what amounts to invest from the IRA owner's account.

STEP FOUR: The self-directed IRA custodian reviews the real estate purchase contract and instructions from the IRA owner to ensure that the investment does not violate rules or laws governing IRAs. In some instances, the IRA custodian may require an attorney to review the documents and offer an opinion as to the nature of the transaction being contemplated and whether such investment is allowed by law.

STEP FIVE: The self-directed IRA custodian executes the real estate purchase contract and signs on the signature line where the IRA is listed as the buyer of the property (e.g., ABC Trust Company FBO John Smith Traditional IRA). The contract is now a legal agreement for the IRA. Pursuant to the terms of the real estate purchase contract, the self-directed IRA custodian will send a check or wire to the title/escrow company for the earnest-money deposit specified in the contract. The IRA owner should *not* use personal funds to make the earnest-money deposit.

STEP SIX: Closing documents are prepared to close the purchase of the rental property in the name of the IRA (e.g., ABC Trust Company FBO John Smith Traditional IRA). The deed vesting title to the property should be vested in the IRA's name (e.g., ABC Trust Company FBO John Smith Traditional

IRA). The IRA owner issues a buy-direction letter or other written instructions to the self-directed IRA custodian instructing the custodian to execute the closing documents and to wire funds or send a check for the balance of the purchase funds to be escrowed by the title/escrow company and paid to the seller at closing.

STEP SEVEN: The IRA owner decides to lease the property and hires a property manager to manage the property, receive rental income, and pay expenses. The IRA owner issues a written instruction to the self-directed IRA custodian to execute a property management agreement between the IRA (as owner of the property) and the property management company. The IRA owner could also have the tenant enter into a lease with the IRA as the landlord directly. Income from the rental income shall be directed and paid to the self-directed IRA custodian and will be credited to the IRA account. If the property manager needs funds to pay for expenses to the property, the IRA owner will instruct the self-directed IRA custodian to pay the amounts necessary to cover the property expenses.

STEP EIGHT: All rental income or gains from the sale of the property shall be paid to the self-directed IRA custodian for the IRA. Additionally, all expenses related to the property shall be paid by the self-directed IRA custodian from the respective IRA. The IRA owner should *not* personally receive any income, *nor* should he or she pay for any expenses out of pocket related to the investment property.

As you can see from the steps outlined above, there are a few important steps you must take when you make an investment with your self-directed IRA. First, make sure that the investment and all documents relating to the investment are in the name of the self-directed IRA and not the name of the IRA owner. Second, the IRA owner cannot sign for the IRA and must instruct the self-directed IRA custodian to sign any investment documents. The custodian and will then sign for the IRA and will send the funds to the seller/issuer of the investment. Third, all income from the investment must be received by the IRA, and all expenses from the investment shall be paid from the IRA. See diagram below.

DIAGRAM 2.1, SELF-DIRECED IRA INVESTMENT PROCESS

IRA Owner   Self-Directed IRA   Rental Property

The IRA owner cannot personally receive income from the IRA's investment, and the IRA owner cannot personally pay for investment expenses of the IRA. The only way the IRA owner can personally receive income from the IRA is by taking a distribution from the IRA. IRA distributions are subject to the early withdrawal and distribution rules found in IRS Publication 590-B.

FREQUENTLY ASKED QUESTIONS

Q. Can I reside in a property owned by my IRA or use it for personal use?

A. No, you cannot personally benefit from your retirement plan's investments. This is a result of the prohibited transaction rules which are discussed at length in Chapters 4-7.

Q. Do I have to use a custodian to make a self-directed IRA investment?

A. Yes, an IRA must be established with a qualified trustee who serves as the custodian for the account and submits reports and filings to the IRS regarding the IRA.

Q. Can I be the real estate broker and receive a commission when using my IRA to purchase a rental property?

A. No. You cannot personally benefit from your retirement account investments. However, brokers may negotiate a lower purchase price in lieu of a commission. This allows the IRA to benefit as opposed to the IRA owner personally.

Q. If I invested my self-directed IRA in a business, can I work for that business and receive a salary for performing services?

A. No, this is considered a prohibited transaction as you could be personally benefiting from your retirement plan's investment by receiving a salary or management fee from the business. There are possible structuring options where compensation to an employee whose IRA is invested in the company is possible. Please refer to Chapter 11 for an extensive explanation.

Q. Can my IRA get a loan to purchase rental property? My self-directed IRA would invest a portion of cash and the loan would fund the balance.

A. Yes, this is possible but the loan must be nonrecourse and there may be a tax known as unrelated debt financed income tax ("UDFI") that is due. These items are both explained at length in Chapters 5 and 14.

CHAPTER 4: The Prohibited Transaction Rule Basics

WHAT IS A PROHIBITED TRANSACTION?

A prohibited transaction is briefly defined in IRS Publication 590-B as any improper transaction between an IRA and a disqualified person. A disqualified person includes the IRA owner and certain family members. For example, a prohibited transaction would occur if you use your IRA to buy real estate that you already own in your personal name, as your IRA is restricted from buying/selling investments that you personally own.

KEY POINTS
▪ *The prohibited transaction rules restrict with WHOM your IRA may transact. They do not restrict what investments an IRA may own.*
▪ *An IRA cannot transact (e.g. buy/sell) with the IRA owner and certain family members of the IRA owner.*
▪ *There are three types of prohibited transactions: 1) per se prohibited transactions, 2) extension of credit prohibited transactions, and 3) self-dealing prohibited transactions.*

The prohibited transaction rules do not specify *what* your IRA may invest in. Rather, they restrict *who* your IRA may transact with.

For example, my IRA can buy a rental property from an unrelated third-party seller, but it cannot buy a rental property from my spouse as my spouse is disqualified by law to my IRA. The subject matter of the transaction (the rental property) is not the problem. The problem is who is on the other side of the transaction with my IRA. When you invest your IRA in mutual funds or publicly traded stocks you don't need to worry about the prohibited transaction rules because you are buying investments from large financial institutions and you aren't typically dealing with family members or persons who can be prohibited to your IRA. In fact, when implementing the Employee Retirement Income Security Act in 1974 ("ERISA") and the Prohibited Transaction Code Section, Congress reasoned the following.

> In general, it is expected that a transaction will not be a prohibited transaction…if the transaction is…the purchase or sale of securities through an exchange where neither buyer nor seller (nor the agent of either) knows the identity of the other party involved. H.R. Rep. 93-1280, 93rd Cong. 2nd Sess., 307 (1974).

As a result, most retirement plan investors have never heard of the prohibited transaction rules, as they are rarely applicable to standard IRA investments.

STATUTORY & REGULATORY HISTORY TO THE PROHIBITED TRANSACTION RULES

Additionally, Congress stated that one of the purposes of the prohibited transaction rules was to ensure that account owners did not engage in transactions for their own current personal benefit at the sake of risking their retirement plan funds. The Senate Report to the prohibited transaction code section stated the following:

> The purpose of section 4975, in part, is to prevent taxpayers involved in a qualified retirement plan from using the plan to engage in transactions for their own account that could place plan assets and income at risk of loss before retirement. *Ellis v. Commissioner*, T.C. Memo 2013–245 (2013), citing, S. Rept. No. 93–383 (1974), 1974–3 C.B. Supp.) 80; H.R. Rept. No. 93–807 (1974).

When an IRA is self-directed, prohibited transaction issues will more commonly arise. The IRS is obviously aware of this and has explained that:

> IRAs that include, or consist of, non-marketable securities and/or closely held investments, in which the IRA owner effectively controls the underlying assets of such securities or investments, have a greater potential for resulting in a prohibited transaction. Internal Revenue Service, Instructions for Forms 1099–R and 5498 (2013), page 2.

In late 2016, the U.S. Government Accountability Office ("GAO") issued a comprehensive report on Self Directed IRAs, which I consulted with the GAO on, and which they used the first edition of this book as a reference tool for. In the report, the GAO concluded that:

> IRA owners who invest in unconventional assets take on a heightened risk of engaging in a prohibited transaction and losing tax-favored status for their retirement savings. GAO-17-02, *Improved Guidance Could Help Account Owners Understand the Risk of Investing in Unconventional Assets.* (December 2016), page 5.

The consequence of a prohibited transaction engaged in by an IRA owner is that the entire IRA becomes disqualified and is no longer an IRA. This disqualification results in a distribution of the total amount in the IRA to the IRA owner personally. The distribution is subject to applicable taxes and penalties. IRC § 408(e)(2)(A), IRS Publication 590-B (2017). Chapter 7 provides an in-depth explanation of the consequences of a prohibited transaction.

There are three different categories of prohibited transactions under the rules: 1) per se prohibited transactions, 2) extension of credit prohibited transactions, and 3) self-dealing prohibited transactions. This chapter will address per se prohibited transactions, and the following two chapters will discuss extension of credit and self-dealing prohibited transactions.

PER SE PROHIBITED TRANSACTIONS

A per se prohibited transaction occurs when an IRA engages in a TRANSACTION with a DISQUALIFIED PERSON. Your IRA may engage in many transactions and those transactions will not be prohibited unless they are with a "disqualified person." Similarly, your IRA may have dealings with a disqualified person but those are not prohibited transactions unless the dealings with the disqualified person constitute a "transaction."

Because a per se prohibited transaction only occurs when an IRA engages in a TRANSACTION with a DISQUALIFIED PERSON, we must understand what constitutes a "transaction" and who is a "disqualified person".

WHAT CONSTITUTES A TRANSACTION?

A transaction is defined in the Internal Revenue Code as a:

sale…, lease…, lending of money or other extension of credit…, furnishing of goods and services…

between an IRA and a disqualified person. This definition is more fully outlined in IRC § 4975 (c)(1). Most investment activities are going to fall under the definition of a transaction. The following actions will always constitute a "transaction":

- Purchase of an investment asset (real estate, stock, LLC, LP, etc.).
- Extension of credit, receipt or payment of loan payments of principal or interest.
- Payment or receipt for services or goods.
- Receipt or payment of rental income.
- Payment of IRA investment asset expenses (e.g. property taxes for real estate owned by the IRA).

The U.S. Government Accountability Office ("GAO") explained that a prohibited transaction arises when an IRA purchases and owns real estate and commits one of the following prohibited transactions.

1. The IRA leases the property to relatives who are disqualified persons.
2. The IRA owner or other disqualified person personally works on the home and provides services beyond administrative and investment oversight tasks.
3. The IRA owner personally pays for expenses for the IRA owned property.

Each of these instances would certainly result in a per se prohibited transaction as the IRA is engaging in transaction with a disqualified person in each situation. The GAO diagram below outlines the three prohibited transaction scenarios.

DIAGRAM 4.1, GAO REPORT
PROHIBITED TRANSACTIONS

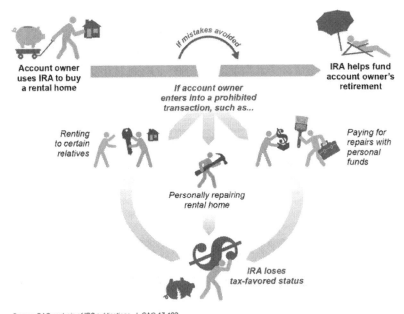

If mistakes avoided

Account owner
uses IRA to buy
a rental home

IRA helps fund
account owner's
retirement

If account owner
enters into a prohibited
transaction, such as...

Renting
to certain
relatives

Paying for
repairs with
personal
funds

Personally repairing
rental home

IRA loses
tax-favored status

Source: GAO analysis of IRS publications. | GAO-17-102

United States Government Accountability Office, GAO-17-102, *Retirement Security Improved Guidance Could Help Account Owners Understand the Risks of Investing in Unconventional Assets*. (Dec. 2016).

WHO IS A DISQUALIFIED PERSON TO MY IRA?

A disqualified person to your IRA generally includes the IRA owner, and the IRA owner's spouse, parents, children, spouses of children, and companies of which the IRA owner or other disqualified persons own or control 50% or more. Specifically, the following persons are disqualified persons to an IRA. This definition is more fully outlined in IRC § 4975 (e)(2):

I.   **IRA OWNER.** IRA account owner as Fiduciary. IRC § 4975 (e)(2)(A). The self-directed IRA account owner is a disqualified person because he or she is a fiduciary to the IRA and makes the investment decisions for the IRA. *Harris v. Commissioner*, 76 T.C.M. 748 (U.S. Tax Ct. 1994); DOL Advisory Opinion 93–33A.

II.   **CERTAIN FAMILY MEMBERS.** Certain members of the IRA owner's family, including the IRA owner's spouse, ancestors, lineal descendants, and any spouse of a lineal descendant. IRC § 4975 (e)(2)(F), IRC § 4975 (e)(6). In other words, the following "family members" of the IRA owner are disqualified to the IRA:

- Spouse
- Ancestors, which by definition includes the IRA owner's parents, grandparents, and great grandparents. It does not include the IRA owner's in-laws or grandparent in-laws. Perhaps the IRS isn't so worried about an IRA owner getting a "sweet-heart" deal from the in-laws.
- Lineal descendant, which includes child, grandchild, great-grandchild, etc.
- Spouse of lineal descendant, which includes son-in-law, daughter-in-law, etc.

III. **COMPANY MAJORITY OWNED/CONTROLLED BY IRA OWNER OR CERTAIN FAMILY MEMBERS.** A corporation, partnership (e.g., LLC), or trust or estate which is owned 50% or more by the IRA owner or other disqualified persons (e.g., disqualified family members).

- 50% or more of the voting power of all classes of stock or of the total shares, or
- 50% or more of the capital interests or profits of such partnership, or
- 50% or more of the beneficial interest of a trust or unincorporated business enterprise. IRC § 4975 (e)(2)(G), IRC § 4975 (e)(4),(5), and (6).

In other words, any company which the IRA owner, disqualified family members, or disqualified business partners own 50% or more is a disqualified person under the rules. For example, if the IRA owner and her spouse own 70% of an LLC then that LLC is a disqualified person to the IRA owner's IRA. If the IRA owner and all other disqualified persons (e.g. spouse, children, etc.) own 49% or less of the company and the other 51% is owned by unrelated third parties then the company is *not* a disqualified person.

IV. **KEY PERSONS IN COMPANY OWNED 50% OR MORE BY DISQUALIFIED PERSONS.** An officer, director, or 10% or more shareholder, or highly compensated employee (earns 10% or more of the company's wages) of a company owned by an IRA owner or other disqualified persons. IRC § 4975 (e)(2)(H)(G).

A company's officers, directors, and 10% or more shareholders are only disqualified to an IRA when the IRA owner and disqualified family members own 50% or more of the company.

For example, if John and Sally own 60% of XYZ Corp and if Julie is a director of XYZ Corp, then Julie is a disqualified person to John and Sally's IRAs. However, if John and Sally own 40% of XYZ Corp (other 60% owned by unrelated persons) and Julie is a director, then Julie would not be prohibited to John and Sally's IRAs because disqualified persons own less than 50% of the company where Julie is a director.

SUMMARY OF DISQUALIFIED PERSONS

In essence, a disqualified person includes the IRA owner, close family members, and certain personal business partners. You'll notice that many family members are not disqualified persons such as brothers and sisters, cousins, aunts and uncles, and nieces and nephews. Also, all friends, co-workers, neighbors, and other third parties are not disqualified. When determining who is disqualified, Congress sought to disqualify persons with whom the IRA owner may enter into an artificial transaction with his or her IRA in an attempt to avoid or unfairly minimize taxes.

TABLE 4.1, WHO IS A DISQUALIFIED PERSON?

Disqualified Persons – Your IRA may NOT engage in a transaction with these persons.	NOT Disqualified – Your IRA MAY engage in a transaction with these persons.
IRA Owner	Non family members
Spouse	Other investors
Children	Step parent (to un-adopted child) or un-adopted step child
Spouses of Children	Aunts and Uncles, Nieces and Nephews, and cousins.
Grandchildren and their spouses	In-laws of the IRA owner
Parents and grandparents	Brothers and Sisters
Companies (corps, LLCs, LPS, partnerships, trusts) where you or family above own or control 50% or more	Companies the IRA owner and other disqualified persons own and control less than 50%
Certain Officers, Directors, or Highly Compensated Employees of companies where the IRA owner owns or controls 50% or more	Everyone else not listed to the left and not disqualified in IRC § 4975 (e)(2)

The diagram below shows that in order for a per se prohibited transaction to occur your IRA must engage in a TRANSACTION with a DISQUALIFIED PERSON.

DIAGRAM 4.2, PER SE PROHIBITED TRANSACTIONS

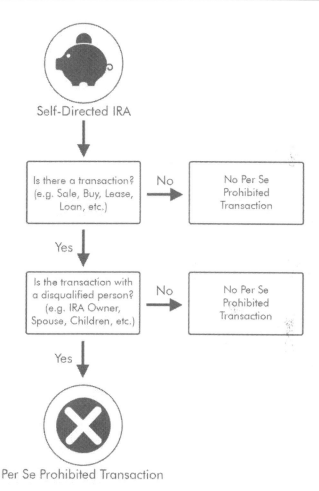

Per Se Prohibited Transaction

Based on what's been discussed, let's say that you own a rental property in your personal name and you want to purchase the property from yourself with your self-directed IRA. Can you do this? No, because the purchase by your IRA would be a transaction (purchase) with a disqualified person (IRA owner). Let's instead say that the rental property is owned by an LLC which is owned by you personally 25%, your wife 25%, and your parents 50%. Can your self-directed IRA purchase the property from the LLC? No, because your IRA would be engaging in a transaction with an LLC that is owned 50% or more by disqualified persons (you 25%, your spouse 25%, and your parents 50%), and the LLC is therefore owned 100% by disqualified persons.

WHAT COMPANIES ARE PROHIBITED TO MY IRA?

What if the rental property is owned by an LLC that is in turn owned 33% by you, 33% by your brother, and 33% by your sister? Can your IRA buy the property from this LLC? Yes, under this example the only disqualified person for the 50% rule is you personally. Brothers and sisters of the IRA owner are not disqualified persons. As a result, the LLC is not disqualified to your IRA, as it is not owned 50% or more by disqualified persons. IRC § 4975 (e)(2)(G), (e)(4). The rationale behind this rule is that the non-disqualified owners of the LLC are in majority control of the LLC, and therefore, they would only decide to sell at a legitimate purchase price and would not allow the property to sell below fair market value to the IRA.

Let's look at another example. Let's say you personally own 20% of a new technology start-up. The other 80% is owned by the founders and other investors who are not family members. The company is issuing more shares and you would like to buy these new shares with your self-directed Roth IRA. By the way, the prohibited transaction rules are the same for Roth IRAs as they are for Traditional IRAs. Can your self-directed Roth IRA purchase these new shares from the company? Yes, since the company is *not* owned 50% or more by disqualified persons your Roth IRA may purchase these new shares.

Let's change the facts a little and instead of purchasing new shares from the company let's say that you want to sell your personal shares (your 20% stake) to your self-directed Roth IRA. Can you do this? No, since the shares you are selling are owned 100% by you personally you cannot transfer/sell the shares you personally own to your Roth IRA. If your Roth IRA is going to invest in the company, it must purchase its shares from the company or from another owner who is selling and who is not a disqualified person to your Roth IRA. You cannot sell shares in any company you own from yourself personally to your IRA.

As you can see, the prohibited transaction rules can be complicated, but they only apply in scenarios where your IRA engages in a transaction where you have personal or family member's interests involved. If the transaction is with unrelated third parties, then you do not need to analyze these rules.

PER SE PROHIBITED TRANSACTION CASE EXAMPLES

Below is a chart that summarizes some per se prohibited transaction cases that have been determined in court or by opinion of the Internal Revenue Service or Department of Labor.

TABLE 4.2, PER SE PROHIBITED
TRANSACTION CASES AND OPINIONS

Citation: *Harris v. Comm'r*, T.C. Memo 1994-22.

Case Facts: IRA owner purchased a home with his IRA and used it as his personal residence. The Tax Court ruled that the purchase was a prohibited transaction since the property was to be used by the IRA owner.

Citation: *In re Hughes*, 293 B.R. 528 (M.D. Fl. Bankr. Ct. 2003).

Case Facts: IRA owner loaned money from his IRA to himself. The loan from the IRA was a transaction with a disqualified person (IRA owner) and the Court ruled that it was a prohibited transaction.

Citation: DOL Advisory Opinion 06-09A

Case Facts: IRA owner planned to enter into a promissory note investment with a company owned 87% by the IRA owner's son-in-law. DOL ruled that it would be a prohibited transaction because the IRA investment would be a transaction with a disqualified person (company owned 50% or more by son-in-law who is a disqualified person).

TABLE 4.2, PER SE PROHIBITED
TRANSACTION CASES AND OPINIONS (CONT'D)

Citation: DOL Advisory Opinion 11-04A

Case Facts: IRA purchased note and deed of trust from bank. The note and deed of trust was for a property where the IRA owner personally lived, and the IRA owner was personally the borrower on the note. The IRA's purchase of the note and deed of trust was not a per se prohibited transaction since the bank was not a disqualified person to the IRA. However, all subsequent loan payments from the IRA owner on the note owned the IRA would be "transactions" with "disqualified persons" and are prohibited transactions.

Citation: DOL Advisory Opinion 93-33A

Case Facts: IRA owner's purchase of a school from a company founded, controlled, and managed by the IRA owner's daughter and son-in-law is a prohibited transaction since the purchase is a transaction with a company controlled 50% or more by disqualified persons (daughter and son in-law).

Citation: *D.E.W. Plumbing v. Domestic Mortgage*, Case 1:10-CV-2593-TWT (U.S. Dist Ct. N.D. Georgia, 2012)

Case Facts: Retirement plan owner directed his company plan to loan money into a company owned by the retirement plan owner and his two children. The court held that the loan was a transaction with a company owned 50% or more by disqualified persons (plan owner and two children).

TABLE 4.2, PER SE PROHIBITED
TRANSACTION CASES AND OPINIONS (CONT'D)

Citation: *In re Daniels*, 452 B.R. 335 (Bankr.D.Mass Ct. 2011).

Case Facts: Retirement plan owner purchased investment property with plan and leased the property to the plan owner's son and daughter-in-law who paid rent to the plan. This was a prohibited transaction as the lease and rent was a transaction with a disqualified person (plan owner's son and daughter-in-law).

Citation: *Morrissey v. Commissioner*, TC 1998-443 (U.S.T.C. 1998).

Case Facts: Retirement plan owner loaned money from plan to himself. The loans and subsequent repayments were transactions (loan and repayment) between disqualified persons (plan owner).

Citation: *Wood v. Comm'r*, 95 T.C. 364 (U.S.T.C. 1990)

Case Facts: Retirement plan owner/trustee sold/transferred real and personal property he personally owned to his retirement plan. The transfer of property to the plan was a transaction by a disqualified person (plan owner).

Citation: *McGaugh v. Comm'r*, 860 F.3d 1014 (7th Cir. 2017)

Case Facts: McGaugh intended to buy shares in a private company with his Merrill Lynch IRA. The Merrill IRA sent the purchase funds but when the shares were sent to Merrill, Merrill refused to hold them as an asset, presumably because they were private stock that was non-publicly traded. The shares were actually titled in the name of Raymond McGaugh

FBO Raymond McGaugh IRA. Merrill eventually considered the funds to buy the shares distributed and issued a 1099-R to Mr. McGaugh. Mr. McGaugh disputed the distribution and prevailed with the 7th Circuit Court of Appeals reasoning that Mr. McGaugh intended the shares to be owned by his IRA and never personally took constructive possession or ownership of the shares.

FREQUENTLY ASKED QUESTIONS

Q. Can my IRA enter into a transaction with myself or another disqualified person if fair market value is paid in the transaction?

A. No. Even if the transaction is at fair market value, your IRA is prohibited from engaging in a transaction with a disqualified person.

Q. Can my IRA loan money to my uncle?

A. Yes, your IRA may make an investment loan to your uncle as your uncle is not a disqualified person.

Q. Can my IRA buy a property and lease it to a company of which I own 60%?

A. No, Your IRA's lease of the property is a transaction, and it is with a disqualified person (company owned 60% by you).

Q. Can my IRA buy a property and lease it to a company of which I own 30% and the remaining 70% is owned by unrelated parties?

A. Yes, this is not a per se prohibited transaction because the lease is a transaction but it is *not* with a disqualified person. However, be careful in this instance because this could constitute a self-dealing prohibited transaction. *See* Chapter 6.

Q. Can my IRA buy newly issued stock from a company that is owned 75% by my son?

A. No, the purchase of stock is a transaction, and the company is a disqualified person since it is owned 50% or more by your son. Consequently, the IRA would be engaging in a transaction with a disqualified person, so there would be a prohibited transaction.

CHAPTER 5: Personal Extension of Credit Prohibited Transactions & Non- Recourse Loans with IRA Investments

An IRA may leverage its investments with debt by using what is called a "nonrecourse" loan. For example, an IRA may use a portion of its funds to make a down payment on a property and can obtain a nonrecourse loan to fund the balance of the purchase price. In a nonrecourse loan, the lender loans against the asset only (e.g. the property). In the event of default, the bank has rights to foreclose against the assets but cannot go after the IRA or the IRA owner to collect the debt. The reason a nonrecourse loan must be used is because the IRA owner cannot guarantee a loan or obtain a loan personally for his or her IRA's investments, as this constitutes an extension of credit prohibited transaction.

KEY POINTS
▪ *An IRA may use debt to leverage its investments but the debt cannot be secured, guaranteed, or extended from the personal assets of the IRA owner as that results in an extension of credit prohibited transaction.*
▪ *If an IRA is obtaining debt, it should get a nonrecourse loan in the IRA's name (or IRA/LLC's name, as applicable).*

PERSONAL EXTENSION OF CREDIT PROHIBITED TRANSACTIONS

The second type of prohibited transaction occurs when a disqualified person, such as the IRA owner, extends credit to an IRA. IRC § 4975 (c)(1)(B) specifically states that a prohibited transaction occurs when there is a "lending of money or other extension of credit between a plan [IRA] and a disqualified person." If you read the language carefully, it uses the words "between a plan and a disqualified person," which means that a loan from the IRA to the disqualified person (e.g. IRA owner) is prohibited as is an extension of credit from a disqualified person to his or her IRA's investments. *Rutland v. Commissioner,* 89 T.C. 1137 (1987). Therefore, extensions of credit going either way between an IRA and a disqualified person create a prohibited transaction.

LEGAL TIP
❖ Loaning money to yourself from your IRA is an extension of credit prohibited transaction.
❖ Personally loaning money to your IRA or personally guaranteeing a loan for your IRA's investment(s) is an extension of credit prohibited transaction.

For example, if the IRA is purchasing an investment property, the IRA owner cannot obtain a standard mortgage using the IRA owner's personal credit and cannot personally guarantee the loan being obtained for the IRA's investment. Extending personal credit or guaranteeing the loan for the IRA would constitute an extension of credit to the IRA by a disqualified person and would result in a prohibited transaction. *Janpol v. CIR,* 101 T.C. 518 (1993). Also, an IRA owner cannot guarantee or obtain a margin trading account for his or her IRA whereby he or she personally agrees to be liable for the amounts loaned to the IRA.

A recent case that illustrates the prohibition on guaranteeing a loan for your IRA was *Peek & Fleck v. Commissioner*, 140 T.C. 12 (2013). In *Peek & Fleck*, Mr. Peek and Mr. Fleck used their self-directed Roth IRAs to form a new company wholly owned by the respective Roth IRAs. This Roth-IRA-owned company then purchased an existing business. The purchase price paid by the Roth-IRA-owned company was funded by cash from the Roth-IRA-owned company and some seller financing from the seller of the business. Under the seller financing, the company agreed to a promissory note with the seller in the amount of $200,000. This arrangement would have been acceptable as the IRA owned company could agree to the promissory note without causing a prohibited transaction. However, the loan became a prohibited transaction because Mr. Peek and Mr. Fleck signed personal guarantees associated with the loan and also offered their personal residences as collateral for the loans. These personal guarantees and the offering of personal assets as collateral violated IRC § 4975 (c)(1)(B) because the IRA owners extended their personal credit for the benefit of the plan's investments.

Unfortunately for Mr. Peek and Mr. Fleck, their Roth IRAs were disqualified as a result of the extension of credit prohibited transactions. As a consequence of the prohibited transactions, the gain of over $1M that they received from the subsequent sale of the business could not be treated under the tax-free Roth IRA rules, but was instead subject to tax on Mr. Peek and Mr. Fleck's personal tax returns.

NONRECOURSE LOAN REQUIREMENTS

Despite the prohibited transaction rule which prohibits the IRA owner or other disqualified person from using his or her personal credit to obtain a loan for the IRA, an IRA can obtain a loan to finance its investments, as long as the financing is considered a nonrecourse loan. A nonrecourse loan does not violate the rules because it is not based on the IRA owner's credit and personal assets and does not require the IRA owner (or other disqualified person) to sign or guarantee the loan. In a nonrecourse loan, the bank extends credit based on the asset or investment being purchased by the IRA, and the bank's money is always secured by the asset on which they lent money.

PRACTICAL TIP
❖ Seek out lenders who specialize in loans to self-directed IRAs. I wouldn't recommend walking into your local credit union to ask about getting a nonrecourse loan for your IRA's purchase of a rental property.

There are a few national banks who offer nonrecourse mortgage loans for IRAs buying real estate, whereby the IRA makes a significant down payment of approximately 30–40%, and the bank finances the difference and records a deed of trust or mortgage against title to the property. Title to the property is held by the IRA. If the IRA defaults on the loan payments to the lender, then the lender will foreclose and take the property back. This type of loan is permissible and does not violate IRC § 4975 (c)(1)(B) because it is based solely on the IRA's assets and investments and not on any disqualified person.

There are a few national banks and many local lenders that offer specialty nonrecourse loan products for self-directed IRAs or

IRA/LLC real estate purchases. The typical qualification requirements to obtain a nonrecourse loan for real estate investments in an IRA or an IRA/LLC are as follows:

- The property must be income-producing (e.g., rental). The property can be single family, multifamily, or commercial, as long as it generates rental income. The lender will look at the expected rental income to determine whether the rental income will be sufficient to cover the loan and other expenses to the property.

- There must be at most 60% to 70% debt-to-equity ratio on the property. In many instances this may require the IRA to put 30 – 40% down. Since the lender's only recourse upon default in a nonrecourse loan is to foreclose and take the property back, lenders requires more equity and down payment on the property than you may see in other investment loan products.

When a loan is in place on the property, the IRA or the IRA/LLC (if that structure is used) receives the rental income and pays the expenses on the property, including the loan payments due under the nonrecourse loan. The IRA owner may not make the loan payments personally, and the loan must be satisfied by the IRA's funds or assets. When the property is sold, the loan is paid off, and the remaining proceeds from the sale go back to the IRA.

LEGAL TIP
❖ Not all nonrecourse loans are in compliance with the rules for retirement plans. IRA owners should be very careful whenever they personally sign "fraud carve-out guarantees."

PERSONAL GUARANTEE ISSUES

IRA owners need to be careful about signing personally on any "carve-out guarantees" that are sometimes required as part of the nonrecourse loan documents for an IRA. Carve-out guarantees are essentially terms that some lenders will use in nonrecourse loan documents to say that even though the loan is nonrecourse, we can go after the carve-out guarantors, which could be the IRA owner, for instances of fraud or misappropriation of funds. While well-crafted carve-out guarantees against the IRA owner won't violate the prohibited transaction rules, they can cause issues if they reach too far and amount to the IRA owner personally extending credit or offering personal assets to satisfy the loan qualification requirements for the IRA.

In all instances where an IRA obtains a nonrecourse loan, the IRA becomes subject to a tax known as unrelated debt financed income tax ("UDFI") on the profits that are returned to the IRA as a result of the debt. IRC § 514. If there is debt on an IRA asset, then the income that is attributable to the IRA's cash investment in the asset is exempt from tax under normal IRA rules, while income that is attributable to the debt is subject to taxes. UDFI tax is explained and covered extensively in Chapter 15.

EXTENSION OF CREDIT PROHIBITED
TRANSACTION CASE EXAMPLES

Below is a chart that summarizes some extension of credit prohibited transaction cases and rulings.

TABLE 5.1, EXTENSION OF CREDIT PROHIBITED
TRANSACTION CASES AND OPINIONS

Citation: *Janpol v. CIR,* 101 T.C. 518 (1993).
Case Facts: Retirement plan owners guaranteed loans from a bank to the retirement plans. The Tax Court held that such guarantees were an extension of credit from a disqualified person to a plan.
Citation: *Janpol v. CIR,* 101 T.C. 518 (1993).
Case Facts: The second prohibited transaction from *Janpol* occurred when the retirement plan owners loaned money from themselves personally to the plan. This was a prohibited transaction, as there was a loan between a disqualified person and a plan.
Citation: *Rutland v. Commissioner,* 89 T.C. 1137 (1987).
Case Facts: Retirement plan fiduciaries and officers of a company plan sold property from themselves personally to the plan. The plan paid cash for the real property and agreed to a note for the balance of the purchase price. The sale of the personally owned property to the plan and the note for the balance of the purchase was a prohibited transaction

TABLE 5.1, EXTENSION OF CREDIT PROHIBITED TRANSACTION CASES AND OPINIONS (CONT'D)

Citation: *Zacky v. Commissioner*, T.C.M. 2004-130 (2004).

Case Facts: Retirement plan owner loaned money from his plan to himself personally to pay off a personal car loan and to pay personal real property taxes. The loans were prohibited transactions as they were extensions of credit from a plan to a disqualified person.

Citation: ERISA ADVISORY OPINION 90-23A

Case Facts: Two attorneys requested approval of a transaction from the Department of Labor ("DOL") in which they would form a new entity and fund it with their self-directed IRAs. The new entity would obtain a loan for the purchase of real estate and the self-directed IRA owners would sign a personal guarantee. The DOL ruled that the guarantees would be an extension of credit from IRA owners to a disqualified person (company entirely owned by their IRAs).

Citation: ERISA ADVISORY OPINION 2006-09A

Case Facts: IRA owner's son-in-law and daughter owned 95% of a corporation. IRA owner wanted to lend money as an investment to the corporation. DOL ruled that the loan would be a prohibited transaction as the company was owned 50% or more by disqualified persons (son-in-law and daughter), and the loan would be an extension of credit.

TABLE 5.1, EXTENSION OF CREDIT PROHIBITED TRANSACTION CASES AND OPINIONS (CONT'D)

Citation: *In Re Daley*, 2013 U.S. App LEXIS 12138 (6th Cir. June 17, 2013).

Case Facts: IRA owner signed documents with his broker whereby his IRA was subject to a lien against any amounts that the IRA owner personally owed to the bank. The Court ruled that this lien language did not constitute a prohibited transaction since the IRA owner did not have any other personal obligations to the bank, and as a result, the language did not burden the IRA or result in an actual extension of credit from the IRA to the IRA owner. This overruled a lower court ruling finding that there was a prohibited transaction.

Citation: *Peek & Fleck v. Commissioner*, 140 T.C. 12 (2013).

Citation: ERISA Opinion Letter 2009-03A

Case Facts: Allowing a security interest of non-IRA assets of by the IRA as condition to opening an IRA is an extension of credit prohibited transaction.

Citation: ERISA Opinion Letter 2011-09A

Case Facts: An indemnification agreement from an IRA owner personally as part of a futures trading account for an IRA results in an extension of credit prohibited transaction.

FREQUENTLY ASKED QUESTIONS

Q. Can I guarantee a loan made to my self-directed IRA?

A. No, the guarantee of a loan by the IRA owner (or a disqualified person to the IRA, spouse, child, parents, etc.) would constitute an extension of credit between a plan (IRA) and a disqualified person and would be a prohibited transaction.

Q. Can I get a loan for a property in my personal name and use my IRA to fund the down payment?

A. No, this would be a prohibited transaction as you cannot personally extend credit for your IRAs investments, nor could you use your IRA to make a down payment (other than by taking a distribution) for a property you buy personally.

Q. What kind of loan can I get when making IRA investments?

A. You essentially have two options: First, you can get a nonrecourse loan. This loan is explained above and does not violate the prohibited transaction rules as it does not include an extension of credit from a disqualified person to the IRA. The second option is that the IRA can participate in a purchase of a property as a cash investor, and other partners (typically LLC members) can serve as the credit partners or can sign the personal guarantees required by the loan, thus avoiding the IRA owner from signing as a guarantor or party to the loan. The credit partner who signs for the loan personally or as the guarantor for an entity (e.g., LLC) cannot be a disqualified person (e.g., can't be the IRA owner's spouse, child, spouse of child, parent, etc.).

Q. Can my IRA invest in an LLC and then others in the LLC as managers or members (and who are unrelated third parties) sign for the loan as the guarantors?

A. Yes. As long as the IRA owner or other disqualified person is not personally signing or offering their credit, this type of loan is acceptable. It is essentially a nonrecourse loan to the IRA and there is only recourse to the other member or person who is signing as the guarantor/credit partner.

CHAPTER 6: Self-Dealing Prohibited Transactions

The third type of prohibited transaction is a self-dealing prohibited transaction. In short, a self-dealing prohibited transaction occurs when the IRA owner or other disqualified person benefits from the IRA's investments. IRC § 4975 (c)(1)(D),(E), and (F). A self-dealing prohibited transaction is also sometimes referred to as a conflict of interest prohibited transaction.

KEY POINTS
▪ *Self-dealing prohibited transactions occur when a disqualified person (e.g., IRA owner) benefits from an IRA's investment.*
▪ *Self-dealing prohibited transactions can arise when an IRA invests into a company where the IRA owner or other disqualified persons are owners or part of management.*
▪ *Self-dealing prohibited transactions are difficult to determine and are based on the facts and circumstances of the IRA's investment and the involvement of disqualified persons.*

Self-dealing prohibited transactions can be difficult to determine as they are based on subjective factors.

The specific definition of a self-dealing prohibited transaction from IRC § 4975 (c)(1) is when an IRA engages in a direct or indirect:

(D) transfer to, or use by or for the benefit of, a disqualified person of the income or assets of a plan; or

(E) act by a disqualified person who is a fiduciary whereby he deals with the income or assets of a plan in his own interest or for his own account; or

(F) receipt of any consideration for his own personal account by any disqualified person who is a fiduciary from any party dealing with the plan in connection with a transaction involving the income or assets of the plan. *Id.*

A careful reading of these sections reveals that paragraph (D) applies to all disqualified persons (e.g., IRA owner, spouse, kids, etc.) while paragraphs (E) and (F) only apply to disqualified persons who are also fiduciaries (e.g., IRA owner). As a result, most self-dealing prohibited transactions are best analyzed under the language of paragraph (D), which essentially gives rise to a prohibited transaction when any disqualified person "benefits" from the income or assets of a retirement plan.

SELF-DEALING PROHIBITED TRANSACTIONS EXPLAINED

Tom W. Anderson, President, Retirement Industry Trust Association, has explained that because of the self-dealing prohibited transaction rules "You can't even buy raw land [with your IRA] and hunt on it with your friends." Anderson, Tom W., *Prohibited Transactions for Investors*, Retirement Industry Trust Association, 2012.

For example, let's say you're a real estate agent, and you act as the agent and purchase an investment property with your self-directed IRA. As part of the purchase, you receive the buyer's agent commission. Since you were the buyer's agent on the transaction, this commission, unfortunately, constitutes a self-dealing prohibited transaction because the IRA owner personally benefitted from the IRA's transaction by receiving the commission. As a result, if you are serving as the real estate agent for your own IRA, then you would need to waive your commission or would need to hire a non-disqualified person to serve as the agent for the self-directed IRA's purchase of the investment property.

There is an argument that a broker commission may be "reasonable compensation" under IRC § 4975 (d)(10), and exempt from the prohibited transaction rules. However, the reasonable compensation exemption for real estate commissions received by a disqualified person, has not been tested in Court nor has it been specifically endorsed by the IRS or DOL. As a result, IRA owners should not rely on it and should avoid commissions or compensation to disqualified persons.

Another common example is a rental property owned by your IRA. While you may lease the property to non disqualified persons, you may not personally stay at or use the property. Use of property violates the self-dealing rules as you end up personally benefiting from your retirement account's investments by getting a free stay. If you paid rent at the same rate that other tenants paid, then you wouldn't be personally benefitting and wouldn't have a self-dealing prohibited transaction. Instead, you would have a per se prohibited transaction because the rent payment would be a payment to the IRA from a disqualified person. Therefore, using the assets of your retirement account for personal use (or use by another disqualified person) will create a prohibited transaction whether you pay for them (per se prohibited transaction) or whether you receive them for free (self-dealing prohibited transaction).

IRA INVESTMENT IN COMPANY WHERE IRA OWNER OR DISQUALIFIED PERSONS WORK

Self-dealing prohibited transactions can arise when an IRA invests into a business where disqualified persons to the IRA (e.g., IRA owner) receive personal compensation. For example, let's say that you manage a business, private equity company, or hedge fund, and that your IRA owns 20% of the company. The other 80% is owned by unrelated third parties who are not disqualified persons. This investment and your employment compensation in the business would not constitute a per se prohibited transaction since disqualified persons own less than 50% but it may result in a self-dealing prohibited transaction if the investment of your IRA results in personal benefit to you in your management or employment duties. Frankly, the cases in this scenario are very inconsistent, and it is very difficult to determine what will constitute a self-dealing prohibited transaction in scenarios where the IRA owner and other disqualified persons have some ownership but own less than 50% of the company in question. The cases and opinions in this situation seem to turn on various facts and circumstances. Please refer to the table at the end of this chapter where I have summarized all relevant cases and opinions regarding self-dealing prohibited transactions.

The following diagram is a useful tool in determining whether there is a self-dealing prohibited transaction:

DIAGRAM 6.1, FINDING SELF-DEALING PROHIBITED TRANSACTIONS

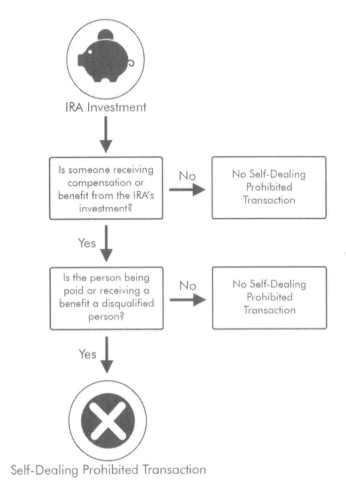

IRA Investment

Is someone receiving compensation or benefit from the IRA's investment?

No → No Self-Dealing Prohibited Transaction

Yes

Is the person being paid or receiving a benefit a disqualified person?

No → No Self-Dealing Prohibited Transaction

Yes

Self-Dealing Prohibited Transaction

SELF-DEALING PROHIBITED TRANSACTION CASE ANALYSIS

The Department of Labor, in Opinion Letter 2006-01A, stated that it is *not* a self-dealing prohibited transaction when a company in which an IRA has invested engages in a transaction with that IRA owner. Rather, it is only a prohibited transaction when there is some unfair benefit taking place or where there is a requirement that the company transact with a disqualified person. The DOL's specifically stated the following:

> The Department's regulation at 29 C.F.R. 2509.75-2(a) (Interpretive Bulletin 75-2) explains that a transaction between a party in interest under ERISA (or disqualified person under the Code, in this case S Company) and a corporation in which a plan has invested (i.e., the LLC) does not generally give rise to a prohibited transaction.

Transactions between a company (owned less than 50% by disqualified persons) where an IRA has invested, and a disqualified person have invested, are not automatically self-dealing prohibited transactions unless there is some unfair benefit taking place in the transaction.

IRA INVESTMENT INTO A COMPANY WHERE DISQUALIFIED PERSONS OWN/CONTROL LESS THAN 50%

When analyzing an investment for a self-dealing prohibited transaction, the IRA owner needs to go further than the objective per se prohibited transaction rules to determine whether a disqualified person is going to benefit personally from the transaction. For example, let's consider a potential scenario where the IRA owner and other disqualified persons own 25% of an LLC, and the remaining 75% is owned by non-disqualified persons. The IRA lends money to this LLC under reasonable market rate terms. Because disqualified persons only own 25% of the borrowing company LLC, there is no per se prohibited transaction since the IRA's transaction is between a non-disqualified person (the LLC). However, there may be a self-dealing prohibited transaction, as the IRA owner may personally benefit as an owner in the borrowing LLC. Since these cases always turn on specific facts and circumstances, it is helpful to understand the primary cases where self-dealing prohibited transactions have been decided.

SIGNIFICANT SELF-DEALING PROHIBITED TRANSACTION CASES

One of the most significant self-dealing prohibited transaction cases affecting self-directed IRAs is *Rollins v. Commissioner*, T.C. Memo 2004-260. In *Rollins*, Joseph Rollins was the trustee and a fiduciary of his company's self-directed 401(k) plan, and he directed the plan's investments. The investments were promissory-note loans from the plan to companies in which Rollins and his wife were owners and officers. The ownership of Rollins and other disqualified persons (e.g. Rollins' wife) in the borrowing companies was at most 33%, with the majority ownership being held by non-disqualified persons. As a result, the receiving companies were not disqualified persons with respect to the loans, and there was not an extension of credit prohibited transaction under IRC § 4975 (c)(1)(B).

Despite the fact that the loans were not extension of credit prohibited transactions, the Tax Court held that there was a self-dealing prohibited transaction pursuant to IRC § 4975 (c)(1)(B).

The facts that doomed Rollins and that led to the self-dealing prohibited transaction were that he was the officer of each of the borrowing companies who signed the promissory note loans with the retirement plan. Additionally, Rollins and his wife, while owning 49% or less of each borrowing company, were the largest individual owners in each of the borrowing companies. As a result of Rollins' apparent control of the borrowing companies receiving the loans from the plan, the Tax Court found that Rollins was using the plan to make loans to companies where he owned enough ownership to personally benefit, in violation of the self-dealing prohibited transaction rules.

LEGAL TIP
❖ If an IRA is engaging in a transaction with a company where a disqualified person (e.g. IRA owner) is an owner or officer, then the disqualified person should not be involved in the decision making for the company regarding the transaction with their own IRA.

Despite the holding in *Rollins*, there are cases where the Courts (or the Department of Labor) have ruled the other way and have not found a prohibited transaction where a retirement plan invests into a company where the retirement plan owner (or other disqualified person) is personally involved as a minority owner or employee. For example, in *Etter v. J. Pease Construction Co.*, the Court held that there was no prohibited transaction when the retirement plan loaned money to a company owned 50% or more by the retirement plan fiduciary. 963 F.2d 1005 (7th Cir. 1992). Even though the borrowing company that received the loan from the retirement plan was a disqualified person (owned, 50% or more by disqualified persons), the Court held that the plan's investment did not violate the prohibited transaction rules because the plan received an excellent return and therefore was a prudent investment decision of the plan fiduciary. This case is a little tricky to understand, but demonstrates the inconsistency that arises when analyzing self-dealing prohibited transactions.

Additionally, in *Greenlee v. Commissioner*, T.C. Memo 1996-378, the retirement plan owner directed the plan trustee, who had final authority for investment decisions, to loan money from the plan to a company owned 18% by the plan owner. The Tax Court held that since the plan owner had an independent trustee who had authority to approve an investment, that the investment was *not* a self-dealing prohibited transaction, as the plan owner was not dealing with the income or assets of the plan for his own benefit. This case is a little unique in that the retirement account owner did not have the final authority to bind the investment, though the account owner did have the authority to make investment recommendations.

And finally, in DOL Opinion Letter 88-018A, the Department of Labor stated that a promissory note from a self-directed IRA to a company in which the self-directed IRA owner owned 48% of the company and was on the board of directors would not result in an extension of credit prohibited transaction under IRC § 4975 (c)(1)(B) since the borrowing company to the transaction was owned 50% or more by non-disqualified parties and was therefore not a disqualified person. However, the DOL cautioned that because of significant ownership in the borrowing company by the IRA owner, there *could* be a self-dealing prohibited transaction under IRC § 4975 (c)(1)(D) or IRC § 4975 (c)(1)(E). As a general rule, the DOL refrains from making conclusions in opinion letters as to self-dealing prohibited transactions when there is nothing specific in the facts and usually just states that there could be a self-dealing prohibited transaction, and that the answer depends on the facts and circumstances of the particular case.

The following table summarizes additional cases and rulings where self-dealing prohibited transactions have been found:

TABLE 6.1, SELF-DEALING PROHIBITED TRANSACTION CASES AND OPINIONS

Citation: Summa Holdings, Inc., et al, v. Commissioner, T.C. Memo 2015-119
Case Facts: James Benenson III and Clement Benenson were brothers and their Roth IRAs wholly owned a c-corporation (JCH), which in turn wholly owned another c-corporation (JCE). JCE then entered into agreements with Summa Holdings, Inc. and its subsidiaries and received commissions. Summa was majority owned and controlled by the Benenson brother's father. Summa or its subsidiaries expensed the payments and the Corporations ended up claiming them as income and paying corporate tax. They then distributed the after-corporate tax profits to the Roth IRAs. IRS argued a "substance over form doctrine" argument to find a prohibited transaction as there was no other business purposes to the Roth IRAs investment/involvement other than to receive dividends and income from the owners controlled companies. Court also analyzed IRS Notice 2004-8 as value shift from the existing business transferred to the Roth IRAs. Court found a self-dealing prohibited transaction since the substance of the Roth IRA investments was a transfer of value from the disqualified person's company (father's company).
Citation: DOL Advisory Opinion 2011-04A

Case Facts: IRA sought to purchase promissory note from third-party bank. The borrower to the note, however, was the IRA owner personally. The DOL stated that the existence of an outstanding note between the IRA and the IRA owner personally would be a self-dealing prohibited transaction.

Citation: DOL Advisory Opinion 2006-01A, 29 C.F.R. 2509.75-2(a)

Case Facts: IRA owned 49% of an LLC that in turn leased a property to a company majority owned by the IRA owner. Even though the IRA owned less than 50% of the LLC and was therefore not a disqualified person, the DOL stated that since the intent of the LLC at formation was to then lease property to a company majority controlled by the IRA owner, that the investment would constitute a per se prohibited transaction and self-dealing prohibited transaction since it would be for the benefit of a company majority owned by the IRA owner. The DOL relied on 29 C.F.R. 2509.75-2(a) in reaching this conclusion, which states that a retirement plan engages in a prohibited transaction when it invests into a company and when that company has an arrangement to then invest with a disqualified person.

TABLE 6.1, SELF-DEALING PROHIBITED
TRANSACTION CASES AND OPINIONS (CONT'D)

Citation: DOL Advisory Opinion 82-08A
Case Facts: Four siblings each owned 45%, 40%, 10%, and 5% of a company. The siblings wanted to make a loan investment from their IRAs to the company. Because siblings are not disqualified persons, the company was not a disqualified person under the rules, and as a result, there was no per se or extension of credit prohibited transaction. However, the DOL reasoned that because of the significant ownership interests of the siblings, who are disqualified to their own IRAs, the loan investments would be a self-dealing prohibited transaction.
Citation: DOL Advisory Opinion 89-03A
Case Facts: An officer and 1% shareholder of a publicly traded company wanted to invest his self-directed IRA into the company for shares equaling less than 1%. The DOL stated that the investment would not constitute a per se prohibited transaction because of the IRA owner's small ownership stake but withheld opinion on whether the purchase would constitute a self-dealing prohibited transaction and cautioned the IRA owner on the issue without expressing an opinion.

TABLE 6.1, SELF-DEALING PROHIBITED
TRANSACTION CASES AND OPINIONS (CONT'D)

Citation: DOL Advisory Opinion 90-20
Case Facts: Company sought opinion as to whether its employees could purchase shares of its parent holding company with their self-directed IRAs. DOL stated that such stock purchases of employee's IRA would not constitute a per se or self-dealing prohibited transaction. DOL cautioned that purchases of stock for employees who are also officers or directors may cause a self-dealing prohibited transaction but refused to express a final opinion as to such.
Citation: DOL Advisory Opinion 2000-10A
Case Facts: IRA owner and family members owned over 50% of an investment partnership, though only about 20–25% was owned by disqualified family members. IRA owner wanted to invest his self-directed IRA into the investment partnership and would reorganize the ownership such that following the investment, his IRA would own 39.38% and disqualified persons to his IRA would own about 11%. The partnership would be managed by an unrelated third party. The DOL ruled that this would not result in a per se prohibited transaction and did not find a self-dealing prohibited transaction at the time of the IRA investment, though they did say it was possible one could arise later because of the involvement of the IRA and disqualified persons.

TABLE 6.1, SELF-DEALING PROHIBITED
TRANSACTION CASES AND OPINIONS (CONT'D)

Citation: TAM 9208001 (IRS, Technical Advice Memorandum)

Case Facts: A disqualified person caused a retirement plan to loan money to a limited partnership where the disqualified person was a 7.5% partner. The IRS wrote that this was a self-dealing prohibited transaction.

Citation: TAM 9119002 (IRS, Technical Advice Memorandum)

Case Facts: A disqualified person and plan owner caused his company plan to loan money to Company Y. The plan owner was a 39% owner of Company Y. According to the facts, the IRS ruled that there was no evidence to refute the assumption that the plan owner participated in the decision to make the loan to Company Y. As a result, the IRS reasoned that because of the plan owner's participation in making the loan with Company Y and because the plan owner benefited as a significant owner of Company Y, the loan was a self-dealing prohibited transaction.

Citation: *Lowen v. Tower Asset Management, Inc.*, 829 F.2d 1209 (2nd Cir. 1987)

Case Facts: A disqualified person to the plan caused the plan to invest in companies where the disqualified person would receive commissions and fees for services. The Court ruled that this was a self-dealing prohibited transaction because the disqualified person would receive financial benefit for the plan's investments in the companies.

TABLE 6.1, SELF-DEALING PROHIBITED
TRANSACTION CASES AND OPINIONS (CONT'D)

Citation: *Flahertys Arden Bowl, Inc. v. Commissioner*, 115 T.C. 269 (2000), *affirmed per curiam*, 271 F.3d 763 (8th Cir. 2001).

Case Facts: A disqualified person caused his retirement plans to loan money to a business substantially owned (over 50%) by the disqualified person. The Court ruled that this was a self-dealing prohibited transaction since the disqualified person's business was benefitting from the investment. This also constituted a per se prohibited transaction.

Citation: PLR 8717079, Department of Labor PRL

Case Facts: IRA owner was a manager and a member of the board of directors of Company. The IRA owner also owned less than 1% of the stock of company. The IRA owner proposed to invest his IRA into Company to buy one hundred shares, which purchase would result in the IRA owner still owning less than 1% between him personally and his IRA. The IRS ruled that this would not be a per se prohibited transaction but reserved to say whether or not it would be a self-dealing prohibited transaction.

Citation: IRS CCA 200952049

Case Facts: IRA owner's receipt of compensation from IRA investments is a self-dealing prohibited transaction even if such amounts are paid indirectly from an LLC in which the IRA invests.

TABLE 6.1, SELF-DEALING PROHIBITED
TRANSACTION CASES AND OPINIONS (CONT'D)

Citation: PLR 8009091, Department of Labor Private Letter Ruling.

Case Facts: IRA owner was a director of Corp A and a former employee of Corp A. Corp B owns 35% of Corp A and the IRA owner was the president of Corp B. The IRA owner proposed to purchase 5% of the shares of Corp A. The DOL ruled that the purchase would not be a prohibited transaction as Corp A was not a disqualified person to the IRA owner. The DOL cautioned that a self-dealing prohibited transaction may occur though, if the "plan's acquisition of the stock insures your [IRA owner's] reelection as a director of Corp A or benefits you in your position as president of Corp B."

Citation: *Rollins v. Commissioner*, T.C. Memo 2004-260.

Case Facts: See case explanation in this chapter.

Citation: *Greenlee v. Commissioner*, T.C. Memo 1996-378

Case Facts: See case explanation in this chapter.

Citation: *Etter v. J. Pease Construction Co.* 963 F.2d 1005 (7th Cir. 1992)

Case Facts: See case explanation in this chapter.

Citation: DOL Opinion Letter 88-018A

Case Facts: See opinion explanation in this chapter.

IDENTIFYING SELF-DEALING PROHIBITED TRANSACTIONS

After considering numerous self-dealing prohibited transaction cases, it is apparent that the IRS, the DOL, and the Courts will analyze the following three key factors to determine whether there is a self-dealing prohibited transaction:

1. What involvement did the IRA owner have in arranging the investment with the other party to the transaction? For example, what seemed to doom the plan owner in *Rollins* was that he was arranging the loan investment on both sides of the table: on his retirement plan side and on the borrowing-company side. In fact, he was the officer that signed the promissory notes back to the retirement plan. As a practical point, always have a non-disqualified person be the company signatory and authorized person to approve any transaction with an IRA.

2. Were the terms of the investment commercially reasonable for the IRA, or did they amount to the IRA owner taking advantage of his or her IRA account? If the terms of the IRAs investment fall outside of what are typical commercially reasonable terms, then the transaction may be scrutinized for how those terms benefit a disqualified person who is involved in the transaction (as a minority owner in a company involved in the transaction or as an indirect beneficiary to the investment). An important question to ask and a great fact in defense is whether the self-directed IRA was simply getting the same investment deal any other investor would have received. For example, if the company was selling stock or LLC units and gave the same terms to

the self-directed IRA as it gave to outside parties (non-disqualified parties), then there is a great defense that the terms were reasonable. If, on the other hand, the IRA received different terms than outside parties were receiving, then it makes the terms appear not to be at market value.

3. The percentage of ownership or amount of control disqualified persons may have in a company involved in a transaction with an IRA. Disqualified person ownership of 50% or more creates a per se prohibited transaction, so obviously the ownership must be below 50%. For purposes of analyzing a company involved in a transaction with an IRA, 49% ownership of disqualified persons would be the most susceptible to a self-dealing prohibited transaction, while ownership below 10% is far less susceptible to a self-dealing prohibited transaction. Facts which show that the entire company considered the transaction and that non-disqualified persons approved the transaction help to demonstrate that the investment was not made for the personal benefit of the IRA owner.

FREQUENTLY ASKED QUESTIONS

Q. I own 25% of a company and non-disqualified persons to my IRA own the other 75%. Can my IRA loan money to or otherwise transact with this company?

A. It depends. Since the company is owned 75% by non-disqualified persons, the company is not prohibited to your IRA. However, there may be a self-dealing prohibited transaction as you may personally benefit from the IRA's investment into the company. This is certainly an area where you'd want to get an opinion from an attorney as to whether the loan or transaction with the company would be appropriate. Keeping the terms of the transaction at commercially reasonable rates and having others in the company handle the negotiations and agreement for the company would be critical.

Q. I'm president of a company and own 5% of the company personally. I have some options to acquire stock at a discounted price. The options were issued by the company to me as part of my compensation as an officer of the company. Can I exercise these options and buy the shares with my IRA?

A. No. Since the shares were earned as part of your personal compensation they are an asset you personally own and cannot be transferred to your IRA. Transferring the options you personally own to your IRA would be a transaction with a disqualified person and that causes a prohibited transaction.

Q. I'm a real estate agent/broker and am using my IRA to buy real estate. Can I serve as the buyer's agent and receive the buyer's agent commission on the transaction?

A. No. When you receive a commission you will personally benefit by receiving a commission for your IRA's investment. Whenever a disqualified person (e.g., IRA owner) benefits from an IRA investment there is a self-dealing prohibited transaction.

Q. I manage an investment fund/company and am paid a management fee based on the total invested assets under management. The have a small ownership stake (under 5%). Can my IRA or my spouses IRA invest into this fund?

A. No. An investment by your IRA or your spouse's IRA will increase the assets under management of the fund and will create additional management income to you personally. Thus, you will personally benefit from your IRA's investment and that results in a self-dealing prohibited transaction. If you are able to waive compensation for the IRA's portion of investment it may be possible for your IRA or your spouse's IRA to invest into the company.

Q. I'd like to buy an apartment building with my IRA. I want my daughter to live in the property and manage it in exchange for her rent. Is this possible?

A. No. Your daughter is a disqualified person to your IRA. Since she is a disqualified person she cannot personally benefit from the IRA's investment, and as a result she cannot reside at the property.

Q. I serve on the board of directors of a company. Directors are paid only nominal consideration for their service. I am also an owner of less than 10% of the company. One of the other existing owners, who are not related to me, wants to sell her shares. Can I buy these shares with my IRA?

A. Yes. So long as you do not personally benefit from the purchase, you may acquire the shares in your IRA. If your acquisition of the shares entitles you to a position of employment in the company (e.g., as an officer) or to certain benefits personally then you will likely have a self-dealing prohibited transaction.

CHAPTER 7: The Consequences of a Prohibited Transactions

The prohibited transaction consequences differ, depending on whether the IRA owner engages the IRA into a prohibited transaction or whether a third party engages the IRA into a prohibited transaction (e.g., broker, financial advisor, etc.). With respect to self-directed IRAs, it is typically the IRA owner who is engaging their IRA into a prohibited transaction since they usually have sole authority to direct the account.

KEY POINTS
▪ *If an <u>IRA owner engages his or her IRA</u> into a prohibited transaction, then the consequence is disqualification of the IRA and distribution of the entire account. The IRA owner is subject to all consequences of distribution, including possible taxes and penalties.*
▪ *If an <u>IRA engages into a prohibited transaction independent of the IRA owner</u> (e.g. broker or advisor engages the IRA), then the consequence is an excise tax of 15% on the amount involved to the disqualified person in the transaction and a potential additional 100% penalty if the prohibited transaction is not corrected.*

First, let's discuss the consequences to the most common type of prohibited transaction for self-directed IRA owners: prohibited transactions engaged in by the IRA owner.

CONSEQUENCES OF A PROHIBITED TRANSACTION ENGAGED IN BY THE IRA OWNER

If an IRA owner engages their IRA into a prohibited transaction, then the consequence is that the entire IRA is disqualified. Disqualification results in distribution of the entire account, based on the fair market value of all assets in the account as of January 1 of the year in which the prohibited transaction occurred. IRC § 4975 (c)(3), IRC § 408 (e)(2)(A). Distribution of an IRA results in possible taxes on amounts distributed, early withdrawal penalties, and revocation of tax-preferential treatment on the IRA's investments that occurred after the prohibited transaction.

In other words, if an IRA owner engages their IRA into a prohibited transaction then he or she no longer has an IRA and the value of the account is distributed and taxable to the IRA owner. Here's a quick breakdown to the consequences.

1. **Distribution & Taxes.** Regardless of the amount involved in the prohibited transaction, *the entire IRA* (including Roth IRAs, SEP or SIMPLE IRAs and HSAs) is deemed distributed and the IRA owner is subject to any applicable taxes from the distribution. The distribution amount is based on the fair market value of the account as of January 1 of the year in which the prohibited transaction occurred.

2. **Early Withdrawal Penalty.** A 10% early withdrawal penalty of the amount distributed (again, on the entire IRA) is applied to any IRA distributed before the IRA owner

reaches age 59 ½. If the IRA owner was over 59 ½ when the prohibited transaction occurred then the 10% penalty will not apply.

3. **Revocation of Preferred Tax Treatment.** Taxes will be applied to the income and gains from the IRA from the time the IRA engaged in a prohibited transaction. The IRA tax-deferred (Traditional) or tax-free (Roth) benefits are revoked, and any taxes owed on income or gains from the IRA after the prohibited transaction occurred are now due.

Let's break down each of these three consequences to a prohibited transaction.

WHAT TAXES ARE DUE FROM DISTRIBUTION?

Whenever you take a distribution from an IRA—whether from a prohibited transaction or voluntarily—the IRA owner is subject to taxes owed on the amounts distributed. The taxes owed upon distribution vary between Roth IRAs and Traditional IRAs, so I will address each separately.

TRADITIONAL IRAs & DISTRIBUTION

For traditional IRAs, the total amount of the distributed IRA is taxable to the IRA owner. The IRA owner will need to include the amount of the taxable distribution on his or her tax return for the year in which the prohibited transaction occurred. The amount of the distribution is the fair market value of the account on January 1 of the year in which the prohibited transaction occurred.

The taxes due from the IRA distribution depend on the IRA owner's personal tax situation. *IRS Publication 590- B*, Distributions from Individual Retirement Arrangements (2017). For example, if the traditional IRA owner engaged in a prohibited transaction in

2012 and if the amount of the taxable distribution was $150,000 then the IRA owner would claim $150,000 on his or her personal tax return and would combine that income with his or her other income in determining the total taxes due for 2012. As this example illustrates, a large taxable distribution can result in an IRA owner being placed into a higher tax bracket for the IRA taxable distribution amount and for the IRA owner's other income.

ROTH IRAs & DISTRIBUTION

For Roth IRAs, the rules on what is taxable from a distribution are a little more complicated. As most Roth IRA owners know, distributions from their Roth IRAs are not subject to taxes. However, this is only the case if the distributions are "qualified distributions" taken at retirement. A qualified distribution from a Roth IRA is not subject to taxes and occurs when; 1) the Roth IRA owner is 59 ½ at the time of distribution, and 2) any Roth IRA has been funded for 5 years at the time of distribution. IRC § 408A(d)(2)(A) & Treasury Reg. §1.408A-6, Q&A-1(b). If you are over 59 ½ at the time of the distribution (time of prohibited transaction for purposes here) and have had the Roth IRA for 5 years, then the distribution will not be taxable.

If the Roth IRA does not meet the qualified distribution rules at the time of the prohibited transaction as defined above, then a portion of the Roth IRA distribution may be taxable. There are two categories to separate out in this situation as one group is subject to taxes and one group is not subject to taxes.

1. Contributions and Conversions, *Not* Subject to Tax. For amounts that were regular Roth IRA contributions or that were part of a Roth IRA conversion (e.g., taxes were paid on these monies when they went into the Roth IRA), these amounts are *not* subject to taxes upon distribution from the Roth IRA as taxes were paid already on these amounts in the account.

2. Income and Gains, Subject to Tax. For amounts that were investment gains and that were not contributions or conversions, these amounts distributed to the Roth IRA owner are taxable and must be included on the Roth IRA owner's personal tax return. IRS Form 8606 is used to determine and declare the taxable portions for these amounts.

If a prohibited transaction occurs and is reported by the IRA custodian, the IRA owner will receive a 1099-R from his or her custodian. The amount of the on the 1099-R is the fair market value of the account as of January 1 of the year in which the prohibited transaction occurred.

HOW IS THE 10% PENALTY APPLIED?

The IRS applies an early withdrawal penalty of 10% on all pre-tax withdrawals from retirement plans that occur before the account owner reaches age 59 ½. This rule applies in the normal fashion for distributions that occur as a result of an IRA prohibited transaction. There are some exceptions to the 10% penalty such as in instances of disability but those likely are not relevant in determining the penalty after a prohibited transaction. Refer to Publication 598 for distribution-rule exceptions if you have a special circumstance or hardship.

For traditional IRA distributions, the 10% penalty is straightforward and applies on the total amount distributed to the IRA owner before the IRA owner reaches age 59 ½. In the case of a prohibited transaction, this would result in a 10% penalty on the amount in the IRA (fair market value of assets) at the time of the prohibited transaction. For example, if the IRA's fair market value as of January 1 of the year in which the prohibited transaction occurred was $250,000 and if the IRA owner was age 45 at the time of the prohibited transaction, then there would be a $25,000 early withdrawal penalty due on the amounts distributed as a result of the prohibited transaction. This penalty is in addition to the taxes that are due on the IRA owner taking $250,000 into income on his or her personal tax return. If the IRA owner was 59 ½ or older at the time of the prohibited transaction, then the 10% early withdrawal penalty would not apply.

For Roth IRA distributions, the analysis of whether a 10% penalty applies centers on whether the Roth IRA owner was 59 ½ or not. The 5 year Roth IRA qualified distribution rule does not come into play when analyzing whether there is a 10% early withdrawal penalty. Treasury Reg. §1.408A-6,Q&A-5(b). The 10% early withdrawal penalty therefore only applies when the distribution was taken before the Roth IRA owner reached age 59 ½.

If the Roth IRA owner was under age 59 ½ at the time of the prohibited transaction, then the amounts distributed must be analyzed further to determine what portions are subject to the 10% early withdrawal penalty. There are two categories to separate out in this scenario as one group is subject to the 10% penalty, and one group is not subject to the 10% penalty. For amounts that were regular Roth IRA contributions and a Roth IRA was in existence for at least 5 years or that were part of a Roth IRA conversion made at least 5 years ago (e.g., taxes were paid on these monies when they went into the Roth IRA), these amounts are *not* subject to the 10% early withdrawal penalty (or to taxes) upon distribution from the Roth IRA.

For Roth IRA purposes and the 10% early withdrawal penalty, there are two 5 year rules to understand. First, a Roth IRA must be in existence for at least 5 years before its contributions can be determined qualifying contributions, which allow the Roth IRA owner to avoid the 10% early withdrawal penalty. And second, for Roth IRA conversions, the conversion must have been in existence for at least 5 years before it will qualify to be exempt from the 10 % early withdrawal penalty. IRS Publication 590-B (2017).

For amounts that were investment gains and were not qualifying contributions or qualifying conversions where taxes were paid, these amounts distributed to the Roth IRA owner are subject to the 10% early withdrawal penalty. For example, a Roth IRA owner had a Roth IRA consisting of $15,000 in Roth IRA contributions and $20,000 of Roth IRA conversions made at least 5 years ago. The Roth IRA also included investment gains or income of $10,000 and the total account balance was $45,000. If a prohibited transaction occurred before the Roth IRA owner was 59 ½ ,then $35,000 (the amount of qualifying contributions and conversions) would not be subject to the early withdrawal penalty, and $10,000 (the amount of gains in the account) would be subject to the early withdrawal penalty. Therefore, the early withdrawal penalty would be $1,000 (10% of $10,000). The following diagram outlines this scenario.

DIAGRAM 7.1, ROTH IRA DISTRIBUTIONS AND TAXES FOLLOWING A PROHIBITED TRANSACTION

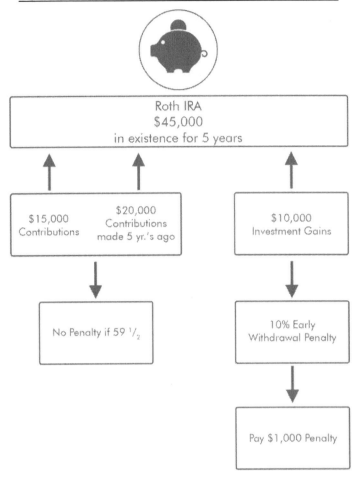

The third consequence of a prohibited transaction is that the transactions that occurred in the IRA after the prohibited transaction are now subject to taxes and must be claimed on the IRA owner's personal tax returns. Since the IRA no longer qualifies for tax-deferred (Traditional) or tax-free (Roth) treatment from the first date of a prohibited transaction, the IRA owner is personally subject to taxes that should have been due from the date the IRA ceased to be an IRA. In many instances, this requires the IRA owner to file amended personal tax returns.

For example, let's say your Roth IRA made separate investment loans of $100,000 to five different people in 2011. The loans accrued interest at 5% and had a lump sum due in five years. Four of the borrowers on the loans were unrelated third parties, and one was the son of the Roth IRA owner. Since the loan to the son is a transaction with a disqualified person, the Roth IRA has engaged in a prohibited transaction.

Let's say that this prohibited transaction is discovered in 2013, and that at this time, the son had made payments of interest to the Roth IRA of $5,000. Let's also assume all the other borrowers had done the same resulting in interest income to the Roth IRA of $25,000. Absent a prohibited transaction, the Roth IRA would receive this interest income tax free since the Roth IRA has preferred tax treatment. However, since a prohibited transaction occurred in 2011, the Roth IRA ceased to be a Roth IRA in 2011, and *all* income that the Roth IRA received since the prohibited transaction occurred is treated as income to the Roth IRA owner personally. It is not just the amount involved in the prohibited transaction that is now subject to personal taxes and is outside of the Roth IRA, but rather all investments there were in the Roth IRA at the time of the prohibited transaction are subject to personal taxation on the Roth IRA owner's tax return. As a result, the Roth IRA owner would have to go back and amend tax returns to claim the $25,000 in interest income the Roth IRA received, but that is now considered personal income as a result of the prohibited transaction. This is in addition to the taxes and potential penalties due from the early withdrawal.

ACCURACY RELATED PENALTY

Since profits and gains from the IRA may end up causing taxes to be owed by the IRA owner personally, the IRS may assess an accuracy-related penalty of 20% on any substantial underreporting of taxes pursuant to IRC § 6662. The IRS can assess this penalty on the amount of taxes that should have been paid by the IRA owner personally on income in the IRA after the prohibited transaction. In other words, since the IRA is no longer an IRA as of the prohibited transaction, any income made would have resulted in taxes being owed by the IRA owner personally, and failure to report that income and pay tax can trigger penalties on top of the tax owed.

The IRS is allowed to assess this penalty when there is negligence or disregard for filing and paying the tax by the IRA owner. For example, in *Peek & Fleck v. Commissioner,* which is discussed in Chapter 5, the IRS was able to obtain an accuracy-related penalty on taxes not paid by the IRA owners personally following a prohibited transaction in their IRAs. 140 T.C. 12 (2013). The IRA owners didn't pay the tax personally because they believed it was not subject to tax since it was in their IRAs. The IRS was successful in obtaining this penalty in *Peek & Fleck* because the IRA owners did not rely on professional advice or a reasonable legal position as to whether the transaction in question was a prohibited transaction. As a result, the IRS was able to obtain an additional penalty of 20% on top of taxes owed personally by the IRA owners.

SEPARATE IRA OR RETIREMENT ACCOUNTS

If you have separate IRAs or retirement accounts that were not involved in the prohibited transaction, those accounts are not distributed and are not subject to the consequences of a prohibited transaction in a separate account. As a result of this separate treatment, many self-directed IRA owners who engage in a transaction where it is unclear whether there is a prohibited transaction under current law benefit by using an IRA that is separate from their other retirement accounts and investments. By using a separate account, the IRA owner can limit the risks of an uncertain prohibited transaction solely to the account involved in the transaction and can isolate his or her other accounts from the possible consequences of a prohibited transaction.

PROHIBITED TRANSACTION CASE EXAMPLE

Let's run through an example of a prohibited transaction to illustrate how the rules work.

CASE EXAMPLE: IRA owner is 45 and uses her traditional self-directed IRA to purchase a rental property in 2009. IRA owner leases the property for 1 year to an unrelated third party and properly collects the income and pays the expenses from the IRA. In 2011, IRA owner leases the property to IRA owner's son and IRA owner's son pays rent to the IRA. Since the lease is a *transaction* and the son is a *disqualified person,* the IRA has engaged in a prohibited transaction.

In 2012, after the prohibited transaction occurred, the IRA sells the property to an unrelated third party, and the IRA receives a gain of $50,000.

In 2013, the IRA owner's self-directed custodian becomes aware of the prohibited transaction and distributes the entire IRA and reports a prohibited transaction by filing IRS Form 1099-R and references the reason for distribution as a prohibited transaction (Distribution Code 5, 1099-R). The 1099-R is issued for year 2011, the beginning date of when the prohibited transaction occurred (lease to IRA owner's son). The value of the distribution is the fair market value of the IRA as of January 1, 2011 (the year of the prohibited transaction). The IRA owner must now complete the following.

1. Report the 1099-R and the taxable distribution amount on the IRA owner's 2011 tax return. If the IRA owner has already filed a 2011 tax return, the IRA owner will need to amend her return to report the income.

2. Pay the taxes and applicable penalty. Since the IRA owner in the example was under age 59 ½ at the time of the prohibited transaction, the IRA owner will also pay a 10% early withdrawal penalty on the amount distributed.

3. The assets owned in the IRA are now the property of the IRA owner. So, for example, the rental property owned by the IRA will need to be deeded from the IRA to the IRA owner personally, and the cash in the IRA will be distributed to the IRA owner personally. Certain amounts of cash in the IRA may also be withheld and paid directly to the IRS by the self-directed IRA custodian for penalties and taxes owed.

4. Calculate and pay any taxes due on income from the property from 2011 to 2012. The taxes will be reported and paid on the IRA owner's personal tax return. For the gain on the sale of the property in 2012, the IRA owner will report that capital gain on the IRA owner's personal return

and will be required to pay capital gains tax on the taxable gain from the sale of the property. Since the property was sold after the prohibited transaction occurred, the taxes on the sale of the property must be paid by the IRA owner personally, and the IRA owner has lost the IRA benefits of having the sale of assets exempt from capital gains taxes.

While prohibited transactions rarely occur, self-directed IRA owners must ensure that they are conducting their transactions in compliance with the rules in order to avoid the negative consequences outlined above.

PROHIBITED TRANSACTIONS ENGAGED IN BY THE IRA OWNER

As more fully outlined above, the consequences of a prohibited transaction depend on the type of account (Roth or Traditional) and the age of the IRA owner. For determining the consequences of Roth IRAs, you must also consider the length of time that the Roth IRA was in existence beginning on the first day of the tax year for which the Roth IRA was funded or converted. For purposes of the chart, the reference below to a Traditional IRA and the consequences are the same for standard traditional IRAs, SEP IRAs, SIMPLE IRAs, and health savings accounts (HSA).

TABLE 7.1, PROHIBITED TRANSACTION CONSEQUENCES

TRAD OR ROTH	AGE OF IRA OWNER	ROTH IRA YEARS	PROHIBITED TRANSACTION ("PT") CONSEQUENCES
Traditional IRA	Under 59 ½	n/a	1. Amount distributed is taxed as income to IRA owner personally. 2. Penalty of 10% is applied. 3. All income from account after PT occurred is taxable personally to the IRA owner.
Traditional IRA	59 ½ or older	n/a	1. Amount distributed is taxed as income to IRA owner personally. 2. *No* 10% early withdrawal penalties. 3. All income from account after PT occurred is taxable personally to the IRA owner.

TABLE 7.1, PROHIBITED TRANSACTION CONSEQUENCES (CONT'D)

TRAD OR ROTH	AGE OF IRA OWNER	ROTH IRA YEARS	PROHIBITED TRANSACTION ("PT") CONSEQUENCES
Roth IRA	Under 59 ½	Over or Under 5 Years, Same Result	1. Amounts distributed are taxed as income to Roth IRA owner, except for amounts that comprise contributions or conversion amounts where taxes were paid. So, in other words, all investment gains and income are subject to taxes and are to be included as income to the IRA owner personally. 2. Amounts distributed are subject to 10% early withdrawal penalties except for amounts that comprise contributions or conversions held 5 years where taxes were paid. So, in other words, only the investment gains and income are subject to the 10% early withdrawal penalty. 3. All income from account after PT occurred is taxable personally to IRA owner.

TABLE 7.1, PROHIBITED TRANSACTION CONSEQUENCES (CONT'D)

ACCOUNT TYPE TRAD. OR ROTH	AGE OF IRA OWNER	ROTH IRA YEARS	PROHIBITED TRANSACTION ("PT") CONSEQUENCES
Roth IRA	59 ½ or older	Over 5 years	1. *No* taxes are due on the amount distributed. 2. *No* 10% early withdrawal penalties. 3. All income from account after PT occurred is taxable personally to IRA owner.
Roth IRA	59 ½ or older	Under 5 years	1. Amounts distributed are taxed as income to Roth IRA owner, except for amounts that comprise of contributions or conversion amounts held 5 years where taxes were paid. So, in other words, all investment gains and income are subject to taxes and are to be included as income to the IRA owner personally. 2. *No* 10% early withdrawal penalties. 3. All income from account after PT occurred is taxable personally to Roth IRA.

PROHIBITED TRANSACTIONS ENTERED INTO BY A
PERSON OTHER THAN THE IRA OWNER

If a prohibited transaction is entered into by a party other than the IRA owner, then the consequence is an initial excise tax of 15% on the amount involved and an additional tax of up to 100% on the amount involved if the prohibited transaction is not corrected within the taxable period. IRC § 4975 (a), IRC § 4975 (b). "Correction" occurs by un-doing the transaction to the extent possible and returning the IRA to the position it was in before the prohibited transaction occurred. IRC § 4975 (f)(5).

The time period to correct the prohibited transaction is the tax year in which the prohibited transaction occurred. IRC § 4975 (b). However, if the taxable year has passed, the IRS allows a prohibited transaction to be corrected within 90 days after the IRS mails a notice of deficiency, alleging the prohibited transaction. IRS, Retirement Plans, *Retirement Plan FAQs Regarding Plan Investments*, Q: 5, (Rev. 11-21-2013).

For example, a financial advisor to the IRA owner independently uses the IRA account to buy stock in XYZ Start-Up Corporation from the financial advisor's personal account for $20,000. Since the purchase of stock by the IRA was from a disqualified person (in this instance the advisor is a fiduciary and is therefore a disqualified person), the IRA has engaged in a prohibited transaction. Since the prohibited transaction was independently engaged in by the financial advisor, and not the IRA owner, the consequence to the prohibited transaction is a penalty of 15% on the amount involved, $20,000, which would result in a penalty of $3,000. This amount is owed by the disqualified person involved in the transaction, which in this case is the financial advisor.

Correction of this prohibited transaction could occur by transferring the stock now owned by the IRA back to the financial advisor's personal account in exchange for the $20,000 paid by the IRA for the stock. If there has been a significant change in value to the stock during the time period when the IRA was the owner, then a third-party professional will likely need to be engaged to determine what value may be retained by the IRA and what must be returned to the financial advisor. The third-party professional's opinion will be subject to the highest fiduciary standards upon audit or examination by the IRS.

PROHIBITED TRANSACTION CONSEQUENCES TO QUALIFIED PLANS SUCH AS SELF-DIRECTED 401(k)s

If you have a 401(k) or other qualified plan, the consequences of a prohibited transaction are an initial excise tax of 15% on the amount involved in the prohibited transaction and an additional tax up to 100% on the amount involved if the prohibited transaction is not corrected. IRC § 4975 (a), IRC § 4975 (b). This 15% excise tax and additional 100% tax are applied to all qualified plan prohibited transactions regardless of whether the disqualified person involved was the account owner or another disqualified person (e.g., spouse, children, etc.).

For example, let's say that your 401(k) owns some land and that the 401(k) owner personally pays the property taxes for the land of $1,000 with personal funds. This $1,000 payment would be subject to a 15% tax, which would be $150. The additional tax of 100%, which would result in an amount due of $1,000, could be applied if the prohibited transaction is not corrected.

In this scenario, it is unlikely that the 100% tax would be applied as correction can be accomplished by having the 401(k) account reimburse the account owner for the $1,000 expense that was paid personally. After the reimbursement correction, the plan is back in the same position that the plan would have been in if the prohibited transaction did not occur and if the 401(k) paid the expense in the beginning.

LEGAL TIP
❖ Prohibited transactions in a 401(k) or other qualified plan are subject to a *15% penalty on the amount involved*. In qualified plans, there is no distinction as to whether the disqualified person was the account owner or not. The entire account is *not* distributed as occurs in a prohibited transaction between an IRA and the IRA owner. There is also a potential 100% penalty if the prohibited transaction is not corrected. Essentially, the qualified plan rule is the same rule that applies to prohibited transaction between an IRA and a disqualified person other than the IRA owner.

HOW ARE PROHIBITED TRANSACTIONS DISCOVERED OR ALLEGED?

A prohibited transaction is usually discovered or alleged in one of three instances: First, the self-directed IRA custodian becomes aware of the prohibited transaction and distributes the account by filing a 1099-R. Second, the IRS audits the IRA or some other party involved in the IRA's investment and discovers a prohibited transaction. Upon discovery of a prohibited transaction, the IRS will recalculate taxes owed by the IRA owner and will issue a notice of deficiency for the taxes due by the IRA owner. Or, third, the IRA owner enters bankruptcy, and the bankruptcy trustee or a creditor seeks to disqualify the IRA by claiming that it engaged in a prohibited transaction. IRAs are generally exempt from creditors in bankruptcy up to certain amounts but can be distributed and can lose their exempt status if the trustee or creditor can show that the IRA engaged in a prohibited transaction. The motivation of the trustee or creditor to allege a prohibited transaction is to disqualify the IRA and its creditor protections. If disqualification is successful, the Trustee can access the funds in the former IRA account, which can be used to pay the creditors of the IRA owner.

STATUTE OF LIMITATIONS
FOR PROHIBITED TRANSACTIONS

The statute of limitations for a prohibited transaction may be 3 years, 6 years, or unlimited. The standard statute-of-limitations deadline is 3 years after the IRA filed a tax return disclosing the prohibited transaction. IRC § 6501(a). IRS Form 5329 or IRS Form 5330 is the applicable return that is filed to declare a prohibited transaction and to pay any applicable taxes and penalties. IRS, *Instructions for Form 5329*, Additional Taxes on Qualified Plan (Including IRAs), pg. 2. (2017), IRS, *Instructions for Form 5330*, Return of Excise Taxes Related to Employee Benefit Plans (Rev. Dec. 2013).

IRS Form 5329 is what is filed if the IRA engaged in a prohibited transaction with the IRA owner or other fiduciary. IRS Form 5330 is what filed if the IRA engaged in a prohibited transaction with a disqualified person who was not a fiduciary (e.g. not making the IRA's investment/transaction decisions).

The 3 year statute-of-limitations can be extended up to 6 years when a return was filed when there was a substantial omission from the return that related to the prohibited transaction. IRC §

6501(e)(1), IRS Tax Exempt and Government Entities, Chapter 11 Statute of Limitations, Training 4213-021 (Rev. April 2002). But what is substantial enough to allow the IRS up to 6 years? In *Thiessen v. Commissioner*, 146 T.C. No. 7 (2016), the Tax Court held that the statute of limitations period may be extended an additional three years for a prohibited transaction when the amount of the prohibited transaction, which was not reported, results in an increase of greater than 25% of the taxpayers gross income for the year in question pursuant to IRC § 6501(e)(1). In other words, if the taxpayer had $100K in annual gross income and if the prohibited transaction would result in a 1099-R of greater than $25K then the IRS will be allowed to pursue the prohibited transaction for an additional three years up to a total of six years.

The worst case scenario, is an indefinite statute of limitations for the IRS to allege prohibited transactions. An indefinite statute-of-limitations applies when there has been a false return, a willful attempt to evade tax, or when no return was ever filed. IRC § 6501(c)(1),(2),(3).

Since the filing of IRS Form 5329 rarely happens, the legal statute-of-limitations for most prohibited transactions is indefinite. This means that the IRS may allege a prohibited transaction at any time.

LEGAL TIP
❖ Unless the IRA files a tax return and discloses the prohibited transaction to the IRS, the applicable statute of limitations for prohibited transactions is indefinite. Practically speaking though, the IRS does not normally investigate prohibited transactions past 6 years except when there is clear evidence of tax fraud or evasion.

According to the *Internal Revenue Agent Field Manual*, IRS agents are instructed to treat all prohibited transactions as if the 3 year rule applied in order to minimize issues with taxpayers who may claim they are subject to the 3 year rule. *Internal Revenue Manual* 4.72.11.6. (8/13/2013, www.irs.gov). In order to pursue prohibited transactions past the 3 year statute of limitations, an IRS revenue agent must obtain approval from IRS Area Counsel. *IRS Tax Exempt and Government Entities Manual*, Chapter 11 Statute of Limitations, Training 4213-021, pg. 5. (Rev. April 2002).

FREQUENTLY ASKED QUESTIONS

Q. What happens if I've engaged in a prohibited transaction with my own IRA? I used my IRA to buy some stock from myself personally in a small privately held company.

A. The IRA is disqualified as an IRA as of the date of the prohibited transaction. All assets owned by that IRA account are deemed personally owned by you as of the date of the prohibited transaction. A distribution and 1099-R from your custodian will be reported to the IRS at the fair market value of the IRA as of January 1 of the year in which the prohibited transaction occurred. You are now responsible for any taxes and penalties from the distribution. Additionally, the assets that were held by the IRA in a tax-favored status are now held personally and are subject to personal taxes.

Q. I've received a notice of deficiency from the IRS where they allege that I engaged in a prohibited transaction with my IRA. I disagree with the IRS. How do I challenge this?

A. You may resolve your case with the IRS Appeals Office and with the U.S. Tax Court. You typically only have 90 days to challenge the IRS written notice of a prohibited transaction and re-determination of tax. In most prohibited transaction instances, you will challenge the prohibited transaction in U.S. Tax Court. While the case is pending in the Tax Court you are given the opportunity to resolve the case administratively with the IRS Appeals Office. If resolution does not occur to your satisfaction, then the case proceeds in Tax Court.

Q. I've had a Roth IRA for 10 years and engaged in a prohibited transaction personally with my Roth IRA. I understand that the Roth IRA is disqualified and that the fair market value of the account is distributed to me as of January 1 of the year of the prohibited transaction. I'm 52 years old; is the Roth IRA distribution taxable to me?

A. Since you are under age 59 ½, the amounts distributed that are investment gains or returns in the Roth IRA will be subject to taxes *and* the 10% early withdrawal penalty. The amounts distributed that are contributions or that were part of a conversion are not subject to taxes or penalties and are received tax free (since tax was already paid on these amounts).

CHAPTER 8: Advanced Self-Directed IRA Investment Issues

In addition to the prohibited transaction rules found in IRC § 4975, there are some additional legal concepts that are applicable in determining whether a self-directed retirement plan's investment is lawful. We've already discussed in Chapter 2 how an IRA cannot own collectibles, life insurance, or s-corporation stock. This chapter outlines some additional restrictions and covers advanced planning topics. This chapter covers the effects of the Exclusive Benefit Rule, the Step Transaction Doctrine, the Plan Asset Rule, and the DOL Interpretive Bulletin on Prohibited Transactions.

KEY POINTS
▪ *IRA investments must be made at fair market value at the time of the investment. Special consideration or unfair terms for the IRA will violate the exclusive-benefit rule.*
▪ *The prohibited transaction rules cannot be avoided by using a "straw person" in the middle of a transaction between a disqualified person and an IRA. These arrangements violate the step transaction doctrine.*
▪ *If the plan asset rule applies to a company then the company is subject to the prohibited transaction fiduciary standards as if it were the IRA transacting with others.*
▪ *Investment structures whereby an IRA invests into a company and the company is then required to transact with a disqualified person, will violate the DOL's Interpretive Bulletin and will likely result in a prohibited transaction.*

EXCLUSIVE BENEFIT RULE

The Exclusive Benefit Rule requires that all investments from a retirement account must be made for the benefit of the retirement account. IRC § 408(a). The IRS has explained that the prohibited transaction rules and the exclusive benefit rule are related rules and that in many instances a violation of the prohibited transaction rules will also result in a violation of the Exclusive Benefit Rule. *Internal Revenue Manual*, Section 4.72.11.1.2, Prohibited Transactions (www.irs.gov, 2013).

For example, if an IRA owner uses his or her IRA to purchase new stock from a business in need of capital and the majority of the company is owned by the IRA owner personally, this purchase of stock would violate the prohibited transaction rules as it would be a transaction with a disqualified person. This purchase would also violate the Exclusive Benefit Rule since the retirement account's investment appears to be used to benefit the IRA owner's personal business as opposed to benefiting the retirement account.

There are a couple of key factors to consider in determining whether the Exclusive Benefit Rule has been violated in an IRA. These factors are outlined in the *Internal Revenue Manual*, Section 4.72.11.1.3, Prohibited Transactions (www.irs.gov, 2013), and are as follows:

1. The cost of an investment must not exceed its fair market value at the time of the investment.
2. A fair return commensurate with the prevailing rate must be provided.

The first rule of self-directed IRA investments is to avoid transactions with disqualified persons, but the second most important rule is to ensure that fair market value is being paid, and transactions are at "arm's length." While a sister, brother, and friend are not disqualified persons under IRC § 4975, any investment with these parties must be scrutinized to ensure that fair market value is being paid. For example, if an IRA owner loans money from his or her IRA to his or her brother at 1%, this loan would violate the Exclusive Benefit Rule since the loan was not at fair market value when the prevailing market rate was 5%.

Additionally, the purchase or sale of company stock, LLC or LP interest, or any other retirement plan asset where fair market value is not being charged would violate the Exclusive Benefit Rule. If the Exclusive Benefit Rule has been violated by an IRA, then the entire IRA is disqualified and it loses its tax exempt status. *Id. at* 4.72.11.1.2. This is the same result that occurs in the event of a prohibited transaction, as discussed in Chapter 7.

In summary, the Exclusive Benefit Rule requires an IRA to pay and receive fair market value when conducting investment transactions. Any special treatment because of a relationship to the IRA owner, regardless of whether the person is a disqualified person, will always violate the Exclusive Benefit Rule.

STEP TRANSACTION DOCTRINE

The Step Transaction Doctrine is a legal principle applicable to structuring IRA investments and prevents an IRA owner from unfairly adding additional steps into a transaction in an effort to avoid a prohibited transaction. This doctrine applies to most provisions of the tax code and was first used in *Gregory v. Helvering*, 293 U.S. 465 (1935). With regard to self-directed IRA investments, the Step Transaction Doctrine typically arises when an IRA owner is trying to benefit from his or her IRA's investments and is using a "straw person" to be part of the transaction in place of the IRA owner or other disqualified owner.

For example, an IRA owner who is a real estate broker wants to receive the buyer's agent commission on the purchase of real estate for his or her IRA. Obviously, the IRA owner could not be the agent and receive the commission payment directly as this would be a prohibited transaction. However, what if the payments were restructured such that the IRA owner instead listed a friend as the agent or broker and had an arrangement with that friend whereby the friend would serve as a "straw person" to simply receive the commission and would then pay that commission to the IRA owner? This arrangement would violate the Step Transaction Doctrine and would result in a prohibited transaction. While you can analyze this transaction on its face and say that the fee from the IRA's investment is being paid to a non-disqualified person and therefore it is not a prohibited transaction, the extra step is being created and implemented solely to defeat the tax code and serves no other economic purpose in the transaction. Consequently, the Step Transaction Doctrine would apply and the extra step would be disregarded.

As a result of the Step Transaction Doctrine, IRA owners cannot create "straw person" steps into their transactions in order to avoid application of the prohibited transaction rules. These "straw persons" or additional steps in the transaction will be disregarded and the courts will typically apply the prohibited transaction and other rules applicable to IRAs as if the extra steps did not occur.

THE PLAN ASSET RULE

The Plan Asset Rule is one of the most commonly

misunderstood rules that can apply to self-directed IRA investments. The Plan Asset Rule is found at Code of Federal Regulations § 2510.3-101 and provides that assets of a company can be deemed assets of a retirement plan, and thus, the laws effecting retirement plan investments apply to the company where the plan is invested.

For example, if my retirement plan invests into an investment company partnership and owns 40% of the equity ownership of the company, then under the Plan Asset Rule, the *company* is subject to the rules affecting my retirement plans investments. The consequence of this is that the company is subject to the prohibited transaction rules and cannot engage in a transaction with a disqualified person to my retirement plan (e.g., IRA). Additionally, the company and its management are subject to fiduciary standards, and the company must meet the highest levels of care applicable to a fiduciary, which include avoiding conflict-of-interest transactions and duties of prudence.

If the Plan Asset Rule applies, this does not mean that my IRA cannot invest into the company. Rather, it simply means that the Company is subject to the following restrictions, among others.

1. The Company must ensure that all activities, expenses, payments, and investments of the Company do not result in a prohibited transaction for any retirement plan member of the Company. In order to comply with this, the Company must know every disqualified person of a retirement plan owner and must avoid transaction between the company and any of these disqualified persons.
2. The Company is subject to fiduciary standards for its conduct, investments and payment of expenses. This is an

extremely high standard and creates significant liability to the company and its management.

WHEN DOES THE PLAN ASSET RULE APPLY

According to 29 C.F.R. § 2510.3-101(f), the Plan Asset Rule applies to a plan when it invests into a company and when that company is owned 25% or more by retirement plans.

While the Plan Asset Rule applies when a company is owned 25% or more by retirement plans, the Plan Asset Rule oftentimes can be disregarded because there are numerous exceptions to the Rule. If an exception applies to a company, then the Plan Asset Rule does not need to be followed by the company.

The exceptions to the Plan Asset Rule are outlined in the chart below.

TABLE 8.1, PLAN ASSET RULE EXCEPTIONS

Exception to Plan Asset Rule	When It Applies
Operating Company	An Operating Company is a company that is "in the production or sale of a product or service other than the investment of capital". 29 C.F.R. § 2510.3-101(c).
Real Estate Operating Company (REOC)	A Real Estate Operating Company is a company that is invested 50% or more into real estate. 29 C.F.R. § 2510.3-101(e).
Venture Capital Operating Company (VCOC)	A Venture Capital Operating Company is a company that is invested 50% or more into venture capital investments. 29 C.F.R. § 2510.3-101(d).
Publicly Traded Company	A publicly traded company is not subject to the Plan Asset Rule.
Debt/Note Investments	If the plan's investment is into a debt instrument (no equity component) or note then the rule does not apply as it only applies to "equity" investments. 29 C.F.R. § 2510.3-101(b).

TABLE 8.1, PLAN ASSET RULE EXCEPTIONS (CONT'D)

SPECIAL RULE	SPECIAL RULE APPLICATION
SPECIAL NOTE: Company 100% Owned by Plan(s)	If a Company is 100% owned by retirement plans, then the Plan Asset Rule exceptions *do not* apply. As a result, in 100% Plan Owned Scenarios, you must always apply the Plan Asset Rule.

As a result of the definitions above, the Plan Asset Rule will not apply to most self-directed retirement plan investments.

Generally speaking, the self-dealing prohibited transaction rules will always be applicable in a company where a self-directed IRA has invested even if the company is owned less than 25% by retirement plans and even if there is an exception to the Plan Asset Rule. Consequently, self-directed IRA investors should always analyze the self-dealing prohibited transaction rules when a company where their retirement plan is an owner does business or conducts a transaction with a disqualified person.

For example, Sally's self-directed IRA owns 35% of a C corp that is a technology start-up company. The company is providing a product, and as a result it is an operating company, and the Plan Asset Rule does not apply to the company. However, this does not mean that the prohibited transaction rules can be forgotten and that Sally could use her IRA's influence as a large shareholder to make herself the president of the company at a significant salary. Rather, the employment of Sally or any transactions with disqualified persons of the IRA and the company must still be considered for any self-dealing prohibited transaction issues.

DOL INTERPRETIVE BULLETIN TO
PROHIBITED TRANSACTIONS

The Department of Labor ("DOL") issued 29 C.F.R. 2509.75-2 to demonstrate how the DOL would apply the prohibited transaction rules to interpret certain structures and investments from retirement plans. The pertinent portion for self-directed IRAs reads as follows:

> ...if a transaction between a party in interest [disqualified person] and a plan [IRA] would be a prohibited transaction, then such a transaction between a party in interest and such corporation or partnership will ordinarily be a prohibited transaction if the plan may, by itself, require the corporation or partnership to engage in such transaction.

For example, if a self-directed IRA invests into a corporation and requires that corporation to hire the IRA owner's spouse, then this would violate the DOL interpretive bulletin and would constitute a prohibited transaction since the IRA "required" the company to engage in a transaction with a disqualified person to the IRA.

The interpretive bulletin was used by the DOL in its Opinion 2006-01A and resulted in the finding of a prohibited transaction. Under this opinion, a self-directed IRA owned 49% of an LLC (the rest was owned by a non-disqualified person) which in turn leased property to a company that was majority owned by the IRA owner. Even though the IRA owned less than 50% of the LLC and was therefore not a disqualified person, the DOL relied on its own interpretive bulletin and stated that since the intent of the LLC at formation was to then lease property to a company majority controlled by the IRA owner, that the investment would constitute a prohibited transaction.

The lesson to be learned from the DOL Interpretive Bulletin is that a company in the middle of a transaction between a disqualified person and a self-directed IRA will be closely scrutinized, and if the company is required or if its purpose is then to engage in a transaction with a disqualified person, then there will likely be a prohibited transaction. The DOL views this as an "indirect" prohibited transaction, and the IRS will likely challenge these investment structures.

FREQUENTLY ASKED QUESTIONS

Q. Can my IRA loan my nephew (who is not a disqualified person) money at 1% interest? I would like to help him attend college.

A. No. This loan investment would violate the exclusive benefit rule as it is below a reasonable market rate and is not being made to benefit the account but rather a family member.

Q. Can my IRA invest into a company owned by my close friend and then my friend will pay me that money as a management fee or other payment so that it can be expensed from his company and so that I can get access to my retirement plan funds without taking an early withdrawal?

A No. This would amount to a step transaction and the IRS would disregard the investment into your friend's business and would instead look at the investment from your IRA being paid to you personally. This would result in a prohibited transaction. It would also likely be a self-dealing prohibited transaction since the only reason your IRA invested was because you understood the that funds would be used to pay you personally.

Q. I personally own shares in a private company and know that I cannot use my Roth IRA to buy my own shares, but could I use my Roth IRA to buy a partner's shares, and then I will sell my shares to my partner, who also wants to own his shares in his Roth IRA? We will use a third-party valuation (409A or other opinion) to set the price for the shares. Can we do this?

A. This cannot be done. While the Roth IRA's purchase of shares from a partner who is not a disqualified person is not a prohibited transaction on its face, the IRS would likely apply to the Step Transaction Doctrine to disregard the purchase from your partner and would instead look at the end result, which is that you personally sold shares and your Roth IRA gained shares. Therefore, this would likely constitute a prohibited transaction.

Q. If I used the Real Estate Operating Company ("REOC") or other exception to the Plan Asset Rule does that mean that an LLC owned by my IRA could pay me management fees or a salary for managing the company?

A. No. While the plan asset rule would not apply and while a payment from the LLC to you personally would not be a per se prohibited transaction, it would likely constitute a self-dealing prohibited transaction as you are personally benefitting from your retirement plan's investment when you take a management fee or other salary for managing the company. Note that where the IRA and other disqualified persons ownership is not significant and is not controlling (certainly below 50%), it is possible for a disqualified person (e.g., the IRA owner) to receive compensation, salary, or wages from the company, but those structures should be closely analyzed and structured.

Q. I would like to use my self-directed IRA to buy 40% of an LLC. The other 60% of the LLC will be owned by other non disqualified persons. The LLC will then buy an office building. I then intend to lease a portion of the space to a company I own 100%. Is this allowed?

A. Under the DOL Interpretive Bulletin, this would constitute a prohibited transaction if the LLC is "required" to then lease the property to your company. If the LLC that owns the building leased the property to others and then it happened to lease the building to a company the IRA owner owns 100%, then it may be permitted as long as the leasing wasn't required by the IRA when it invested into the LLC. However, if the LLC immediately leases the property to the IRA owner's company then it would likely fall under the DOL Interpretive Bulletin as a Prohibited Transaction as it appears that the sole reason for the IRAs investment was to benefit the IRA owner's own personal company.

CHAPTER 9: Self-Directed IRAs and Real Estate

Real Estate is the most common investment made by self-directed retirement plan investors. IRAs may invest in all types of real estate, including: residential and commercial properties, apartment complexes, land, water or mineral rights, and new construction and development. Real estate owned by a retirement plan must always be held for investment, and the IRA owner and disqualified persons (e.g., certain family) cannot live in or benefit from the property. Additionally, all income derived from the property should be paid directly to the IRA custodian for the benefit of the IRA, and all expenses for the property should be paid from the IRA (except when an IRA/LLC is used).

KEY POINTS
• *All contracts, deeds, and legal documents must be in the name of the IRA and not the IRA owner's name. When applicable, documents may be in the name of an IRA/LLC.*
• *The IRA owner and other disqualified persons may not receive a commission or other personal financial compensation for the IRA's purchase, management, or sale of real estate.*
• *Any loan in connection with the IRA's purchase must be nonrecourse and may result in UDFI tax.*
• *The IRA owner and certain family members (disqualified persons) may not reside at or personally benefit from the real estate. The real estate must be held for investment.*
• *The IRA owner and disqualified persons may oversee and direct repairs or management of the property through their IRA (or IRA/LLC as applicable) but the IRA owner and disqualified persons are prohibited from physically working on the property.*

PURCHASING REAL ESTATE WITH AN IRA

When purchasing real estate with an IRA, the IRA must be listed on the contract as the buyer, and it is the custodian of the IRA and not the IRA owner who signs the contract to bind the IRA. For example, the buyer to the contract would be ABC Trust Company FBO Sally Jones IRA. Once the contract is ready to be signed, the IRA owner will send it to his or her self-directed IRA custodian with a direction of investment form, instructing the custodian to sign the contract for the IRA. In most instances, the custodian of the IRA will require the IRA owner to sign the contract as "read and approved" so that the custodian is certain that the IRA owner has read the terms and approved them for his or her IRA. Remember, that the IRA is buying the property and not the IRA owner, so all contracts must be signed by the IRA custodian, who is the only party that can legally bind the IRA.

All funds due by the buyer and relating to the purchase of the property must be paid by the IRA, including: earnest money deposit or down payment, closing costs, inspection and due diligence costs, and the final funds necessary to close the property. Since the IRA owner is a disqualified person to his or her own IRA, the IRA owner (and any other disqualified person) cannot make the earnest money deposit and cannot cover other expenses to the property with personal funds outside of the IRA.

The purchase contract for a property cannot be assigned from a disqualified person (e.g., IRA owner) to an IRA. Similarly, the IRA cannot assign a property to the IRA owner or other disqualified persons. Assignment of a contract between an IRA and a disqualified person is a per se prohibited transaction. So, for example, it is *not* acceptable to get a property "under contract" in your personal name or under a company you own and then later assign it to your IRA.

LEGAL TIP
❖ The IRA is the party to all contracts and pays all money to acquire the property.
❖ The IRA owner should not use personal funds to acquire the property.
❖ The IRA needs to be on the initial contract to purchase the property. The IRA owner cannot assign the contract from the IRA owner to the IRA as that is a prohibited transaction.

A real estate contract could be assigned to the IRA from someone else who is not a disqualified person; conversely, any assignment from a disqualified person will likely constitute a prohibited transaction. In the event that an IRA owner mistakenly enters into a contract in their personal name, then the IRA owner should seek to unwind the contract in his or her personal name with the seller and should obtain a new contract, properly listing the IRA as the buyer. Any earnest money or deposits made by the IRA owner personally should be returned to the IRA owner personally and the IRA should then bear those expenses and contract requirements in the new contract.

If the contract cannot be undone in the IRA owner's personal name, then an addendum to the contact can be added, clarifying that the buyer is the IRA. The addendum should not transfer or assign the contract but shall instead clarify who the buyer is. For example, if John Smith is intending to use his IRA to buy a property and mistakenly listed himself as the buyer, then an addendum to the contact can be added, clarifying that the buyer is not John Smith but is ABC Trust Company FBO John Smith IRA. This should be done only as a second resort and in the case of mistake as there are some prohibited transaction issues involved when doing an addendum such as this. Again, the first attempt to correct the contracts should always be unwinding the contract in the IRA owner's name and obtaining a new contract with the IRA correctly listed as the buyer. The addendum practice should only be used in the case of mistake and when completing a new contract in the IRA's name is not possible.

NONRECOURSE LOANS & REAL ESTATE

It is possible for an IRA to obtain a loan in connection with its cash investment to purchase real estate. However, the loan must not result in an extension of credit prohibited transaction under IRC § 4975 (c)(1)(B). As discussed in Chapter 5, an extension of credit prohibited transaction will occur when an IRA owner's credit qualifies the IRA for the loan or when the IRA owner (or other disqualified person) personally guarantees a loan for the IRA.

As a result of the prohibited transaction issues, any loan obtained by the IRA to purchase real estate must be a nonrecourse loan. A nonrecourse loan is a loan where the lender's sole recourse in the event of default is to foreclose and take the property back. The lender does not have any additional recourse against the IRA or the IRA owner. Additionally, the qualification rules and criteria for an IRA compliant nonrecourse loan are solely based on the property being used to secure the loan.

MULTIPLE OWNER TITLE HOLDING OPTIONS

As discussed earlier, title to the investment must be held in the IRA's name. For example, the grantee and owner on the deed will be ABC Trust Company FBO Sally Jones IRA.

If the IRA is going to be on title to real property with other owners, then the multiple-party form of ownership must be tenants in common. Other forms of multiple-party title ownership, such as joint tenancy and tenants by the entirety, should *not* be used because those ownership interests have characteristics whereby ownership passes to the other party on title following the death of the owner. Because the IRA cannot die and because the IRA's ownership following the death of the IRA owner is determined based on the IRA beneficiary designations, the IRA's ownership cannot be transferred via joint tenancy or survivorship methods. Tenants in common, on the other hand, is a form of holding title whereby upon the death of an owner, the title to their ownership passes to his or her heirs. In the case of the death of the IRA owner, the heirs to the IRA pursuant to the IRA beneficiary designation forms will receive the ownership to the property. This change of ownership upon death of the IRA owner may occur by an inherited IRA to the beneficiary or via distribution to the beneficiary.

LEGAL TIP
❖ If the IRA is on title to real property with other parties the form of multiple-party ownership to the property should be tenants in common.

LEASING THE REAL ESTATE & MANAGEMENT STRUCTURES

When IRA-owned property is held for rent, it must be structured such that rental income is received by the IRA, and expenses are paid by the IRA. The IRA owner and other disqualified persons cannot personally be the "middle man" by paying expenses personally or by collecting the rent in their personal account and then forwarding the funds to the IRA. There are essentially three different methods whereby the IRA may be structured to properly collect rent and pay expenses.

TABLE 9.1 METHODS TO MANAGE REAL PROPERTY OWNED BY A SELF-DIRECTED IRA

3 METHODS TO MANAGE THE PROPERTY
❖ *Manage directly through the IRA.* Money goes to the IRA custodian, and expenses are paid by the custodian at the direction of the IRA owner.
❖ *Property manager.* The IRA hires a property manager who manages the property and receives the income and pays property expenses. Cash flow is returned to the IRA.
❖ *IRA/LLC.* Under the IRA/LLC, the IRA owner is the manager of the IRA/LLC and receives income and pays expenses from an IRA/LLC checking account. The IRA/LLC structure is very common in IRA-owned real estate investments.

First, the IRA may be receiving the income directly and paying the expenses. This method involves a lease between the IRA and the tenant directly. Under this method, the tenant pays rental income to the IRA (e.g., ABC Trust Company FBO Sally Jones IRA) and sends the actual payment to the IRA custodian. The custodian then deposits that income into the respective IRA. If expenses are due, the IRA owner will need to direct the custodian to pay them by completing a written form (e.g., payment authorization letter) and instructing the IRA custodian as to the expenses to be paid from the IRA. There is usually a fee each time an instruction letter is issued to a self-directed IRA custodian. This method can be tedious and can be fee intensive ,and as a result, it is not the most common way of managing a rental property held by an IRA. This method does work well for properties that do not have on-going transactions or liability issues such as raw land.

Second, the IRA hires a property management company who receives the rental income to the property and pays the expenses to the property. The property management company cannot be a disqualified person to the IRA owner, and the property management company will typically take a percent of the rental income collected as payment for their services. Under this method, the IRA enters into an agreement with the property management company, and the property management company then enters into leases with respective tenants. The IRA receives rental income minus property expenses and fees charged by the property management company.

Third, many IRA owners with rental property decide to use a structure known as an IRA/LLC. This structure is more fully outlined and explained in Chapter 13. Under the IRA/LLC structure, the IRA invests into a newly created specialty LLC, and the IRA's investment is then the ownership of the LLC. The IRA will invest an amount designated by the IRA owner into the LLC, and then funds are typically deposited into an LLC checking account at a bank selected by the IRA owner. See the following

DIAGRAM 9.1, IRA/LLC STRUCTURE FOR REAL ESTATE

Self-Directed IRA   IRA/LLC   Rental Property

The IRA owner then, as manager of the LLC, signs the contract for the LLC to purchase the real estate. The property should close in the LLC name with funds from the LLC bank account, and the LLC then, in turn, rents the property, receives the income, and pays the expenses all from the LLC checking account. The LLC is entirely owned by the IRA, and all funds in the LLC checking account must eventually be returned to the IRA when the IRA owner desires to take a distribution. Please refer to Chapter 13 for an extensive discussion as to the IRA/LLC structure.

Regardless of the method used to own and manage the IRA-owned rental property, the property cannot be leased to a disqualified person. So, for example, the IRA cannot purchase a property and allow the IRA owner's son to lease the property as that lease would be a transaction with a disqualified person, which results in a prohibited transaction.

In addition to prohibited transactions that are involved in leasing the property to family members, the IRA owner should closely analyze any leasing arrangement to a company where the IRA owner or other disqualified persons are owners of the IRA or company. For example, any lease to a company that is owned 50% or more by the IRA owner or other disqualified persons would constitute a prohibited transaction. IRC § 4975(e)(2)G). Additionally, any investment structure whereby the IRA invests into a company (even when the IRA owns less than 50%) and the company is then required (or its sole purpose is) to lease to a disqualified person would constitute a prohibited transaction as the IRA's investment cannot be made with the intent to benefit a disqualified person. DOL Advisory Opinion 2006-01A, 29 CFR 2509.72-2.

MANAGING THE REAL ESTATE

When managing IRA investment assets, the IRA owner should limit his or her activities to administrative and investment-oversight tasks. While it is permissible to administer the investment, it is generally viewed impermissible to physically work on investment assets (such as rental real estate) since such actions can constitute a per se prohibited or self-dealing prohibited transaction. IRC § 4975(c)(1)(C).

A Bankruptcy Court Judge recently interpreted the prohibited transaction rules to determine whether an IRA owner, who managed real estate owned by his IRA, committed a prohibited transaction. *In Re Cherwenka*, Case 13-57592-MGD (Bankr. N.D. 2014). The Court held that the IRA owner did not commit a prohibited transaction when he did the following.

- Researched and identified properties to buy
- Appointed and approved work on properties
- Oversaw payments on the property for work paid by the self-directed IRA.

The Court reasoned that these actions do not constitute a "transaction" between the IRA owner and the IRA and therefore cannot be a prohibited transaction. The Court further stated that,

...self-directed IRAs as qualified IRAs, necessarily implies that a disqualified person (the owner as fiduciary) will make investment decisions regarding the plan. *In Re Cherwenka,* Case 13-57592-MGD (Bankr. N.D. 2014).

The following table breaks down what activities are permissible and what activities are prohibited.

TABLE 9.2 PERMISSIBLE AND PROHIBITED MANAGEMENT ACTIONS BY DISQUALIFIED PERSONS

PERMISSIBLE	PROHIBITED
Making decisions as to the property manager or tenants. Making all decisions for the property. When to buy, sell, at what price, etc.	Taking title or entering into contracts in the IRA owner's personal name as opposed to the IRA (the IRA custodian should sign all contracts).
Setting terms for the lease or other legal agreements. When the property is owned directly by the IRA, any contract must be signed by the IRA custodian.	Receiving rental income in the IRA owner's personal account or paying IRA expenses from a personal account of the IRA owner.
Visiting the property and overseeing repairs and maintenance. Hiring contractors to do repair and maintenance.	Physical work on the property. Work by the IRA owner or other disqualified person (s) on the property is prohibited.

REAL ESTATE DEVELOPMENT & SHORT-TERM FLIPPING

An IRA may invest into real property that is being developed and may also purchase properties on a short-term basis and flip them for profit. A retirement plan's investment into real estate development or on real estate flips, however, can subject the IRA to a tax known as unrelated business income tax ("UBIT tax"). IRC § 511, 512. The UBIT tax applies to the net profits that arise from the development of real property or from property held without any investment intent (e.g., bought and held immediately for sale). Real property held for investment (e.g., rental, or held for 1 year or more) is exempt from UBIT tax so all efforts should be made to holding the property for investment as opposed to holding for development or acquiring and holding for immediate sale. Please refer to Chapter 15 for an extensive discussion as to when UBIT tax applies.

LEGAL TIP
❖ Significant short-term real estate transactions in an IRA can subject the IRA to UBIT tax.

AVOID OVER-EXTENDING THE IRA

The IRA owner should avoid overextending the IRA into an investment where the IRA may end up being unable to cover unexpected property expenses. For example, if the IRA owner has $300,000 in his or her IRA to purchase real property, he or she should avoid buying a $300,000 property as there may be unexpected repairs or costs, which the IRA may need to pay and that it would be unable to afford should those costs arise. The IRA could use rental income from the property, or the IRA owner may be able to make an annual contribution to the IRA to cover the shortfall. However, if those funds are inadequate, the IRA is left in a difficult position and may be unable to cover its own expenses.

The IRA owner (and other disqualified persons) cannot just pay the expenses owed by the IRA personally to cover the shortfall as that would constitute a transaction from a disqualified person and would be a prohibited transaction. I typically recommend that the IRA maintain 10% of the purchase price of the property on hand in a liquid investment to cover unexpected expenses. In other words, if the IRA buys a $250,000 property it would be well-served by having an additional $25,000 available in the self-directed IRA (or in other IRAs that could be transferred) to cover unexpected costs or expenses.

In the event that an IRA becomes overextended and cannot pay its obligations, the IRA owner may rely on Department of Labor Prohibited Transaction Exemption 80-26, which allows the IRA owner to loan money to his or her IRA so that his or her IRA may pay obligations that it owes. DOL PTE 80-26, 71 CFR 17917 *Amendment to Prohibited Transaction Exemption 80-26* (April 7, 2006).

Tom W. Anderson explained that PTE 80-26 (and related 2002-13) can be used "...if you held a rental property in your IRA that you had a mortgage on and you lost your tenant, you could lend money to your IRA to pay the mortgage." Anderson, Tom W., *Prohibited Transactions for Investors*, pg. 17, Retirement Industry Trust Association, 2012, http://ritaus.org.

This loan from the IRA owner to the IRA is specifically exempt from the prohibited transaction rules in IRC § 4975 and is permissible so long as the following conditions are present:

1. *The proceeds of the loan to the IRA must be for the payment of ordinary operating expenses of the plan, including the payment of benefits in accordance with the terms of the plan (e.g., required minimum distributions) or a purpose incidental to the ordinary operation of the plan.* Many practitioners take the position that a loan or other obligation incurred from an investment asset meets the criteria of an operating expense to the plan.

2. *The loan must be interest free and un-secured.* The loan should not cost the IRA money or jeopardize its assets.

3. *Any loan over 60 days must be in writing.* Most custodians who will allow an IRA owner to utilize PTE 80-26 will require a written agreement, regardless of the duration of the loan.

A PTE 80-26 loan from the IRA owner to the IRA must be coordinated and documented with the IRA custodian. It should not be used to fund new obligations or to make new investments but can be used as a last resort when the IRA owner can only save an investment asset by using PTE 80-26 and by loaning funds to his or her IRA.

CHECKLIST FOR IRA OWNERSHIP OF REAL ESTATE

✓ Is the contract and deed/title in the IRA's name (e.g., ABC Trust Company FBO Sally Jones IRA)?

✓ Did the IRA custodian sign the contract and legal agreements for the IRA, or, where applicable, did the manager of the IRA/LLC sign them?

✓ Did the IRA owner refrain from using personal expenses in purchasing and maintaining the property?

✓ If the IRA obtained a loan to purchase the property, was the loan nonrecourse, and is the IRA owner aware of possible UDFI taxes on any net profits from the debt?

✓ Is the IRA custodian, the property manager, or a properly established IRA/LLC, receiving the rental income and paying the expenses for the property?

✓ Does the IRA have sufficient capital available to cover an unexpected property expense?

✓ Is the IRA owner holding the property for investment, and are the IRA owner and other disqualified persons avoiding personal use or benefit from the property?

✓ Was the broker or agent in the transaction (when applicable) a non-disqualified person? Did the IRA owner refrain from personally benefitting from the IRA's purchase?

FREQUENTLY ASKED QUESTIONS

Q. Can I buy real estate with my IRA, hold it as a rental property, and then later move into that property and live in it during my retirement?

A. Yes, this is possible, however, before the IRA owner may live in the property he or she must first distribute the property from the IRA to the IRA owner personally. Once the property is distributed from the IRA to the IRA owner, it is owned personally and is not subject to the IRA rules that prohibit personal use. While many IRA owners consider this strategy, I frankly don't think it is that great of a structure for traditional IRAs because the property must first be distributed from the IRA, and upon distribution, the IRA owner will pay taxes (if Traditional; no tax if Roth) on the fair market value of the property. This type of distribution is called an in-kind distribution (distribution of property other than cash) and is acceptable for an IRA to do but requires an appraisal of the property at the time of the distribution to set the value of the distribution. The value of the distribution is what will be taxable to the IRA owner. Also, if the property is distributed before age 59 ½, then there is an additional 10% early withdrawal penalty.

Q. What do I do if I own property in my IRA and have to take a required minimum distribution ("RMD") from my IRA because I have turned 70 ½? I do not want to sell the property and don't have other cash in my IRA to take my RMD.

A. If you do not want to sell the property or if you are unable to sell, you can take a portion of the property owned by the IRA as an in-kind distribution to satisfy the RMD. For example, if the property is worth $100,000 and if your RMD for the year is $5,000, you would take a 5% tenant in common interest in the property as an in-kind distribution from the IRA to yourself personally. This is not a prohibited transaction because it is part of a distribution which is not a transaction. In the end, you would own 5% personally, and your IRA would own the remaining 95%. You need to be careful moving forward to make sure that you properly share expenses and income in this scenario. This is not the easiest course to satisfy RMD, but is an option if all others are unavailable.

Q. I'm obtaining a loan for a property with my IRA, and I live in California. The state law does not allow a mortgage lender to go after a borrower for any deficiency still left after foreclosure of the property. Does this anti-deficiency statute mean that any loan I obtain in California will be a nonrecourse loan?

A. No, a standard loan written in a state with anti-deficiency terms will still violate the rules for retirement plan nonrecourse loans, and as a result, will result in a prohibited transaction. This is because these loans still require the IRA owner's credit to be used or require a personal guarantee for the debt. As a result, they end up being a personal extension of credit to the IRA.

Q. My daughter is moving away to college. I'd like to buy a rental property in her college town with my IRA to let her stay at the property. Is this allowed? What if her friend is the tenant on the lease, and my daughter lives in the property as her roommate?

A. No, the daughter of an IRA owner is a disqualified person, and the leasing to her would be a prohibited transaction. Additionally, even if a non-disqualified person (the daughter's friend) was the tenant on the lease with the IRA, if the daughter is living at the property, she is a disqualified person benefitting from the IRA's property, which results in a self-dealing prohibited transaction.

CHAPTER 10: Promissory Notes and Loan Investments with a Self-Directed IRA

A self-directed IRA may lend money to another as an investment. In a loan investment, the IRA is the lender, and the party receiving the loan funds is the borrower. The borrower cannot be a disqualified person (e.g., IRA owner or certain family) as a loan to a disqualified person would result in a prohibited transaction. IRC § 4975(c)(1)(B). A loan from a self-directed IRA must be evidenced by written loan documents—such as a promissory note—and may be secured by real estate or other assets or may be un-secured.

KEY POINTS
▪ *A self-directed IRA may loan money to non-disqualified persons as an investment. An IRA cannot loan money to the IRA owner or family members of the IRA owner as they are disqualified persons.*
▪ *The loan from the IRA may be secured by real estate or other assets or may also be un-secured.*
▪ *Un-secured loans can be risky investments for an IRA, and the IRA owner must closely evaluate the borrower's credit worthiness.*
▪ *Equity participation notes, where the IRA gets a share of profits from a loan, can result in UBIT tax to the IRA.*

NOTE/LOAN INVESTMENTS WITH A SELF-DIRECTED IRA

A loan investment from a self-directed IRA is evidenced by a promissory note. A promissory note is the legal obligation between the IRA (the lender) and the borrower. The promissory note is typically only signed by the borrower. The terms of the promissory note will indicate, among other things, the amount loaned, the interest rate charged, the monthly payment amounts, and the due date of the loan.

In order to complete a loan investment from the self-directed IRA, the IRA owner will need a properly drafted promissory note with the pertinent terms included in the note. The borrower will sign the promissory note and any related loan documents, and the IRA owner will instruct the IRA custodian to fund the loan and to send the loan amounts to the borrower. If the promissory note is secured, additional documents will be required. For example, if your IRA is loaning money to someone who is purchasing real estate, then the loan should also include a deed of trust or mortgage.

A deed of trust or mortgage is a lien recorded against title to the real estate and protects the IRA (lender) against default. If the borrower defaults on a promissory note that is secured by a deed of trust or mortgage, then the IRA may foreclose and force the sale of the property to satisfy the amounts owed on the defaulted promissory note. Because a secured promissory note provides assets which an IRA may recover against, secured promissory notes are less susceptible to losses and default.

A promissory note may require monthly payments of principal and interest, or it may instead have one lump-sum payment due at the end of the note. A lump-sum promissory note, also known as a balloon note, usually includes a shorter term and allows the borrower to avoid monthly payments. Under a lump-sum promissory note, the principal and all accrued interest are due on the "balloon date" or final due date of the note.

Payments on a promissory note are typically received and processed by a third-party payment servicer or escrow company. The servicer receives and tracks payments from the borrower and sends them to the self-directed IRA custodian for deposit into the self-directed IRA. The servicer can also send missed/late payment notices to the borrower and can charge the borrower fees for late payments. The self-directed IRA custodian may receive monthly payments directly from the borrower for the benefit of the IRA but usually charges a nominal fee to receive the monthly payments.

The IRA owner should not personally receive the payments for the IRA as the IRA owner cannot deal with the income or assets of his or her IRA. IRC § 4975(c)(1)(E).

LEGAL TIP
❖ The interest rate charged on a loan by a self-directed IRA must be commercially reasonable and must be based on an arm's-length transaction.

The interest rate charged on the promissory note must be commercially reasonable. As discussed in Chapter 8, the interest rate charged on a promissory note must be based on an arm's-length transaction and must be at fair market value in order to be in compliance with the Exclusive Benefit Rule. IRC § 408(a). For example, an annual interest rate of 1% is not commercially available in the market and as a result a loan at 1% interest would likely violate the Exclusive Benefit Rule as it is not at fair market value.

On the other hand, a loan at 20% that is fully secured against real property could violate the Exclusive Benefit Rule as such a rate could exceed the current prevailing rates in the market. Excessively low or excessively high rates are suspect and may raise compliance questions with your custodian.

PROMISSORY NOTE TERMS & CHECKLIST

At a minimum, a promissory note should include the following terms:

- ✓ Amount loaned.
- ✓ Date of loan.
- ✓ Monthly payment amount and due date, or lump-sum due date.
- ✓ Interest rate being charged and type of rate. Annual, simple, or compounded interest, etc. Including an amortization table of the interest and payments is helpful to clarify the interest being charged and the payments due.
- ✓ Name of borrower. If the borrower is a company, it is helpful to obtain the personal guarantee of the owner(s) of the company.
- ✓ The IRA should be listed as the lender (e.g., ABC Trust Company FBO Sally Jones IRA).
- ✓ Default clause, stating what constitutes default.
- ✓ Acceleration clause, which allows the lender to call the entire note due if the borrower defaults on a payment.
- ✓ Attorney's and collection fees provisions, allowing the lender ("IRA") to re-coup expenses incurred in collecting on a defaulted loan.
- ✓ Place of payment. To a payment processor or escrow company or to the IRA custodian directly.

✓ Late payment fee/penalty.

✓ Description of collateral securing the loan (e.g., real estate or equipment) if the loan is secured. A deed of trust or mortgage should be included when the loan is secured by real property. If the loan is secured by equipment or other personal property, the loan is typically secured by a UCC-1 filing.

✓ If the loan is secured by real estate, obtain a title insurance policy in favor of the IRA (lender) protecting the title position of the deed of trust/mortgage.

✓ If the loan is secured by real estate, issue lender instructions to the title company or attorney handling the closing.

✓ Obtain a loan application from the borrower and collect the borrower's SSN, date or birth, address, employer, income, and assets. This information is vitally important in the event of default as it will assist in collection efforts. It is also helpful in the event that the loan is cancelled as a 1099-C should be issued to the un-collectible borrower.

✓ Loan document drafting fees and title insurance costs, which protect the lender (IRA), should be paid by the borrower at closing. This is the customary practice of lenders.

✓ Signature of the borrower and any guarantors to the loan. The lender to a loan typically does not sign the loan.

When drafting the promissory note, the IRA owner should rely on an attorney and/or a title company who is experienced in private lending transactions. There are many laws that apply to loans and the IRA owner needs to make sure that the loan is drafted properly so that is in compliance with these laws. For example, California has a usury law which restricts the interest charged on a loan to a maximum rate of 10 % annually. Calif. Const. Art. 15. California's 10% usury interest-rate restriction contains numerous exceptions, such as an exception when the loan is arranged by a broker and is secured by real property. These exceptions require strict compliance with certain procedures. Because of the strict compliance requirements an IRA owner should seek the guidance of competent professionals when drafting promissory notes and related loan documents for his or her IRA's investment.

SECURED NOTES

A secured promissory note is a loan whereby the borrower pledges certain assets (e.g., real property) to the lender as collateral for the loan. If the borrower defaults, the lender is able to sell the collateral to satisfy the amounts owed. Under a promissory note secured by real estate, the borrower allows the lender to place a lien (deed of trust or mortgage) against real property. Under a promissory note secured by personal property, a UCC-1 filing is the lien used. In the event of default by the borrower, the lender has rights to foreclose and sell the real estate at a foreclosure auction and can use the proceeds from the foreclosure sale to satisfy the amounts owed by the borrower.

NOTE SECURED BY REAL ESTATE

The document securing a promissory note against certain real property is either a deed of trust or a mortgage. Both a mortgage and a deed of trust are liens against title and secure a lender's loan. Whether a deed of trust or mortgage is used depends on the state where the real property subject to the lien is located. Some states only allow mortgages, and some states allow for deeds of trust. Both are liens against real property and secure the lender against default by the borrower; however, under a mortgage, the lender must go to court to enforce the default, whereas, under a deed of trust, the lender can foreclose after giving certain notices to the borrower and without having to get court approval. Regardless of whether the IRA is obtaining a deed of trust or a mortgage, the IRA owner needs to understand what other liens (e.g., other mortgages or deeds of trust) are already recorded on title as prior liens recorded before the IRA's lien have first priority to collect against the property. Make sure you work with a local title company or attorney to determine whether title is clear or not. Some custodians require that a title/escrow company, or an attorney is involved when an IRA loans money against real property.

Lastly, IRA owners should also use a lender instruction letter, which should be issued to the title company handling the closing. The instruction letter to the title company should include conditions which must be met before the loan funds are released to the borrower. Those conditions usually include confirmation that the borrower has signed the documents and confirmation that the deed of trust or mortgage is recorded in the lien position required (e.g., 1st lien position).

The following table breaks down the typical documents involved when an IRA loans money for the purchase of property.

TABLE 10.1, LOAN DOCUMENT EXPLANATIONS

Document	Purpose	Parties
Promissory Note	This is the legal obligation between the IRA (lender) and the borrower.	IRA is the lender. The lender can also sometimes be called the payee or the holder.
Deed of Trust	Secures the loan against certain real estate. Must be recorded on title. Watch out for liens in place ahead of the deed of trust.	The IRA is the beneficiary in the documents and the borrower is the trustor. There is also a trustee who is party to a deed of trust. The trustee is typically a title company or attorney in the state where the property is located.
Mortgage	Secures the loan against real estate. Must be recorded on title. Watch out for liens in place ahead of the mortgage.	The IRA is the mortgagee. The borrower is the mortgagor.

NOTES SECURED BY PERSONAL PROPERTY

Promissory notes can also be secured by personal property—such as equipment or stock—of the borrower. To properly secure personal property, there must be a security agreement and a UCC-1 filing. The security agreement is a contract between the borrower and lender that outlines the property being secured by the promissory note, and states the process in which the IRA (lender) may take the property from the borrower upon an event of default on the promissory note. A UCC-1 filing is a form document signed by the borrower and filed typically with the Secretary of State (or state corporation division, varies by state) where the property and/or the borrower is located. The UCC-1 filing should identify the borrower, the loan, the secured party (e.g., the IRA), and the property subject to the UCC-1 lien (e.g., equipment VIN, stock/unit share numbers, or other pertinent property description).

Secured promissory notes are preferred to un-secured notes because under a secured note, the lender has collateral to collect against in the event of default of the borrower.

UNSECURED NOTES

An IRA may loan money via an un-secured promissory note. An un-secured promissory note is a loan that is not secured by any real or personal property of the borrower. Un-secured promissory notes can be risky investments, and as a result, an un-secured loan should only be pursued after the IRA owner has properly analyzed the borrower's ability to re-pay the loan.

AVOIDING PROHIBITED TRANSACTIONS
IN PROMISSORY NOTES

A per se prohibited transaction occurs whenever an IRA lends money to a disqualified person. IRC § 4975(c)(1)(B). For example, a prohibited transaction would occur if the IRA owner issued a loan from his IRA to his daughter since children are disqualified persons.

A self-dealing prohibited transaction can occur when a disqualified person to an IRA benefits from an IRA's loan. IRC § 4975(c)(1)(D), (E). For example, in *Rollins v. Commissioner,* a retirement plan made a loan investment to a company where the retirement plan owner and his spouse were minority shareholders. T.C. Memo 2004-260. The borrowing company was owned 49% or less by disqualified persons (account owner and his spouse) and as a result was not a per se prohibited transaction. IRC § 4975(e)(2)(G). Although a per se prohibited transaction was avoided, the Tax Court still found a self-dealing prohibited transaction occurred since the account owner and his spouse (disqualified persons) would benefit indirectly as owners of the borrowing company.

PROFIT/EQUITY PARTICIPATION IN PROMISSORY NOTES

Under most promissory notes, the amounts payable to the lender are the principal amount of the loan plus interest. However, some loan investments contain clauses whereby the lender is also entitled to a share of the profits from the borrower's business. Another variation occurs when, in addition to a flat rate of interest, the lender is entitled to a share of the appreciation that occurs on a property acquired by the borrower with the loan. Both of these loan structures (share of profits, share of appreciation) are acceptable investments for an IRA. However, the payments to the IRA for profit/equity participation can result in UBIT tax. IRC § 511. UBIT tax is more fully explained in Chapter 15.

Let's first analyze loans that involve profit sharing clauses. For illustration purposes, an IRA loans XYZ, LLC $100,000 at 6% annual interest. XYZ, LLC is a new clothing company using the loaned funds to purchase new inventory. In addition to XYZ, LLC, paying interest, it also agrees to pay the IRA 10% of its profits for the first year of the loan. XYZ, LLC ends up with $200,000 in profit the first year.

Under the above scenario, XYZ, LLC will owe $6,000 in interest (6% annual rate) and $20,000 in profit sharing to the IRA. The $6,000 is interest income and is exempt from UBIT tax pursuant to the interest-income exemption. IRC § 512(b)(1). Unfortunately, the $20,000 in profit sharing is considered ordinary income; and as a result, the IRA is required to pay UBIT tax on the profit-sharing income.

Another variation of these types of loans is a promissory note that contains interest and also a share of the profits from the sale of property purchased with the loan. This type of a loan is sometimes referred to as an "equity kicker," shared appreciation mortgage, or a participating loan. For example, an IRA loans a borrower funds to buy a property at a fixed rate of interest of 5%. In addition to the fixed rate of interest, the borrower also agrees to pay the IRA (the lender) a 20% share of the profits from the sale of the property. The borrower intends to hold the property for five years before selling, and the term of the note is 5 years.

Under this scenario, the 20% share of profits paid to the lender would be a share of the capital gain income from the sale of the property and would be exempt from UBIT tax under the capital gain exemption to UBIT tax. IRC § 512(b)(5). Thus, both sources of income to the IRA are exempt from UBIT tax. The 5% of interest income is exempt under the interest income exemption and the 20% share of gains from the sale is exempt under the capital gain exemption. Consequently, UBIT tax would not apply to the IRA's income.

If, however, the borrower sold the property with a hold time of less than one year the gains from the sale of the property may be considered ordinary income as opposed to capital gain income, and as a result, the capital gain exemption may not apply when the borrower sells the property after a hold period of less than one year. Consequently, participating loans should not be pursued on short-term real estate ventures as the income from the profit sharing may be subject to UBIT tax.

DOES UBIT APPLY IF MY IRA MAKES NUMEROUS LOANS WITH DIFFERENT BORROWERS?

In Rev. Ruling 79-349, the IRS was asked whether UBIT would apply to a large employee retirement plan who makes hundreds of loans to individuals. The concern from the plan was that they make so many loans that their income may be considered to be income from a trade or business and thus subject to UBIT. The IRS determined that even though the number of loans would constitute a trade or business that the interest income exemption to UBIT, IRC § 512 (b)(1) and Reg 1.512(b)-1(a), would exclude that income from UBIT as it is still "interest income" and is thus exempt from UBIT tax. The IRS cautioned, however, that the interest income exemption only applies to interest income and points charged for the loan and that any application fees or other fees from the loan would fall outside the interest income exemption. In summary, self-directed IRAs who make numerous loans to different borrowers where interest and points are all that is charged will not be subject to UBIT on the income earned.

Please refer to Chapter 15 for a more in-depth discussion of the UBIT tax exemptions.

FREQUENTLY ASKED QUESTIONS

Q. Can I loan myself money from my IRA? I was able to take a loan from my 401(k) account. Can I do the same thing with my IRA?

A. Unfortunately, no. A loan from the IRA to the IRA owner is a prohibited transaction. There is a special rule and procedure available to employer plans like a 401(k) that allows you to loan yourself half the balance of the 401(k), not to exceed $50,000. This rule does apply to IRAs though.

Q. Can I loan my sister money at 0% interest. She needs the money to get caught up on her mortgage?

A. No, while you sister is not a disqualified person, your IRA can only make investments on commercially reasonable terms, and a loan at 0% isn't any kind of an investment but is a gift. If the loan were commercially reasonable (e.g., what a bank would loan her money at), then it is possible to loan her money from your IRA.

Q. I'd like to loan money to a start-up company. The promissory note terms will allow me to convert the loan to ownership in the business. Can I do this?

A. Yes, this is possible. This arrangement is often times referred to as a convertible note because it allows the lender to convert the note (debt) to company ownership (equity). Be aware that if you do convert to ownership and if the company is a pass-through company (e.g., LLC) operating an ordinary-income business (e.g., selling goods and services), then the IRA may incur UBIT tax on its profits.

Q. What happens if the borrower defaults and if the note becomes un-collectible? I'd like to just write off the loan in my IRA. Can I do this?

A. If the borrower defaults then the IRA needs to make collection attempts before a custodian will allow the loan to be "written off." You'll typically need to document these attempts. The IRA can hire a lawyer to make collection attempts. If there is a bankruptcy notice from the borrower and if the loan was discharged, then those documents can be supplied to the custodian, and they will typically write off the investment. If there isn't a bankruptcy, the IRA owner will need to otherwise document the un-collectability of the borrower (e.g., lawyer collection efforts). Some custodians also require that the borrower be issued a 1099-C for cancellation of debt before the IRA can write off the loan. This 1099-C to the borrower results in income to the borrower.

Q. Can my self-directed IRA make a loan investment into a company where I work and where I (and all disqualified persons) own 20% of the company?

A. This is possible. The IRA owner should not be involved in the negotiation of the note from the company/borrower side and should not be involved in the company decision making to enter into the loan. Also, the loan proceeds should not be used to compensate the IRA owner (or any other disqualified person). There are self-dealing prohibited transaction issues in an investment to a company where an IRA owner is employed or is a shareholder. Please refer to Chapter 6 for an extensive discussion of self-dealing prohibited transactions.

CHAPTER 11: Private Stock and Self-Directed IRAs: Start-Ups, LPs, LLCs, Hedge Funds, Private Equity, PPMs, and Crowdfunding

Retirement accounts may invest into publicly traded stock as well as non-publicly traded stock. IRAs may invest into corporations, limited liability corporations, or limited partnerships. The only restriction to company ownership for IRAs is that IRAs may not own shares of S corporations as an IRA does not qualify as an S corporation shareholder. IRC § 1361 (b)(1), IRS Letter Ruling 199929029, April 27, 1999.

KEY POINTS
■ *All stock certificates, LLC membership certificates, or LP interests should be in the name of the IRA (e.g., ABC Trust Company FBO Sally Jones Roth IRA).*
■ *An IRA typically cannot buy shares/units of a company owned 50% or more by disqualified persons (e.g., IRA owner and certain family).*
■ *IRAs invested into operational businesses (e.g., restaurant, tech company) that do not pay corporate taxes (e.g. not C corps) can be subject to UBIT tax. UBIT tax does not disqualify the IRA from investing it just means that the IRA has to report and pay some tax.*
■ *IRAs could potentially cause a self-dealing prohibited transaction when they invest into a company where the IRA owner (or other disqualified persons) has significant ownership or serves as an officer, director, or highly compensated employee.*

When an IRA invests into private-company stock or units, the IRA receives all the rights and responsibilities of owners of the company pursuant to the company documents. Because private-company ownership rules and responsibilities vary widely, the IRA owner must examine the legal documents of the private company prior to investing to ensure that the IRA is not subjecting itself to a prohibited transaction.

IRA INVESTMENT INTO COMPANY WHERE DISQUALIFIED PERSONS ARE EXISTING OWNERS

If the IRA owner and family members (e.g., disqualified persons) are not owners or are not part of management of the planned investment, then the IRA may invest into the company without having to analyze the prohibited transaction rules. However, when the company consists of disqualified persons as owners or members of management, then the IRA owner needs to analyze the participation of disqualified persons in the company to determine if the IRA's investment would result in a prohibited transaction.

An IRA should not invest into a company that is owned 50% or more by disqualified persons as the purchase of stock or units would constitute a transaction with a disqualified person and would result in a per se prohibited transaction. IRC § 4975 (e)(2)(G). For example, if John and his mother Sally each owned 50% of a company, neither John nor Sally could purchase new stock in the company with their IRAs as the company is owned 50% or more by disqualified persons.

If the company is owned 49% or less by disqualified persons, then it is possible for the IRA to invest into the company, but such investment still must be analyzed to ensure that there is not a self-dealing prohibited transaction. In DOL Advisory Opinion 2000-10A, Mr. Adler desired to invest his IRA into an investment partnership company where he and disqualified persons owned 20-25%. The company was managed by an unrelated third party to Mr. Adler's IRA. The DOL ruled that the investment of Mr. Adler's IRA into the company would not be a per se prohibited transaction since the company was owned less than 50% by disqualified persons. The DOL also did not find a self-dealing prohibited transaction but also declined to issue an opinion as to such.

In many instances, the shares or units being purchased by an IRA will be issued and sold by the company. When the shares or units are being sold by an existing owner, the IRA cannot buy the shares if the existing owner selling to the IRA is a disqualified person as that would result in a transaction with a disqualified person and would be a prohibited transaction.

For example, let's say that Steve owns 10% of a technology company and wants to sell his ownership to his daughter Kathryn's Roth IRA. Even if Steve is the only owner of the technology company that is disqualified to Kathryn's IRA and even if the company is owned 90% by non-disqualified persons, the purchase by Kathryn's Roth IRA of her father's stock is a per se prohibited transaction since Kathryn's father is disqualified to her Roth IRA. Kathryn's Roth IRA may purchase from any of the other owners of the company who are not disqualified to her Roth IRA, but her father's ownership is prohibited to her Roth IRA.

The following diagram outlines when an IRA may invest into a private company.

DIAGRAM 11.1, WHEN CAN AN
IRA INVEST INTO A PRIVATE COMPANY?

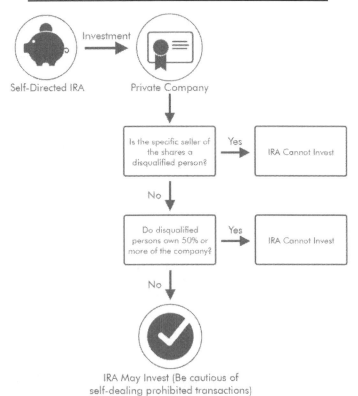

IRA May Invest (Be cautious of
self-dealing prohibited transactions)

IRA INVESTMENT INTO COMPANY WHERE DISQUALIFIED PERSON(S) ARE OFFICERS, DIRECTORS, OR EMPLOYEES

If the IRA owner or a disqualified person is an officer, director, or highly compensated employee of a company where his or her IRA plans to invest, the IRA's investment may constitute a self-dealing prohibited transaction if the IRA owner personally benefits by having his or her IRA invest.

LEGAL TIP
❖ If an IRA invests into a company where a disqualified person is employed or serves as an officer or director, the IRA investment cannot benefit the disqualified person's employment or compensation.

For example, in DOL Private Letter Ruling 8009091, an IRA owner planned to invest his IRA into a company where he was on the board of directors. In addition to being a director of the company, he also held a personal minority ownership stake in the company. The DOL ruled that the investment from the IRA would not constitute a per se prohibited transaction since the company was not a disqualified person to the IRA. Additionally, the DOL did not find a self-dealing prohibited transaction in the facts but stated one could occur if the IRA's purchase of stock in the company helped to secure the IRA owner's position as a director of the company. In other words, if the IRA's investment into the company where the IRA owner works results in the IRA owner receiving an increase in salary, a promotion, or any other additional financial compensation or benefit, then the IRA's investment will result in a self-dealing prohibited transaction.

There are a number of techniques and structures which may be implemented to avoid a self-dealing prohibited transaction occurring when the IRA owner (or other disqualified person) is a part of management and when his or her IRA is an owner of the company. The goal is to ensure that the IRA owner is unable to use his or her rights and powers as a shareholder to personally benefit himself or herself in his or her position as a director, officer, or employee. In many instances this can be accomplished by establishing boards or committees of non-disqualified persons who are independent and who have authority over the IRA owner in his or her personal position with the company.

IRA INVESTMENT INTO HEDGE FUND OR PRIVATE OFFERINGS

An IRA may invest into hedge funds, private offerings, regulation D investments and other offerings of company ownership that are in compliance with state and federal securities laws. In many instances, a PPM or hedge fund is established in accordance with Regulation D of the US Securities and Exchange Commission, whereby the company files a notice document with the SEC and prepares numerous offering documents which outline the investment, describe the background of the company and its management, and list the risk factors of the offering company. Many of these investment structures are only available to accredited investors. Accredited investors are investors who either have sufficient assets or annual income whereby the law determines that they can bear the risk of loss in certain non-publicly traded investments. By law, an accredited investor includes the following:

- Annual income of over \$200,000 single, or \$300,000 married, in each of the past 2 years.
- Net worth in excess of \$1,000,000, not including equity in investor's personal residence. 17 CFR 230.501.

In order for an IRA to qualify as an accredited investor, the IRA owner must qualify. For example, if the IRA owner has a qualifying \$1.5M net worth, then he or she may invest his or her IRA into a PPM, hedge fund, or Regulation D offering that is only available to accredited investors. If the investment is only available to accredited investors and if the IRA owner does not qualify as an accredited investor, then the IRA cannot invest into the offering.

There are numerous types of private stock/unit purchases that do not require an SEC notice filing. However, the IRA owner should seek legal counsel in reviewing any company documents to ensure that the offering company is in compliance with securities laws.

IRA INVESTMENT INTO HEDGE FUND OR PRIVATE OFFERING WHERE A DISQUALIFIED PERSON IS PART OF MANAGEMENT

If an IRA owner is part of management that runs the hedge fund or private offering company, then the investment from his or her IRA into the company that he or she (or other disqualified persons) manages may constitute a self-dealing prohibited transaction under IRC § 4975 (c)(1)(F). In a common hedge fund structure, the management of the hedge fund receives compensation under a 2/20 structure, whereby they receive an annual fee of 2% of assets under management and 20% of any profits. If the IRA of a member of management invests \$100,000 into the fund then this will result in an additional \$2,000 paid annually to management (2% fee) and also allows management to personally obtain a share of the profits that are derived from their own IRAs. As a result, the typical fee structures of a hedge fund will lead to a self-dealing prohibited transaction if management (or disqualified persons to management) were to invest their IRAs into the fund. Typically the ownership of a hedge fund or private offering is comprised 50% or more by non-disqualified persons (e.g., other investors), and as a result there usually is not a per se prohibited transaction that will occur when a member of management's IRA invests into the company.

A self-dealing prohibited transaction may be avoided in certain offerings if management is able to waive management compensation from their own IRAs investment. Under certain fund documents, management may be able to accomplish this waiver, which should be in writing, and as a result may be able to invest their own IRAs into the offering. However, offerings which require the members of management to make certain personal investments into the fund should not be accomplished through a member of management's IRA. An IRA owner needs to keep his or her personal obligations and compensation separate from his or her IRA's investments. Additionally, members of management should not invest their IRAs into a company fund during the initial raise of capital or in order to meet any minimum funding amounts. Investment from a member of management's IRA during initial raises or capital calls can be seen as unfairly benefiting the IRA owners.

In summary, a member of management's IRA may be invested into a hedge fund or investment company under limited circumstances and only when the compensation paid to management excludes fees or profits from their own IRAs.

IRA INVESTMENT INTO HIGH RISK/HIGH RETURN CLASSES
OF STOCK, PRIVATE EQUITY & THE ROMNEY/BAIN MODEL

There has been much reporting by the *Wall Street Journal* and other financial publications as to Mitt Romney's IRA which was valued between $20M—$101M. A basic analysis reveals that the significant returns he achieved in his IRA were a result of self-directed investments into companies where his company, Bain Capital, was involved as a consultant and private equity investor. A thorough analysis on the subject was conducted by Mark Maremont of the *Wall Street Journal*, who analyzed and reported on Bain Capital's IRA investment structures in an article titled *Bain Gave Staff Way to Swell IRAs by Investing in Deals*, dated March 28, 2012.

The article analyzed certain publicly available reports which showed how Bain structured certain deals with two different classes of stock which were available to its employees and investors. The first class, the safe-preferred class, received a preferred annual return of, say, 10—12% and received all of their capital (e.g., what they invested in) back before any other class of investors were paid. After their return of capital and preferred payments, the safe-preferred class received a limited portion of the profits payable above the preferred returns. In other words, if the company did poorly, or only reasonably well, the safe-preferred class got paid and was protected. If the company, however, received significant returns, the safe-preferred class would still receive their preferred return (10—12%) but would only participate in a minority portion of returns above the preferred amount. The safe-preferred class, therefore, had the lowest risk but also carried a diminished ability for significant up-side returns.

The second, risky, high-return class did not receive any profits or return of capital until the safe-preferred class was first paid. After the safe-preferred class was paid, however, the high-return class received the vast majority of the profits that exceeded the preferred return amounts. As a result, if you were an investor in the risky high-return class shares, you could lose your investment if the company did poorly or only marginally well. Conversely, if the company did exceptionally well, your shares would receive the vast majority of the significant returns.

A Bain employee's investment into Sealy Corp was analyzed in the *Wall Street Journal* article by Mr. Maremont and showed that the employee invested $3,000 from his IRA into the risky high-return class and $27,000 of his personal funds into the safe-preferred class. When Sealy Corp was sold years later, the $27,000 investment of personal funds in the safe-preferred returns was worth of $58,000, and the $3,000 IRA investment into the risky high-return shares was worth $102,000. Since the risky high-return deal produced a significant return above the safe-preferred rate, it resulted in an incredible return being paid to the high-risk and high-return shares.

The IRAs involved in the Bain example were traditional IRAs, and as a result, the IRA owners received tax-deferred treatment such that the IRA owner only paid taxes when money was distributed from the IRA at retirement.

In 1998, Roth IRAs became available. Roth IRAs do not receive a tax deduction on contributions, but the investment gains are not subject to tax, *and* the qualifying amounts withdrawn at retirement (age 59 1/2) are not subject to tax. Consequently, Roth IRAs can produce entirely tax-free returns.

While Roth IRAs were first only available to lower and middle-income taxpayers, the Tax Increase Prevention and Reconciliation Act (TIPRA) allowed all taxpayers (starting in 2010) to convert traditional IRAs and other retirement accounts to a Roth IRA, subject to paying taxes on the amount converted to the Roth IRA.

As a result of the availability of Roth IRAs, most high-risk/high-return structures today are implemented with Roth IRAs, where the Roth IRA owner is typically more interested in taking high-risk in hopes of receiving a significant tax-free return in a Roth IRA account that can be entirely tax free.

CONSIDERATIONS WHEN AN IRA OWNS PREFERRED OR HIGH RISK CLASSES OF UNITS/SHARES

An IRA may invest into a company that holds different share/unit classes and where there are high-risk and high-return characteristics. At a minimum, the company should adhere to the following guidelines when offering different classes of shares to IRAs:

- The different share classes must be available to *all* investors. For example, company founders or management could not create a special share class only available to their IRAs as this would likely result in a self-dealing prohibited transaction.
- The share class structure must be reasonable and the risk/reward metric must be based on actual market factors and investor interest. A lop-sided structure (whereby IRAs received a lion's share of the profits while only having minimal risk) would likely violate the self-dealing prohibited transaction rules and the exclusive benefit rule.

- The company documents should clearly outline the different classes. An IRA investment cannot be split between different ownership classes unless all other investors are offered and allowed the same opportunity.

Companies (corporations or LLCs) with two or more share classes require special consideration and legal advice as there are self-dealing prohibited transaction land-mines that must be avoided.

IRS NOTICE 2004-8, PROHIBITION ON ROTH IRA VALUE SHIFTING

In 2004, the IRS issued Notice 2004-8, Abusive Roth IRA Transactions. This Notice made certain investment structures with Roth IRAs whereby Roth IRA owners were unfairly shifting value/income to their Roth IRA's listed transactions. A listed transaction is one which requires special disclosure to the IRS and generally will trigger an audit of the activities being conducted. The notice was specific to Roth IRAs as such accounts can receive tax-free treatment for their investments. While the types of transactions the IRS is seeking are also problematic for Traditional IRA's the Notice and disclosure obligations only apply to Roth IRAs.

IRS Notice 2004-8 was issued by the IRS so that the IRS may be able to more easily audit certain transactions whereby Roth IRA owners were unfairly shifting income and/or assets from their personal businesses to their Roth IRAs. Transactions where a Roth IRA (or Roth IRA-owned company) unfairly shifts value or income will typically result in a prohibited transaction. This unfair value shifting to a Roth is of additional interest to the IRS as it can result in tax avoidance.

The IRS wants to ensure that the only income being paid to a Roth IRA-owned corporation is income that the Roth IRA corporation has earned and is entitled to. The IRS does not want to see income that should be paid to a company owned by the IRA owner personally instead of being paid to the Roth IRA corporation as a way of unfairly avoiding taxes.

The IRS describes that:

> ...these transactions involved the following parties: (1) an individual (the taxpayer) who owns a pre-existing business such as a corporation or a sole proprietorship (the Business); (2) a Roth IRA within the meaning of § 408A that is maintained for the Taxpayer, and (3) a corporation (the Roth IRA Corporation), substantially all the shares of which are owned or acquired by the Roth IRA. The Business and the Roth IRA Corporation enter into transactions as described below. The acquisition of shares, the transactions or both are not fairly valued and thus have the effect of shifting value into the Roth IRA. IRS Notice 2004.

The IRS explains further that the following transactions are examples of what the IRS is seeking to uncover:

> ...the Roth IRA Corporation acquires property, such as accounts receivable, from the Business for less than fair market value....or any other arrangement between the Roth IRA Corporation and the Taxpayer, a related party [aka, disqualified person] that has the effect of transferring value to the Roth IRA corporation comparable to a contribution to the Roth IRA. *Id.*

The notice states that the following structures must be

disclosed as a listed transaction by a Roth IRA owner via IRS form 8886.:

> ...arrangements in which an individual, related persons described in § 267(b) or 707 (b), or a business controlled by such individual or related persons [aka, disqualified person], engage in one or more transactions with a corporation, including contributions of property to such corporation, substantially all the shares of which are owned by one or more Roth IRAs maintained for the benefit of the individual, related persons described in § 267(b)(1), or both. *Id.*

If you break down the language of the Notice, it requires disclosure when the following items occur.

1. A Roth IRA or the Roth IRAs of related parties (aka, disqualified persons) owns substantially all the shares of a corporation (a Roth IRA corporation). The term "substantially" is not defined but presumably it means at least a majority.
2. The Roth IRA corporation engages in at least one transaction with the Roth IRA owners or related parties to the Roth IRA owners (aka, disqualified persons).

If a transaction meets the notice requirements for disclosure, it will almost always result in a prohibited transaction. This is because transactions between a Roth IRA-owned corporation and a disqualified party will usually result in a per se or a self-dealing prohibited transaction. This is certainly the case if fair market value is not being paid. As a result, it is unadvisable to set up such a structure. In other words, if you have to report under the notice, you have probably engaged in a prohibited transaction.

IRA INVESMENT INTO CROWDFUNDING OFFERING

Crowdfunding is a new exemption to the securities laws signed into law by President Obama in 2012 as part of the Jumpstart Our Business Startups Act ("JOBS Act"). Crowdfunding investments will likely be very popular among self-directed IRA investors as they provide opportunity for investors to take ownership in businesses or investment projects at start-up or early funding levels where there is opportunity for significant growth and returns. There is also, of course, a significant risk, and as a result, the amount of money that may be invested into a crowdfunding offering is limited by law, whether it is a personal investment or an IRA investment.

The crowdfunding exemption allows entrepreneurs and investment sponsors to raise small sums of money from large groups of people without having to complete a public securities offering with the SEC. The concept of crowdfunding is to loosen the restrictive securities laws so that new or existing companies can raise small sums of money from large groups of people. By limiting the amount of money raised by each person, the law limits each investor's risk. Crowdfunding can be used to fund any type of business or venture, including a real estate business or investment, a new movie, restaurant, or a technology business. The crowdfunding rules are found in 15 U.S.C. 77d(6) and are summarized below.

- The issuer of the investment cannot sell more than $1M of securities in a 12 month period.
- The amount that can be invested from an IRA depends on the income or net worth of the investor. For investors with net worth or annual income less than $100,000, they can

invest the greater of $2,000 or 5% of their annual income or net worth. For investors with annual income or net worth greater than $100,000, they can invest up to 10% of their annual income or net worth not to exceed $100,000. There is no requirement that investors are "accredited investors," and anyone can invest at least $2,000 in a "crowdfunding transaction."

- The transaction must also be conducted through a broker or a "funding portal" that provides risk disclosures and other information to investors. A funding portal is a new system of exchange that has been used in recent years by many small companies but has only recently been recognized in law under the JOBS Act. A funding portal is defined as a person or entity that acts as an intermediary in a transaction involving the offer or sale of securities for the account of others. There are a number of restrictions placed upon funding portals such as: prohibitions on investment advice or recommendations; they cannot solicit offers or transactions; they cannot compensate employees based on the sale of securities; and they cannot hold, manage or possess investor funds or securities. Funding portals must register with the SEC as a funding portal, but they do not have to be registered as a broker-dealer.

In summary, an IRA may invest in a crowdfunding investment and the amount an IRA can invest depends on the income or net worth of the IRA owner. If an IRA owner has already invested a maximum amount from his or her non-retirement funds into a crowdfunding investment, then he or she cannot invest their IRA into the investment. In other words, the total amount that an IRA may invest into a crowdfunding offering is comprised of amounts invested from the IRA owner personally and his or her IRA.

UBIT TAX & IRA PRIVATE COMPANY OWNERSHIP

There is a tax called Unrelated Business Income Tax ("UBIT") which applies to the ordinary income received by an IRA. IRC § 511. An extensive discussion of UBIT tax can be found in Chapter 13. For purposes of private stock/unit investment, IRA owners need to be aware of investments which can cause UBIT tax to their IRA. The UBIT tax rate ranges from 0—37% with the 37% rate occurring once there is $12,500 in annual net income that is subject to the UBIT tax. As a result, IRA owners will typically avoid investments which may subject the IRA to UBIT taxes. In general, UBIT tax will likely occur in investments into private companies where the business is an operational business and does not pay corporate tax. The best way to understand when UBIT tax is owed is to first understand what is specifically exempt from UBIT tax. The exemptions are found in IRC § 513 and are as follows:

- rental income;
- capital gain income (except from real property held immediately for sale);
- interest income;
- royalty income;
- dividend income from a C corporation, also certain qualifying dividends from REITs.

The following table outlines some examples of private company structures and shows whether the company's IRA owners are subject to UBIT tax.

TABLE 11.1, PRIVATE COMPANY
OWNERSHIP SUBJECT TO UBIT TAX

SUBJECT TO UBIT TAX	NOT SUBJECT TO UBIT TAX
Restaurant that is an LLC or other pass-through company.	Restaurant that is a C corporation and pays corporate taxes.
Software company that is an LLC and sells technology services or products.	LLC or LP that owns rental property and receives rental income.
Real estate development LLC who conducts non-passive real estate activities.	LLC or LP that lends money and receives interest income.
Real estate company that consistently buys and sells real property on a short-term (less than a year hold) basis.	LLC or LP that owns software or other intellectual property and licenses it for royalty

For example, if an IRA invests into a new technology start-up company that is an LLC and does not pay corporate tax, then the net income from that business that is payable to the IRA will be subject to UBIT tax. If, on the other hand, an IRA invests into Apple stock, which is a C corporation, then there is no UBIT tax owed on the dividends/profits paid to the IRA since Apple is a C corporation and pays corporate tax before issuing its dividends. In other words, the tax is coming off for C corporations at the company level. The LLC technology company, on the other hand, does not pay a corporate tax and instead distributes its income to the underlying owners who pay whatever taxes are due on its profits. So, in the end, there will always be a tax paid on profits made in an ordinary-income business owned by an IRA. If the company is a C corp, the taxes paid will be at the company level and then profits are paid to owners. If the company is an LLC or other pass-through company, the tax will be paid at the owner level. For an IRA that is an owner, this will result in UBIT tax, unless the income meets an exception to the UBIT tax.

CHECKLIST FOR IRA INVESTMENT INTO PRIVATE COMPANY STOCK/UNITS

- ✓ Is the stock/units registered in the name of the IRA (e.g., ABC Trust Company FBO Sally Jones IRA)?
- ✓ Will the IRA be subject to UBIT tax as a result of the company's operation business and flow-through tax status?
- ✓ Is the company majority owned and controlled by non-disqualified persons?
- ✓ Do the company documents anticipate IRAs as owners? Do the documents ensure that prohibited transactions are avoided and that the IRA owner will get the necessary information to report its annual fair market value?

FREQUENTLY ASKED QUESTIONS

Q. I currently own a business and want to get some cash out personally. Can my IRA buy some of my personal ownership?

A. No, the purchase of your own shares with your IRA would be a transaction with a disqualified person and is a prohibited transaction.

Q. I've been involved in providing services/work in a new business start-up and will receive 20% of the company ownership for my efforts. Can I take this ownership in my IRA?

A. No, your IRA can only make investments of its capital in exchange for ownership. It cannot receive a share of the company that is due to you personally for work performed. Transferring such ownership you are personally due over to your IRA would be a prohibited transaction. It is possible for your IRA to invest some capital into the business under terms that other capital investors may be offered.

Q. I currently own 15% of XYZ Company personally. I do not work in the business and am solely an owner/investor. The company is offering additional units of ownership. Can I purchase some additional units with my IRA?

A. Yes, you can buy new units from the company; however, don't sell any of your personal units around this same time as that could be deemed an indirect prohibited transaction whereby you exchanged personal ownership for ownership in your IRA.

CHAPTER 12: Precious Metals Investments and IRAs

Precious metals have been a popular investment for retirement plans since the financial market collapse in 2008. Most standard IRAs with financial institution custodians will typically only offer precious metals through funds or other complex structures whereby the IRA does not directly own the precious metals. A self-directed IRA can hold actual precious metals as long as those metals are not considered collectibles under law and as long as they are properly stored.

KEY POINTS
▪ *An IRA may own gold, silver, platinum, or palladium that meets certain fineness requirements or which are specifically approved coins.*
▪ *Certain precious metals that are deemed "collectible" items may not be owned by an IRA.*
▪ *The IRA owner cannot have personal possession of the precious metals, and they must be stored with a financial institution, bank, or trust company.*

WHAT PRECIOUS METALS MAY BE OWNED BY AN IRA

Only precious metals which meet the requirements of IRC § 408(m)(3) may be owned by an IRA. All other metals or coins are

considered collectible items and cannot be held by an IRA. IRC §
408(m)(2)(C), and (D). IRC § 408(m)(3) reads as follows:

(3) Exception for certain coins and bullion. For purposes of this
subsection, the term "collectible" shall not include

(A) any coin which is
(i) a gold coin described in paragraph (7), (8), (9), or (10) of
section 5112 (a) of title 31, United States Code,
(ii) a silver coin described in section 5112 (e) of title 31,
United States Code,
(iii) a platinum coin described in section 5112 (k) of title 31,
United States Code, or
(iv) a coin issued under the laws of any State, or
(B) any gold, silver, platinum, or palladium bullion of a
fineness equal to or exceeding the minimum fineness that a
contract market (as described in section 7 of the
Commodity Exchange Act, 7 U.S.C. 7) requires for metals
which may be delivered in satisfaction of a regulated
futures contract, if such bullion is in the physical
possession of a trustee described under subsection (a) of
this section.

Precious metals may be owned in either bullion (e.g., bars)
form, meeting minimum purity requirements—or in certain
approved coin form. The following precious metals meet the
bullion requirements of IRC § 408(m)(3) and may be held by an
IRA:

- Gold, meeting minimum fineness requirements of 99.5%.
- Silver, meeting minimum fineness requirements of 99.9%.
- Platinum, meeting minimum fineness requirements of
99.95%.

- Palladium, meeting minimum fineness requirements of 99.95%

The fineness requirement is based on what is required under a futures contract under law. IRC § 408(m)(3)(B). The futures contract fineness requirements is what I have outlined above. If the bullion is not one of the approved four metals or if the bullion does not meet the fineness requirements, then the bullion is considered a collectible item and cannot be owned by the IRA.

WHAT COINS MAY BE OWNED BY AN IRA

In addition to bullion, certain approved coins may be owned by an IRA. Coins with a value based on a collectible quality (such as rare coins) cannot be owned by the IRA.

IRS Publication 590-A, pg. 35 (2017), states that an IRA can invest in the following approved coins:

> ...one, one half, one quarter, or one tenth ounce U.S. gold coins, or one ounce silver coins minted by the Treasury Department.

American Gold Eagle coins, in the specifications outlined above, are common coins owned by self-directed IRAs. Additionally, if the precious metals meet the fineness requirements outlined above for bullion, they may be bought in bar or coin form. As a result, coins may either be from the group specifically approved such as those in Publication 590-A or they may be bullion meeting the metal type and fineness requirements.

The following table outlines specifically what precious metals may be owned by an IRA. Potts, Jon, *Retirement Industry Trust Association Certified SDIP Course Book*, Chapter: Precious Metals, Page 37, (2017).

TABLE 12.1, ACCEPTABLE PRECIOUS METALS FOR IRAs

GOLD	
American Eagle bullion and/or proof coins	American Buffalo bullion coins
Australian Kangaroo/Nugget bullion coins	Austrian Philharmonic bullion coins
Canadian Maple Leaf bullion coins	
Bars and rounds produced by a refiner/assayer/manufacturer accredited/certified by NYMEX/COMEX, NYSE/Liffe, LME, LBMA, LPPM, TOCOM, ISO 9000, or national government mint and meeting minimum fineness or 99.5%.	

SILVER	
American Eagle bullion and/or proof coins	America the Beautiful bullion coins
Australian Kookaburra bullion coins	Austrian Philharmonic bullion coins
Canadian Maple Leaf bullion coins	Mexican Libertad bullion coins
Bars and rounds produced by a refiner/assayer/manufacturer accredited/certified by NYMEX/COMEX, NYSE/Liffe, LME, LBMA, LPPM, TOCOM, ISO 9000, or national government mint and meeting minimum fineness or 99.9%.	

TABLE 12.1, ACCEPTABLE PRECIOUS METALS FOR IRAs (CONT'D)

PLATINUM	
American Eagle bullion and/or proof coins	Australian Koala bullion coins
Canadian Maple Leaf bullion coins	Isle of Man Noble bullion coins
Bars and rounds produced by a refiner/assayer/manufacturer accredited/certified by NYMEX/COMEX, NYSE/Liffe, LME, LBMA, LPPM, TOCOM, ISO 9000, or national government mint and meeting minimum fineness or 99.95%.	

PALLADIUM
Canadian Maple Leaf bullion coins
Bars and rounds produced by a refiner/assayer/manufacturer accredited/certified by NYMEX/COMEX, NYSE/Liffe, LME, LBMA, LPPM, TOCOM, ISO 9000, or national government mint and meeting minimum fineness or 99.95%.

STORAGE RULES FOR PRECIOUS METALS OWNED BY AN IRA

Precious metals must be stored with a licensed financial institution or trust company. Personal storage of precious metals owned by an IRA is not allowed. A broker-dealer, third-party administrator, or any company not licensed as a bank, credit union, or trust company may not store precious metals owned by an IRA. IRS Private Letter Ruling 200217059.

Pursuant to IRC § 408(m)(3)(B), bullion must specifically be stored by a "bank." The term "bank" is defined in the code as including a national or state-chartered bank or credit union as well as a state-chartered trust company. IRC § 408(n).

A literal interpretation of IRC § 408(m)(3)(A) is that the specifically approved coins under Section (A) are not subject to the bank or trust company storage requirements. However, this code section and the possibility of personally storing the specific coins exempted in Section (A) has not been clarified by the IRS, DOL, or in court and as a result, most practitioners and self-directed custodians will recommend that all precious metals be stored domestically with a bank or trust company.

CONSEQUENCES OF VIOLATION OF PRECIOUS METALS IRA RULES

If an IRA purchases precious metals that do not meet the specific requirements of IRC § 408(m)(3), then the precious metals are deemed collectible items. As a result, they are considered distributed from the IRA at the time of purchase. IRC § 408(m)(1). Similarly, if the storage requirement is violated, then the precious metals are also deemed distributed as of the date of the storage violation. IRS Private Letter Ruling 20021705. The consequence of distribution is that the value of the amount involved is deemed distributed and is subject to the applicable taxes and penalty.

For example, if a traditional IRA bought precious metals for $10,000 and if those metals did not meet the purity requirements, then those assets would be deemed as distributed from the IRA to the IRA owner personally, and the IRA owner would receive a 1099-R from their IRA custodian for $10,000. This $10,000 1099-R is taxable and must be claimed as income on the IRA owner's personal tax return. Additionally, if the IRA owner is under age 59½, then the IRA must also pay an early withdrawal penalty of 10% of the amount involved (in this example, $1,000). The other cash or investments in the IRA remain unaffected, and only the metals that are "collectibles" or that were improperly stored are subject to distribution.

CAUTION REGARDING PROOF COINS

There are certain specifically approved coins which an IRA may buy known as "proof coins", which are sold and offered though the U.S. Mint and precious metals dealers. The most common proof coins are American Gold Eagle proofs or American Silver Eagle proofs. The only thing that makes these proof coins different from say a non-proof coin is a certificate and a fancy box. Clearly, these coins are meant for collection and not for investment and should be avoided by self-directed IRA investors. As reported by the Wall Street Journal, many self-directed IRA investors have used their IRAs to purchase proof coins only to see them drop significantly in value as the price of a proof coin is far above the per ounce price of the metal. Rothfeld, Michael, (2017, Nov 26). U.S. Mint's Gold and Silver Coins Turn to Lead for Some Retirement Investors, *Wall Street Journal*. Additionally, selling a proof coin at the same price your purchased it is difficult as the secondary market for proof coins isn't as high as the retail market you encounter when buying the proof coins in the first place.

CHECKLIST FOR PURCHASING
PRECIOUS METALS WITH AN IRA

✓ Is the precious metal in question acceptable bullion or coins for IRAs?

✓ Are the precious metals being stored by a federal or state-regulated bank or trust company?

✓ Are the precious metals being purchased from a non-disqualified person (e.g., not the IRA owner or disqualified family members)?

FREQUENTLY ASKED QUESTIONS

Q. I currently own some precious metals personally. Can I assign or sell them to my IRA?

A. No, the transfer of the precious metals from you personally to your IRA would be a prohibited transaction as it is a transaction with a disqualified person (IRA owner).

Q. Can I store the precious metals owned by my IRA in a safe in my home or business?

A. No, personal storage is typically prohibited. Precious metals should be stored at a financial institution or trust company. While there is an arguable position that certain specifically approved coins do not have to be stored in with a bank or trust company, personal storage is still not recommended.

Q. Can I buy bronze metals or foreign coins with my IRA?

A. No, only gold, silver, platinum or palladium metals that meet certain requirements may be owned by your IRA. As to foreign coins, most of them do not meet the bullion purity requirement, and none of them are the type of coins that are specifically approved by law.

Q. If I have an IRA/LLC, what rules apply to storage of the precious metals owned by the IRA/LLC?

A. An IRA/LLC may obtain a safe deposit box with a financial institution in the name of the LLC, and such safe deposit box may store acceptable precious metals. Such IRA/LLC-owned safe deposit boxes would most likely meet the storage requirements for IRAs as the deposit box is a form of storage at a licensed financial institution (e.g., bank).

CHAPTER 13: The IRA/LLC Structure

The IRA/LLC investment structure is accomplished when an IRA invests into a newly created limited liability company ("LLC") and owns 100% of the membership units of the LLC.

KEY POINTS
■ *An IRA may own 100% of an LLC and that LLC may be managed by the IRA owner, subject to certain restrictions.*
■ *The IRA/LLC must be a newly created LLC that is clearly owned by the IRA. The IRA owner cannot use an existing LLC they personally own.*
■ *The IRA/LLC documents must be tailored to the IRA as an owner and must take into account the numerous IRA ownership issues.*
■ *IRA/LLCs are subject to the prohibited transaction rules. An IRA/LLC should not be used as a method of circumventing the prohibited transaction rules.*
■ *Multiple IRAs or a combination of IRAs and individuals can own an IRA/LLC, but careful attention must be paid towards the set-up and funding of the IRA/LLC. Multiple ownership options are outlined in Chapter 14.*

The IRA owns the LLC company units just like your IRA can own shares of Coca-Cola, Inc. stock. The IRA will be listed on the LLC documents as the owner (e.g., ABC Trust Company FBO Sally

Jones IRA), and the IRA owner will typically be listed as the non-compensated manager of the IRA/LLC. A third party may also be the manager. Once the IRA/LLC is properly established, it will open an LLC checking account at a bank selected by the IRA owner. The self-directed IRA custodian then issues a check in the name of the newly created IRA/LLC, and this amount is the investment from the IRA.

For example, if the new IRA/LLC is called XYZ Investments, LLC, then the self-directed IRA custodian will issue a check in the name of XYZ Investments, LLC in the amount determined by the IRA owner. The IRA owner, as manager of the IRA/LLC, will receive that check and will deposit it into a new LLC bank account.

The diagram below outlines the IRA/LLC structure.

DIAGRAM 13.1, IRA/LLC STRUCTURE

Self-Directed IRA — Investment, Owns 100% of LLC → IRA/LLC — Receives Rent, Pays Expenses ← / Buys Property → Rental Property

The IRA owner may serve as the manager of the IRA/LLC, subject to certain restrictions in the LLC documents. When the IRA owner is the manager of the IRA/LLC, he or she is able to manage the IRA/LLC's affairs, including the bank account, and can also sign contracts and make decisions on behalf of the IRA/LLC.

Under the IRA/LLC structure, the self-directed IRA invests into the IRA/LLC and the IRA owns 100% of the IRA/LLC. (See the diagram at the beginning of this chapter.) The IRA/LLC then purchases and owns a rental property. The property is owned by the IRA/LLC, the contract to purchase will be in the IRA/LLC's name (e.g., XYZ Investments, LLC), and the bank account will be in the IRA/LLC's name. When the tenants to the rental property pay rent, they pay it to the IRA/LLC, and the amounts are deposited into the IRA/LLC bank account. When expenses for the property need to be paid, they are paid from the IRA/LLC bank account, with the IRA owner signing as the Manager. Additionally, when leases or other agreements relating to the IRA/LLC and its property need to be signed, the manager of the LLC, which may be the IRA owner, will sign on behalf of the IRA/LLC.

The example above and many of my explanations in this chapter relate to real estate owned by an IRA/LLC. However, the rules apply in the same way regardless of the actual investments held by the IRA/LLC. I use real estate as an example because it is a common investment asset held by an IRA/LLC and because it is easy to understand.

TAX REPORTING FOR THE IRA/LLC

When there is one IRA that owns 100% of the IRA/LLC, the IRA/LLC is considered a single-member LLC and is disregarded for tax purposes. IRS Publication 3402 (2012) and Treasury Regulations § 301.7701-3. If the IRA/LLC is disregarded for tax purposes, then it does not need to file a federal tax return with the IRS.

TABLE 13.1, ADVANTAGES OF THE IRA/LLC

ADVANTAGES OF THE IRA/LLC
❖ Protect the IRA owner, the IRA, and the IRA custodian from liability that arises from the self-directed IRA investments.
❖ Allow the IRA owner to more easily manage his or her IRA's investments by being able to accomplish investments as manager of the LLC (e.g., can sign contracts and checks, and receive income and pay expenses).

ADMINISTRATIVE BENEFITS OF THE IRA/LLC

A significant benefit of the IRA/LLC is that it allows the IRA owner, as manager of the IRA/LLC, to more easily execute and perform on investments for the IRA. For example, if an IRA owner wanted to purchase real estate at a trustee's sale, the IRA owner would be unable to actually perform on such an investment as the IRA owner would have to identify the property at auction, submit documents to the IRA custodian for approval, and then would need to wait for the self-directed IRA custodian to approve the purchase before funds would be invested from the IRA. These procedural obstacles essentially make it impossible to purchase real property at auction. Additionally, rental properties, hard-money lending, tax liens/deeds, trust deed investing, and real estate property rehab projects all benefit from the administrative conveniences of the IRA/LLC as the IRA owner is able to sign the contracts and manage the bank account's income and expenses.

ASSET PROTECTION ADVANTAGES OF THE IRA/LLC

The IRA/LLC provides an important level of asset protection that protects the IRA, the IRA owner, and the custodian of the IRA from liabilities that can arise on assets and investments owned by the IRA/LLC. The common characteristic of all LLCs is that they protect the owner of the LLC, in this case the IRA, from the liabilities and claims that arise from the LLC's assets or activities. For example, if the IRA/LLC owns a rental property and if there is a slip-and-fall accident or some other liability that arises, the injured party would be forced to sue the IRA/LLC but could not sue the IRA, the IRA owner, or the custodian of the IRA. This "limit to liability" for the owners of limited liability companies ("LLCs") is a key characteristic of LLCs in all fifty states. As a result, self-directed IRA investments that can produce liability are best accomplished in an IRA/LLC where liability can be limited to the LLC and can be separated from the rest of the IRA's assets and from the IRA owner.

Rental real estate, real estate rehab projects, and other investments which can create potential liability benefit from the asset protection characteristics of an IRA/LLC. Other assets such as raw land, private stock, or promissory notes and trust deed investments do not typically create liability (other than the investment risk) and as a result do not benefit as significantly from the asset protection characteristics of an IRA/LLC.

There is much misconception and incorrect information about the asset protection characteristics of self-directed IRAs. Many websites claim that an IRA is exempt from the collection efforts of creditors and is "bullet-proof" from liabilities that can arise from the IRA's investments. These claims are incorrect and are based on a misunderstanding of the laws affecting IRAs. While most state laws and the federal bankruptcy laws provide protections to retirement accounts for liabilities of the IRA owner, those exemptions are meant to protect the IRA from being subject to creditors of the IRA *owner* who is described in the laws as the "debtor." 11 USC § 522. However, this protection does not extend to the investments and activities of the IRA. The IRA needs to bear investment rewards and risks. As a result, an IRA is subject to losses and liabilities that can occur in its investments.

SELF-DIRECTED IRA OWNER MAY PERSONALLY BE LIABLE FOR THE ACTIONS OF THE IRA

In addition to the IRA being subject to liabilities that occur on its investments, the self-directed IRA owner can also personally be subject to liabilities. IRC § 408 states that an IRA is a trust created when an individual establishes an IRA by signing IRS Form 5305. IRS Form 5305 is completed, with some variations, when an IRA custodian establishes an IRA on behalf of an IRA owner. The courts have analyzed what an IRA is under law and have stated that an IRA is a trust or special deposit of the individual for the benefit of the IRA owner. *First Nat'l Bank v. Estate of Thomas Philip*, 436 N.E. 2d 15 (1992). The IRA is *not* a separate entity or irrevocable trust which can keep its liabilities separate from its owner. Since the IRA is a trust that is revocable and terminated at the discretion of the IRA owner, each investment in fact is truly controlled by the IRA owner as he or she could terminate the IRA at any time and take ownership of the IRAs assets in his or her personal name.

The IRA is akin to a revocable trust, which is commonly understood by lawyers and courts to provide no asset protection and no prevention of creditors from pursuing the trust creator and owner from liabilities and judgments that arise in the trust. Following this same rationale, a self-directed IRA owner would likely be subjected to a similar downfall in the event of a large liability which is not satisfied by the assets of the IRA. As a consequence, the personal assets of the IRA owner may be at risk.

The IRA/LLC provides an important level of asset protection that protects the IRA, the IRA owner, and the custodian of the IRA from liabilities that can arise on assets and investments owned by the IRA/LLC. It is important to note, again, that not every self-directed IRA investment can create liability, and as a result, every self-directed IRA does not need an IRA/LLC. That being said, self-directed IRA owners investing their IRA into assets that can create liability should consider using an IRA/LLC to limit that liability risk.

CASES AND LAWS AFFECTING THE IRA/LLC STRUCTURE

There are numerous sources of law that affect the IRA/LLC structure and govern how an IRA/LLC may be established and operated. The first and most significant body of law is the prohibited transaction rules found in IRC § 4975. There are two types of prohibited transactions that an IRA must avoid: The first type is a per se prohibited transaction and occurs when an IRA engages in a transaction with a disqualified person. The second type is a self-dealing prohibited transaction and occurs when the IRA owner (or other disqualified person) benefits from the IRA's transactions.

The primary concern when establishing an IRA/LLC is that it must be created and operated in compliance with the prohibited transaction rules. A prohibited transaction could occur during the creation of the LLC, in the change of ownership, in the management of the IRA/LLC, or in the investments or transactions that the IRA/LLC enters into.

THE SWANSON CASE

The most cited and referenced case regarding the IRA/LLC structure is *Swanson v. Commissioner*, 106 T.C. 76 (1996). This case involved a self-directed IRA and a newly formed corporation. The IRA owner was a director and the president of the new corporation. The IRA purchased 100% of the shares of the corporation in exchange for a cash investment. The corporation was taxed as a foreign sales corporation. It is important to note that the corporation could not have been taxed as an S corporation as an IRA does not qualify as an S corporation shareholder. The IRA-owned corporation received income from its business activities and distributed approximately $600,000 in profits to the IRA.

The IRS challenged the IRA-owned corporation structure on two fronts: First, the IRS claimed that a per se prohibited transaction occurred when the IRA purchased shares of the corporation. IRC § 4975 (c)(1)(A). The rationale from the IRS was that the new corporation was a disqualified person to Mr. Swanson's IRA, and therefore, the purchase of shares by the IRA was a transaction with a disqualified person. The U.S. Tax Court disagreed with this analysis and ruled that:

> ...a corporation without shareholders does not fit within the definition of a disqualified person...accordingly, the issuance of stock to the IRA#1 did not, within the plain meaning of section 4975 (c)(1)(A), qualify as a "sale or

exchange, or leasing, of any property between a plan and a disqualified person." *Id. at 89.*

In other words, the corporation is not a disqualified person upon formation: and therefore, the IRA's purchase of 100% of the initial ownership was not a prohibited transaction as there was no transaction with a disqualified person. It is important to note though, that if Mr. Swanson had established the company and had listed himself personally as the initial owner, it would have been a prohibited transaction for his IRA to then acquire the shares from himself personally as that would have resulted in an IRA transaction with a disqualified person. As a result, in the IRA/LLC context, it is important that an IRA become the owner of the company upon formation of the IRA/LLC to avoid ownership transferring from the IRA owner to the IRA.

LEGAL TIP

❖ An IRA investment into a company as the initial owner is not a prohibited transaction as a newly created company without owners cannot be a disqualified person to an IRA.

The second claim by the IRS in the *Swanson* case was that a self-dealing prohibited transaction occurred when the IRA-owned corporation returned profits and dividends to the IRA in violation of IRC § 4975 (c)(1)(E). The Tax Court ruled that there was no evidence of self-dealing and ruled that:

> ...the only direct or indirect benefit that the petitioner [Swanson] realized from the payments of dividends [profits] by Worldwide [the corporation] related solely to

his status as the participant of IRA#1. In this regard, petitioner benefitted only insofar as IRA#1 accumulated assets for future distribution...[which is not a prohibited transaction]. *Id. at 89-90.*

As a result of the court's ruling, a self-dealing prohibited transaction does not occur when an IRA receives income and profits that result from an IRA-owned company's activities.

LEGAL TIP
❖ The return of profits or dividends from an IRA-owned company to the IRA is not a prohibited transaction.

In addition to ruling in favor of Mr. Swanson, the IRA owner, the Tax Court also ruled that the challenges brought by the IRS against Mr. Swanson were not "substantially justified" in law and ordered the IRS to pay Mr. Swanson's attorney's fees in defending the case pursuant to IRC § 7430. *Id. at 91.*

Since the *Swanson* case was decided in 1996, limited liability companies ("LLC's") have become a much more preferred entity structure for business and investment companies, including those used by self-directed IRA investors. While *Swanson* and many other cases applicable to the IRA/LLC structure have involved 100% owned corporations, the legal ramifications and the court's rulings as to prohibited transactions have the same effect and application to LLCs as IRC § 4975 makes no distinction between corporations and LLCs.

THE HELLWEG CASE

In 2011, the Tax Court decided the case of *Hellweg v. Commissioner*, T.C.M. 2011-58 (2011). *Hellweg* involved the creation of four 100% owned C corporations which were owned by Roth IRAs of family members and the Roth IRA owners each served as the president of their respective Roth IRA-owned company. The IRS challenged the structures and alleged prohibited transactions. The Tax Court dismissed the IRS's challenges and stated in its opinion:

> Congress has enumerated the types of transactions which IRAs are prohibited from making in section 408(e)(2) through (5) and (m). No part of the Transaction here is prohibited under any of those provisions....Section 4975 (c)(1) prohibits a list of self-dealing prohibited transactions between a plan and disqualified persons. We have previously held that a similar transaction was not a prohibited transaction under section 4975 (c)(1(A) or (E). See *Swanson v. Commissioner*, 106 T.C 76 (U.S. Tax Ct. 1996). *Id. at pg. 24-25.*

Hellweg is one of the most recent cases addressing the legal issues applicable to the IRA/LLC and is consistent with *Swanson*. As a result of the legal history and unsuccessful challenges by the IRS, the IRA-owned company structure is becoming well-settled law and is becoming more widely used by self-directed IRA investors.

THE ELLIS CASE

The most recent case addressing the IRA/LLC structure is *Ellis v. Commissioner*, No. 14-1310 (8th Cir 2015). In *Ellis,* the Court of Appeals upheld the Tax Court's decision that an IRA can acquire substantially all of the initial membership interest of an LLC (e.g., 98%) in exchange for a cash investment. The Court also ruled that it is a prohibited transaction for the IRA owner to be paid compensation for managing the IRA/LLC.

As to the first question, the Tax Court held that Mr. Ellis' IRA did *not* engage in a prohibited transaction when it acquired 98% of the ownership of a newly established LLC called CST, LLC. The other 2% was owned by an unrelated person who was not part of the case and whose ownership did not have an impact on the decision. The IRS contended that a prohibited transaction occurred when the IRA bought ownership of CST, LLC. The Court disagreed, however, and held that the IRA's purchase of the initial membership interest of the LLC was *not* a prohibited transaction. The Court stated that the IRA's purchase of membership interest in a new LLC is analogous to prior holdings of the Court whereby the Court held that an IRA does not engage in a prohibited transaction when it acquires the initial shares of a new corporation. Similarly, the court held that a new LLC is not a disqualified person to an IRA under the prohibited transaction rules, and as a result, an IRA may invest and own the ownership of the LLC. IRC § 4975(e)(2)(G), *Swanson V. Commissioner*, 106 T.C. 76, 88 (1996). The Court's ruling means that it is *not* a prohibited transaction for an IRA to acquire substantially all or all of the ownership of a new LLC.

As to compensation to the IRA owner for managing the IRA/LLC, as was expected, the Tax Court held that it was a self-dealing prohibited transaction for the LLC owned substantially by Mr. Ellis's IRA to pay compensation to Mr. Ellis personally. The court reasoned that:

> In causing CST [the IRA/LLC] to pay him [IRA owner] compensation, Mr. Ellis engaged in the transfer of plan income or assets for his own benefit in violation of § 4975 (c)(1)(d).

In deciding the case, the Court looked to the operating agreement of the LLC which authorized payment to Mr. Ellis for serving as the general manager. The Court also looked to the actual records of the LLC, which showed the company expensing payments to Mr. Ellis. When using an IRA/LLC, one of the many important clauses in the operating agreement is one which restricts compensation to the IRA owner or any other disqualified person (e.g. IRA owner's spouse or kids).

LEGAL TIP
❖ Compensation to the IRA owner or any other disqualified person is a prohibited transaction. Compensation to the IRA owner is not exempt from the rules under the reasonable-compensation exemption found in IRC § 4975 (d)(10).

It is also important to note that the Tax Court rejected Mr. Ellis's argument that the compensation payments he received were exempt from the prohibited transaction rules under IRC § 4975 (d)(10). Section (d)(10) provides an exemption to the prohibited transaction rules for payments of reasonable compensation from an

IRA to a disqualified person (e.g., IRA owner) for services rendered to manage the IRA.

The Tax Court rejected application of the reasonable-compensation exemption and ruled that the payments from the IRA/LLC were not for management of the IRA but for management of the IRA/LLC and its business activities. In *Ellis*, the IRA owner was actively involved as the general manager of the IRA/LLC, which was in the business of buying and selling cars. As a result, the exemption did not apply, and the payments were a prohibited transaction.

IRA OWNER OR DISQUALIFIED PERSON AS IRA/LLC MANAGER

Most IRA/LLCs are established with the IRA owner as the manager of the LLC. While the IRA owner could select whomever he or she wants to serve as manager, most IRA owners will list themselves as the manager. The manager of an LLC is akin to the president of a corporation as both positions have the authority to act for the company. Under the laws effecting LLCs, the manager does not need to be an owner. So, in the basic IRA/LLC structure, the IRA is the 100% owner/member (owners of an IRA are called members) of the LLC, and the manager is the IRA owner.

An IRA owner or other disqualified person may provide certain services as manager of the IRA/LLC. As a result of the Tax Court's ruling in *Ellis*, it is clear that an IRA owner (or other disqualified person) cannot receive compensation from the IRA/LLC.

In addition to the *Ellis* case, the IRS in 2009 determined that compensation from the IRA/LLC to the IRA owner is a self-dealing prohibited transaction. The IRS Chief Counsel's Office wrote in response to questions from internal revenue agents that:

> Yes you are correct the payment of salary to the IRA owner, even indirectly by an IRA owned LLC, is a prohibited transaction. IRS Chief Counsel Advice Number (CCA) 200952049 (12/24/2009).

LEGAL TIP
❖ If the IRA owner or other disqualified person is serving as manager of an IRA/LLC, then the LLC must restrict the manager from receiving compensation.

Additionally, in the CCA response from the IRS, the IRS clarified questions regarding IRC § 4975 (d)(10), which provides an exemption to the prohibited transaction rules for "receipt by a disqualified person of any reasonable compensation for services rendered." In the CCA, the IRS stated that this exemption to the prohibited transaction rules would avoid a per se prohibited transaction but reasoned that it would not exempt a self-dealing prohibited transaction under IRC § 4975 (c)(1)(E) and (F) as the IRA owner is in a conflict of interest situation when paying himself or herself as manager of the IRA/LLC. This is also the position adopted by the Tax Court in *Ellis*.

The plain language of the reasonable compensation exemption to the prohibited transaction rules found in IRC § 4975 (d)(10) is that the exemptions apply to all prohibited transactions including self-dealing and per se prohibited transactions. The IRS and the Tax Court, however, seem to view the matter differently and have taken the position that any compensation, whether reasonable or not, from the IRA/LLC to the IRA owner results in a prohibited transaction. Consequently, the IRA/LLC documents must restrict an IRA owner (or any disqualified person) from receiving any type of compensation from the IRA/LLC.

While compliance with the Tax Court and IRS/DOL positions are the course I recommend to clients, many experts believe that IRS's interpretation of IRC § 4975 (d)(10) is incorrect. Experienced IRA attorney Noel C. Ice, explained regarding the IRS CCA:

> ...the CCA reasons that the IRC § 4975(d) exemptions only apply to some of the § 4975 (c)PTs [prohibited transactions]. This is a total re-writing of the statute. Ice, Noel C., *When Can an IRA or Qualified Plan Invest in a Closely Held Business?*, Fort Worth, Texas (March 2012).

Compensation to an IRA owner (or other disqualified persons) is strictly enforced by self-directed IRA custodians. When IRA/LLC documents are sent to a self-directed custodian for investment, those documents are reviewed by the custodian's compliance department and will be rejected if the IRA/LLC is able to pay compensation to the IRA owner or any other disqualified person.

EXTENT OF SERVICES PROVIDED BY AN IRA OWNER AS MANAGER

In addition to the compensation restriction, the IRA/LLC should also restrict the services that an IRA owner or other disqualified person may provide to the IRA/LLC. As a general rule, the IRA owner or other disqualified person should restrict his or her activities as manager to administrative and investment oversight functions. These functions include the following:

- Signing contracts or agreements as manager of the IRA/LLC.

- Paying bills, receiving income, and signing checks as the manager of the IRA/LLC business bank account.
- Making decisions as to investments, expenses, tenants, vendors, employees, contractors, and other business activities.

An IRA owner or other disqualified person should be restricted from providing services to the IRA/LLC that would result in a contribution of value. For example, if an IRA/LLC owned a property that was being renovated and if the IRA owner did the physical work to remodel the kitchen, then such work could be deemed a contribution of value from the IRA owner to the IRA. Contributions are governed by IRC § 408(a)(1) which states that "...no contribution will be accepted unless it is in cash...." If a contribution to an IRA is made in a form other than cash, then it is considered an excess contribution and is subject to penalties. As a result, a contribution of services that exceeds administrative or investment oversight functions could create an excess contribution, and the value of said services would be subject to penalties under IRC § 4973. There has not been an IRS or DOL pronouncement addressing this point, nor am I aware of a case addressing this issue. Until such guidance arises, IRA owners and disqualified persons are best advised to limit their actions as manager of an IRA/LLC to administrative or investment oversight functions and should avoid physical work which adds value to an IRA asset.

LEGAL TIP
❖ The IRA owner and other disqualified persons should not physically work on assets if that work adds value to the IRA/LLC's investments (e.g., can't remodel the kitchen on a property owned by the IRA/LLC).

GETTING MONEY INTO THE IRA/LLC

When an IRA/LLC is established, it is usually funded with an initial investment contribution from the IRA. This amount is determined by the IRA owner based on the amount of money, he or she wants to invest into the IRA/LLC. As has been discussed in *Swanson, Hellweg, and Ellis*, the initial funding and capitalization of the IRA-owned company is not a prohibited transaction. But what about additional investments from the IRA to the LLC—is that allowed? In the *Swanson* case, the Tax Court noted that they were not ruling or deciding on whether a subsequent investment from the IRA to the LLC would be a prohibited transaction.

One year following the Tax Court's ruling in *Swanson*, the Department of Labor issued Advisory Opinion 97-23A. In the Advisory Opinion, the DOL stated that subsequent investments from a retirement plan to a company owned 100% by the plan would not result in a prohibited transaction as the funding of money between a retirement plan and a company the plan owns 100% is an "intra plan" transfer of money and not a "transaction" for purposes of the prohibited transaction rules. As a result, additional investment from an IRA to the IRA/LLC is acceptable.

IRA/LLC OPERATIONAL TIP
❖ All money *invested* into the IRA/LLC bank account must be from the IRA and must be recorded by the IRA custodian. All money distributed to the IRA owner must first go to the IRA and then it is distributed from the IRA to the IRA owner.

GETTING MONEY OUT OF THE IRA/LLC

The IRA/LLC bank account must be carefully maintained and should be strictly used for the IRA/LLC's investments. It should receive all income of the IRA/LLC, should pay all expenses of the IRA/LLC, and should not be used for personal purposes. The account should also not be comingled with the personal funds of the IRA owner or other disqualified persons.

The IRA owner cannot take distributions from the IRA/LLC as distributions must be handled at the IRA level. If an IRA owner wants to take a distribution of funds from the money in the IRA/LLC bank account, then the IRA/LLC will need to send a check (return on investment/capital) to the IRA custodian for deposit into the IRA. The IRA owner will then take a distribution from the IRA directly. Since distributions need to be tracked and reported by the IRA custodian and since it is a prohibited transaction for the IRA/LLC to pay the IRA owner, the funds distributed by the IRA must always go through the IRA custodian and will be subject to any applicable distribution taxes or penalties.

PRACTICAL TIP
❖ Not all self-directed IRA custodians allow an IRA/LLC structure where the IRA owner is the manager. This is usually because of concerns regarding prohibited transaction issues after the IRA/LLC is established. This is not because the structure is illegal, rather, it is because of how the structure could potentially be abused. That being said, most self-directed IRA custodians allow the IRA owner to be the manager subject to certain rules and restrictions in the IRA/LLC documents and operation.

NON RECOURSE LOANS & IRA/LLCs

An IRA/LLC can obtain a nonrecourse loan that can be used to purchase real estate or other investment assets. The same nonrecourse loan restrictions apply to the IRA/LLC as apply to the IRA. UDFI tax is also applied in the same ways as is described in Chapters 9 and 15. Most major loan programs offered to self-directed IRAs have the same terms and funding requirements when an IRA/LLC is used instead of an IRA.

PRECIOUS METALS & IRA/LLCs

An IRA/LLC is subject to the same rules regarding the types of acceptable precious metals and storage requirements as the IRA. These rules are more fully laid out in chapter 12. However, an additional storage option is available to an IRA/LLC. An IRA/LLC may obtain a safe deposit box with a financial institution in the name of the LLC, and such safe deposit box may store acceptable precious metals. Such IRA/LLC-owned safe deposit boxes would most likely meet the storage requirements of IRC § 408(m)(3)(B) for IRAs as the deposit box is at a financial institution (e.g., bank). This form of storage has not been addressed by the IRS, the DOL, or the courts, but it is a reasonable application of the storage requirements. Storage at the office address of the IRA/LLC would not meet the storage requirement rules for precious metals.

OPERATING THE IRA/LLC

When operating an IRA/LLC, the IRA owner needs to ensure that the company is abiding by the prohibited transaction rules and other laws affecting the IRA's investment into the LLC. Many IRA/LLC structures are properly established but run into prohibited transaction issues because the IRA owners fail to operate it properly.

For example, in *Repetto, et al v. Commissioner*, Mr. Repetto's Roth IRA owned 98% of a company, and a third-party partner owned 2%. T.C.M. 2012-168 (U.S. Tax Ct. 2012). Mr. Repetto was also the president of his Roth IRA-owned company. Additionally, Mrs. Repetto's Roth IRA owned 98% of a separate company and a third-party partner owned 2%. Mrs. Repetto was the president of her Roth IRA-owned company.

The transactions in question were payments from the Repettos' personally owned construction company to their Roth IRA-owned companies. The actual Roth IRA-owned company structure was not in question in the case and the Tax Court wrote that,

> The [IRS] agrees that generally an entity in which substantially all of the interest is owned or acquired by a Roth IRA may be recognized as a legitimate business entity for Federal tax purposes. However...the resulting payments [from the Roth IRA owners personal construction company to the Roth IRA owned companies] were nothing more than a mechanism for transferring value to the Roth IRAs [since there was no legitimate business purpose for the payments to the Roth IRA owned companies].

The Roth IRA-owned company structure was not put into question by the IRS in *Repetto*. However, the activities that the companies engaged in clearly violated the prohibited transaction rules as well as IRS Notice 2004-8 as the structure was an unfair transfer of value from a disqualified person to a Roth IRA-owned corporation.

The IRA owners should keep the IRA/LLC separate from their personal assets and personal companies. In *Niemann v. Commissioner*, T.C. Memo 2016-11 (2016), Niemann had and IRA/LLC which he managed and used to buy and sell real estate. Unfortunately, while conducting transactions Niemann transferred properties or assets from the IRA/LLC to his personal name or to companies he personally owned. These actions clearly violated the prohibited transaction rules and the Tax Court held that the prohibited transaction rules to apply to the IRA/LLC in the same way as if his IRA had transferred property to him personally (or to companies Niemann personally owned).

The following table outlines a list of do's and don'ts that should be followed by every IRA/LLC. This list applies to IRA/LLCs described in this chapter as well as multi-member IRA/LLCs described in the next chapter.

TABLE 13.2, IRA/LCC DO'S & DON'Ts

DO's	DON'Ts
• Maintain the registration of your Company in whichever State it is registered.	• Allow your Company to lend cash to a disqualified person.
• Provide Annual Valuations to the Custodian of your self-directed retirement account.	• Pay yourself or other disqualified person for performing management to your Company.
• Make distributions from your Company pro-rata according to the ownership percentages established at the initial formation of your Company.	• Allow yourself or other disqualified persons to Contribute sweat equity (labor) to your Company (for example make repairs to property owned by your Company).
• Perform rigorous due diligence on the investments in which your Company intends to participate.	• Enter into a contract in your personal name or a disqualified person's name when the contract should be with your Company.
• Set up a bank account for the Company and maintain separate bookkeeping.	• Sign a personal guarantee or give personal credit on behalf of your Company.

TABLE 13.2, IRA/LCC DO'S & DON'Ts (CONT'D)

DO's	DON'Ts
• Unless your Company is a "Single-Member-LLC," file your annual partnership tax return for the Company (Form 1065).	• Take a "retirement distribution" directly from your Company. This must be done through your IRA Custodian.
• Report any UBTI or UDFI that arises from the operations of your Company (reported on Form 990 for IRAs and form 5500 for 401(k)s.	• Rent, live in, or otherwise use or benefit from any property or assets owned by the Company.
• Update your Beneficiary Designation forms with the Custodian of your self-directed retirement account(s).	• Transfer ownership in the Company to or from a disqualified person.
	• Co-mingle personal or other non-retirement assets or expenses within Company.
• Consult with your CPA or Attorney for your specific situation in order to avoid prohibited transactions or unintended tax consequences related to your Company's investments.	• Use Company funds to pay for personal expenses, even if those expenses are somewhat related to the company.

Some self-directed IRA owners run into problems when they fail to do the little things and when they fail to properly consult with experienced attorneys or professionals. self-directed IRA investors can be "do it yourself" (DIY) type persons, but sometimes a DIY mentality can result in unintended mistakes that can have significant consequences when tens or hundreds of thousands of dollars from an IRA are involved.

ESTABLISHING AN IRA/LLC

When establishing an IRA/LLC, a self-directed IRA owner should consider the following:

1. Engage an experienced attorney to prepare the IRA/LLC documents and provide a written opinion as to the legality of the IRA/LLC. Most self-directed IRA custodians require an attorney to establish the IRA/LLC. Some custodians also require an attorney or CPA to be listed as a designated advisor to the IRA owner with regard to prohibited transactions and operational compliance for the IRA/LLC. A basic IRA/LLC structure does not need to be extremely expensive, and IRA owners should avoid attorneys who charge exorbitant fees for establishing the IRA/LLC. As a point of reference, my law firm currently charges $750 plus state filing fees for establishing a 100% IRA-owned IRA/LLC and charges $1,500 plus state filing fees for a multi member IRA/LLC. IRA owners should avoid on-line business set-up services or IRA/LLC "facilitators" who promote the IRA/LLC structure but who cannot offer you advice or opinion as to the transactions you intend to engage in. In addition to not being able to offer an opinion, these unlicensed providers of legal services regularly have their documents rejected by self-directed IRA custodians.

2. Appropriately plan for the investments the IRA/LLC intends to undertake. Decide which state to establish the IRA/LLC, taking into account the state where the IRA

owner resides and the state where the IRA owner intends to acquire assets. For example, if the IRA owner lived in Arizona but intended to buy Florida real property with his IRA/LLC, I would recommend a Florida IRA/LLC.

3. Verify that your self-directed IRA custodian will allow you as the IRA owner to serve as manager of the IRA/LLC. Most self-directed custodians will allow for this if they receive appropriate documents; however, there are a few self-directed IRA custodians who will not allow an IRA owner or other disqualified person to serve as manager of the IRA/LLC. Those who do not routinely allow an IRA/LLC with an IRA owner as a manager can sometimes be convinced otherwise, as I have done for a few clients. However, it requires special work and exceptions to their procedures, and as a result, self-directed IRA investors are better off using a custodian who allows IRA/LLCs where the IRA owner is the manager.

4. Appropriately plan for who the owners of the IRA/LLC will be. As is discussed in the next chapter, the IRA/LLC can consist of multiple IRAs or individuals, and it is always best to determine who the owners will be upon set- up and formation of the IRA/LLC as there can be restrictions in transferring ownership around following establishment of the IRA/LLC.

5. A properly established IRA/LLC should contain the following items. These items must be supplied to the IRA custodian upon a request for investment from the IRA to the IRA/LLC:

   a. Properly created articles of organization with the IRA as the member and the IRA owner or other person/company as the manager.

b. An operating agreement tailored to the IRA being an owner. All major IRA custodians review submitted IRA/LLC operating agreements to ensure that they are drafted in compliance with the laws effecting IRAs. A standard LLC operating agreement which was not drafted with an IRA owner in mind will not be acceptable and will be rejected. A standard LLC operating agreement will contain numerous clauses which would result in a prohibited transaction and will also not contain sections which most custodians require.

c. Properly obtained Tax ID or EIN with the Tax ID appropriately listing the IRA as the owner. The Tax ID should not be obtained in the personal name of the IRA owner.

d. A subscription document and agreement that outlines the amounts being invested into the IRA/LLC and the units exchanged. In many instances, these terms can be outlined in the operating agreement, but they are also sometimes listed in a separate document.

e. A buy direction letter directing the self-directed IRA custodian to invest the IRA funds into the IRA/LLC.

f. An opinion letter or designated advisor agreement from the attorney establishing the IRA/LLC for the IRA.

In summary, an IRA/LLC can be an excellent tool for certain self-directed IRA investments. However, the IRA owner should receive legal advice and guidance to ensure that the IRA/LLC is property established and operated. Failure to properly establish the IRA/LLC will result in your self-directed IRA custodian rejecting your IRA/LLC documents and could also result in a prohibited transaction and disqualification of your self-directed IRA.

FREQUENTLY ASKED QUESTIONS

Q. I have an existing LLC that I set up and haven't used yet. Can I use that as my IRA/LLC?

A. No, a transfer of ownership of the company from the IRA owner to the IRA is a prohibited transaction.

Q. I set up an IRA/LLC and submitted it to my custodian, and they rejected it and told me it was not set up properly, but they won't advise on how to fix it. What do I do?

A. Most IRA/LLC's established by IRA owners or attorneys, who are unfamiliar with the IRA laws affecting self-directed IRAs, will be rejected by the self-directed IRA custodian. self-directed IRA custodians are also reluctant to give their customers legal advice, so they generally will not tell you what to fix or how to fix it. You will need to consult with an experienced attorney.

Q. Does my IRA/LLC need to file a tax return?

A. When the IRA/LLC is owned by one IRA it does not need to file a tax return to the IRS. If the IRA/LLC is a multi-member IRA/LLC, as discussed in the next chapter, then the IRA/LLC needs to file a tax return annually to the IRS.

Q. I live in California and want to use an IRA/LLC to buy California real estate. Does the IRA/LLC have to pay the annual $800 California Franchise Tax Board fee?

A. Yes, unfortunately, when any LLC does business in California, including an IRA/LLC, it must pay the annual $800 California Franchise Tax Board fee. If the IRA/LLC is not doing business in California, you do not need to worry about this fee, as this fee is unique to California.

Q. If I set up an IRA/LLC now with my IRA owning 100% of the IRA/LLC, can my wife's IRA later invest into that same IRA/LLC?

A. No, the transfer of ownership from your IRA to your wife's IRA would be a prohibited transaction. It is possible to have each IRA invest at the formation of the IRA/LLC and to take ownership at formation according to the amounts invested from each IRA (rather than it transferring from one to the other). This co-investment of IRAs and the options possible are discussed in the following chapter.

Q. Can the IRA/LLC open a brokerage account and trade stocks?

A. Yes, this is possible as an IRA/LLC can own a brokerage account. The IRA owner will want to make certain that the IRA/LLC does not use margin (e.g., debt) for trades. Additionally, from my experience, I think IRA owners are better off trading stocks in an IRA with a brokerage account rather than in an LLC brokerage account. It's just more efficient from a fee standpoint to trade stocks in an IRA brokerage account as opposed to an IRA/LLC brokerage account. Additionally, many brokers are not familiar with IRA/LLCs and can take weeks to process basic account set-up documents.

Q. What do I need to do each year to properly maintain my IRA/LLC?

A. You will need to keep the IRA/LLC active in the state where it is registered, which requires a fee of approximately $100 in most states (fee ranges from zero a year in AZ to $800 a year in CA). You will also need to provide annual valuation figures to your IRA custodian, outlining the fair market value of investments owned by your IRA/LLC at the end of each year. You should also keep accurate records of income and expenses for the IRA/LLC. Although a tax return is not required for an IRA/LLC owned by one IRA, your IRA could be subject to an audit and the better records you have to document the activities of the IRA/LLC, the easier it will be to respond to and answer any questions in an audit. And lastly, we also recommend that IRA/LLC complete an annual set of minutes outlining the activities of the IRA/LLC for the prior year.

Q. I've been asked to complete a W-9 for the IRA/LLC so that the title company or investment sponsor can issue a 1099, how do I complete that when my IRA owns the LLC 100% and is a single-member LLC?

A. For single-member IRA/LLCs, a W-9 is completed using the name of the IRA on line 1 (e.g. ABC Trust Company FBO Mat Sorensen IRA), then line 2 is the name of the LLC, Box 3 would have single-member LLC checked and then in Part I you would input your custodians EIN that they provide for their IRA accounts for tax reporting purposes. You'll have to contact your custodian for this EIN but most provide it regularly for their customers. You can include your IRA account number if you'd like in box 7. If this was a multi-member IRA/LLC, you would simply check partnership in section 3 and would use the IRA/LLCs EIN in Part I and your IRA account would not be listed on line 1.

CHAPTER 14: The Multi-Member IRA/LLC Structure

The multi-member IRA/LLC structure consists of an IRA as a member and at least one other owner. The additional owner may be another IRA, or it may be an individual. There are unique issues that arise in multi-member IRA/LLCs, and the possibilities and restrictions are usually a result of the prohibited transaction rules in IRC § 4975.

The benefit of a multi-member IRA/LLC is that multiple IRAs or individual investors can pool investment capital and/or resources into one multi-member IRA/LLC. The down side is that the multi-member IRA/LLC is more difficult to establish and to administer than the 100% IRA-owned IRA/LLC.

KEY POINTS
▪ *An IRA/LLC can be owned by multiple IRAs or a combination of IRAs and individuals, but careful attention must be paid towards the set-up and funding of the IRA/LLC.*
▪ *A federal partnership tax return must be filed annually by the multi-member IRA/LLC.*

The following diagram outlines the multi-member IRA/LLC structure.

DIAGRAM 14.1, MULTI-MEMBER IRA/LLC STRUCTURE

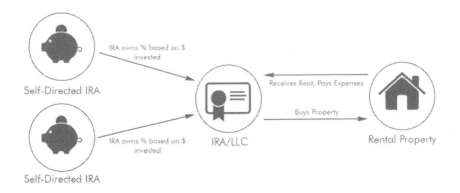

TAX REPORTING FOR A MULTI MEMBER IRA/LLC

As discussed in the previous chapter, if an IRA/LLC is owned by one IRA it does not have to file a tax return with the IRS. However, if there is more than one owner of the IRA/LLC, a partnership tax return will need to be filed by the IRA/LLC claiming the income made by the LLC and showing the amounts of profit and/or loss attributable to each member of the LLC. There is no tax paid on an IRA/LLC's partnership tax return and the K-1 tax reports (the tax form showing each member's share of profit or loss) for IRA members should be reported to the IRA via his or her custodian's Tax ID and not to the IRA owner personally.

IRA AND DISQUALFIED PERSON CO-OWNERSHIP

An IRA and a disqualified person may have an ownership interest in the same asset so long as the ownership is fairly allocated, is separate, and does not unfairly benefit the disqualified person. A Bankruptcy Court was asked whether co-ownership of real estate between an IRA and disqualified person constituted a prohibited transaction. *In re Cherwenka,* Case 13-57592-MGD (Bankr. N.D. GA 2014).

The property in question was owned 45% by the IRA and 55% by the IRA owner. The Court rejected the bankruptcy Trustee's argument that such co-investment purchase resulted in a prohibited transaction and stated that the interests appeared to have been treated distinctly and that the HUD documents from the purchase and sale of the property show that the IRA and the IRA owner's proceeds from the sale were treated separately and that they were apportioned properly. As a result, the Court concluded that no prohibited transaction occurred since there was no evidence of un-fair benefit between the IRA owner and his IRA. In its reasoning, the Court referenced DOL Opinion 2000-10A which addressed an IRA and the IRA owner co-investing into a partnership. In the Opinion the DOL states that, "a violation of section 4975 (c)(1)(D) or (E) will not occur merely because the fiduciary [IRA owner] drives some incidental benefit from the transaction involving IRA assets." The Court referenced this opinion and stated that unless there is evidence of some un-fair benefit that no prohibited transaction occurred merely because of co-investment into the same property.

If you are buying property or others assets (e.g. LLC interests) between your IRA and yourself personally (or another disqualified person) those interests must be carefully calculated and treated such that there is no benefit going unfairly between the IRA and the disqualified person (e.g. IRA owner). In sum, get advice and plan carefully as there are many land-mines you could encounter when investing IRA funds with your own personal funds.

Ownership allocated between owners in a multi-member IRA/LLC should be based on the amount of money invested. Ownership allocations

OWNERSHIP ALLOCATION IN A MULTI MEMBER IRA/LLC

Ownership allocated between owners in a multi-member IRA/LLC should be based on the amount of money invested. Ownership allocations for services or for "finding the deal" should *not* be made when such ownership is being allocated away from an IRA to a disqualified person as that would result in a transaction with a disqualified person. IRC § 4975 (c)(1)(A). Also, an IRA must receive the same ownership percentage share per dollar that an individual who invests receives in the multi-member IRA/LLC. For example, it is not possible to form a multi-member IRA/LLC where a Roth IRA invests $10,000 for 50% ownership and where the Roth IRA owner personally invests $90,000 for 50% ownership. This allocation example is unacceptable because it is clearly being based on something other than dollars invested and would certainly result in a prohibited transaction. Instead, the Roth IRA should receive 10% ownership for a $10,000 investment, and the Roth IRA owner should receive 90% ownership for the personal investment of $90,000. Additionally, it is impermissible to special allocate profits and losses between an IRA member and a disqualified person.

GETTING MONEY INTO A MULTI-MEMBER IRA/LLC

There is much disagreement in the self-directed IRA industry about whether additional contributions or investments into a multi-member IRA/LLC may be made after formation of the IRA/LLC. Subsequent or additional investment into a 100% IRA-owned IRA/LLC is much more commonly accepted among self-directed IRA custodians. However, the multi-member IRA/LLC structure does have some different treatment in the industry as it relates to additional investments into the IRA/LLC after formation and the initial investment or capital.

For example, if a husband's IRA owns 50% of an IRA/LLC and if the wife's IRA owns the other 50%, then is it a prohibited transaction for them to invest an additional $10,000 into the IRA/LLC after formation? What if they both invested their requisite share of the needed capital, which would be $5,000?

Despite the disagreement in the industry, the DOL addressed this issue in Advisory Opinion 2003-15A. This opinion involved numerous Verizon retirement plans that were invested into a company and owned various portions of ownership. The DOL was asked whether additional contributions and distributions between the company and the different retirement plans would result in a prohibited transaction. The DOL stated the following.

> Therefore, transactions between the Verizon Plans [retirement plans] and the CIV [company, e.g. IRA/LLC], including the initial and subsequent contributions to the CIV by the Verizon Plans and distributions from the CIV to the Verizon Plans, would not be prohibited under section 406(a) of ERISA [or under IRC § 4975].

Additionally the DOL stated,

> Consistent with section 3(14) of ERISA, a plan's ownership of fifty percent or more of a partnership entity will not cause that partnership to become a party in interest [aka, disqualified person] with respect to that investing plan.

While this specific factual scenario was discussed under ERISA, which applies to company plans such as 401(k)s, the rules under ERISA are nearly identical to the rules for IRAs under IRC § 4975, and the DOL stated in its opinion that its opinion should be read with the same effect under IRC § 4975. As a result, this ruling can be relied on in the IRA context and makes clear that subsequent investment from owners in a multi-member IRA/LLC will not result in a prohibited transaction. That being said, it is still important to ensure that the additional contributions are pro-rata (e.g., dollars invested are based on ownership share) to protect against any ownership transferring between an IRA and a disqualified person.

MULTI MEMBER IRA/LLC STRUCTURING OPTIONS

The first IRA/LLC structuring option is the 100% IRA-owned IRA/LLC discussed in the previous chapter. The second IRA/LLC structure option is the first multi-member IRA/LLC option and consists of multiple IRAs owning one company. The IRAs could be from disqualified persons or could be unrelated third parties. For example, this structure could consist of someone's Roth IRA and their Traditional IRA. Or, it could be a husband's IRA, a wife's IRA, and son's Roth IRA. Or, It could be the IRAs of two friends who want to invest together.

DIAGRAM 14.1, MULTI-MEMBER IRA/LLC STRUCTURE

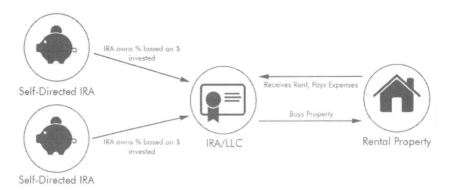

There are prohibited transaction concerns when an IRA invests into a company owned 50% or more by disqualified persons. IRC § 4975 (e)(2)(G). This "50% rule," however, only applies to an IRA investing into an *existing entity*. For example, a prohibited transaction would not occur when an IRA/LLC is established and the initial owners are a husband's IRA and a wife's IRA as there was no disqualified person who owned the multi-member IRA/LLC when it was formed.

An IRA may co-invest into a company with other disqualified persons at formation and such investment will not result in a prohibited transaction since the company formation and initial ownership allocation do not result in a transaction between disqualified persons. A prohibited transaction does not occur because the husband's IRA and the wife's IRA are not transacting between each other. Rather, they are co-investing into a common investment. Again, since there isn't a transaction that is taking place between the disqualified persons and their IRAs, there is not a prohibited transaction.

LEGAL TIP

❖ Multiple IRAs of disqualified parties may co-invest and own shares of an IRA/LLC at the time of formation and initial ownership allocation.

Under option #2, Diagram 14.1, the ownership percentages between the IRAs must be allocated based on dollars invested. For example, if my Roth IRA invests $20,000 into a new IRA/LLC and my traditional IRA invests $80,000, then my Roth IRA should receive 20%, and my traditional IRA should receive 80% of the IRA/LLC ownership. Remember, the primary situation that must be avoided is an instance where ownership changes between a disqualified person and an IRA. A change of ownership between an IRA and a disqualified person's account will result in a prohibited transaction under IRC § 4975 (c)(1)(A). A prohibited transaction occurs because ownership transfer is a transaction, and it is occurring between an IRA and a disqualified person (an IRA owned by a disqualified person).

Changes of ownership can occur when one owner over-contributes into the IRA/LLC. For example, let's say an IRA/LLC needs an additional $10,000 to cover an unexpected expense. If the Roth IRA owns 20% and the Traditional IRA owns 80% of the IRA/LLC, then the Roth must invest an additional $2,000, while the Traditional must invest an additional $8,000. If the traditional is out of funds and cannot invest, the Roth cannot just invest the $10,000 to cover the expense as that would result in an over-contribution based on ownership. This typically results in an increase of ownership to the Roth from the Traditional as the Roth now has $30,000 of the total $110,000 invested and will need to have more than 20% of the ownership (or profit/loss allocation).

As a result of the change of ownership concerns between disqualified IRAs, all additional investments to the IRA/LLC must be made by *all* members of the multimember IRA/LLC, and must be pro-rata based on the ownership percent share of the respective IRAs.

LEGAL TIPS FOR STRUCTURE #2

❖ All additional investments/contributions into the IRA/LLC (following the initial contributions) must be made pro-rata, based on the ownership percentages of the IRAs.

> ❖ A multi-member IRA/LLC is a partnership (more than one owner) and must file a partnership tax return to the IRS.

The IRA/LLC structure option #2 concept was discussed by the IRS in *IRS Field Service Advisory* #2002128011.

IRS FIELD SERVICE ADVISORY #2002128011

Five years after *Swanson*, the IRS issued *IRS Field Service Advisory (FSA)* #2002128011 (April 6, 2001). In the FSA, which is disseminated to IRS personnel, the IRS analyzed a scenario where a father and his three children's IRAs invested into a newly formed corporation. The IRAs each owned 25% of the company and invested equal amounts of capital. The company also returned dividends/profits to the IRAs as the company's business activities allowed. The IRS stated that based on *Swanson*, "...this case should not be pursued as one involving prohibited transactions." *Id. at pg.* 7. The IRS went on to explain, however, that prohibited transactions could occur if the IRA-owned company entered into transactions that benefitted disqualified persons. For example, it would clearly be a prohibited transaction if the company in the IRA-owned company in the FSA bought a car or other asset that was used personally by one of the IRA owners.

IRA/LLC STRUCTURING, OPTION #3

IRA/LLC structuring option #3, Diagram 14.2, consists of an IRA as an owner and an individual investor (non-retirement plan funds) as an owner.

DIAGRAM 14.2, MULTI-MEMBER IRA/LLC STRUCTURE WITH AN INDIVIDUAL INVESTOR AND AN IRA

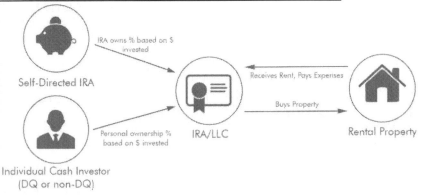

The only change from Option #2 to Option #3 is that one owner is an IRA, and one owner is an individual. When the individual investor in option #3 is a disqualified person, then the rules outlined in Option #2 apply in the same way, and additional investments into the IRA/LLC must be made pro-rata.

This option allows an IRA owner to combine personal funds into an LLC with IRA funds. Nevertheless, this structure should only be utilized when the IRA owner is fully informed of the laws and procedures applicable to this structure as there can be complications if ownership needs to change, or distributions need to occur, or if more money is required in the LLC. As Noel C. Ice explained regarding this type of structure: "After the entity has been formed, there is a mine field left in the wake." Ice, Noel C.,

When Can an IRA or Qualified Plan Invest in a Closely Held Business?, Fort Worth, Texas (March 2012). The best way to avoid these mines is to seek legal counsel before the structure is established so that you are aware of the rules and boundaries upon formation of the new company.

When the individual investor is *not* a disqualified person, the pro-rata additional contribution rules do not apply. For example, if John's IRA invests $50,000 into an IRA/LLC and if his friend Mark invests personal funds of $50,000, the ownership would be set at 50% to John's IRA and 50% to Mark personally. If the IRA/LLC later needed an additional $5,000 and if John did not have money in his IRA to cover his $2,500 portion, it is possible for Mark to invest the $5,000 and for some ownership to transfer from John's IRA to Mark. This transfer of ownership is not a prohibited transaction since Mark is a friend and is not disqualified as to John's IRA. If, however, John and Mark were respectively father and son, then Mark would be disqualified as to John's IRA, and the change of ownership would be a prohibited transaction. IRC § 4975 (e)(2)(F).

DOL ADVISORY OPINION 2000-10A

In some instances, an IRA/LLC may consist of an IRA and the IRA owner (or other disqualified person). A somewhat similar situation occurred in DOL Advisory Opinion 2000-10A. The facts in the Opinion are a little different from the structure diagrammed above, but the company did consist of ownership between an IRA, the IRA owner personally, and disqualified family members who owned less than 50% of the company. In the Advisory Opinion, the DOL stated that the investment from the IRA into the existing company would not be a per se prohibited transaction since the existing company was not owned 50% or more by disqualified parties. The DOL cautioned, though, that when a company is owned by disqualified persons

> ...the fiduciary [IRA owner, disqualified person] must not rely upon and cannot be otherwise dependent upon the participation of the IRA in order for the fiduciary to undertake or to continue his or her personal share of the investment.

As a result of the Opinion above, many professionals recommend that when an IRA co-invests with disqualified persons (such as IRA owner personally), that the investment from the IRA cannot be seen as enabling or saving the IRA owner's personal share of the investment. For example, if an IRA owner wanted to purchase an investment asset for $300,000 but only had $200,000 in personal funds, the IRA owner should not then create an IRA/LLC with his or her personal funds of $200,000 and then rely on his or her IRA to bring in the additional $100,000 as the IRA's investment could be seen as enabling the IRA owner's personal investment.

A conservative analysis of this "enabling" language leads one to conclude that an IRA should only co-invest with the IRA owner (or other disqualified persons) when the end investment was something which the IRA owner could have accomplished personally and without the assistance of the IRA's investment.

LEGAL TIP

❖ If an IRA's investment enables a disqualified person to make an investment they otherwise could not have made without the IRA, then the IRA has engaged in an enabling transaction. Enabling transactions can result in prohibited transactions.

This "enabling" restriction has not arisen again in a case or opinion since the DOL issued the above-referenced opinion, so it is unclear how it would apply to a newly formed IRA/LLC and a new investment asset. The concern of an IRA being used to rescue an IRA owner's personal investment is clearly valid and would likely result in a self-dealing prohibited transaction under IRC § 4975 (c)(1)(E) and (F). However, I'm not so certain it is applicable in a new investment context where the IRA and the IRA owner (or other disqualified person) are taking proportionate risk and burden in the investment, when they are investing at the same time, and when they are receiving ownership and rights to profit and loss based on their specific dollars invested. That being said, the law has not been clearly established on the enabling transaction and co-investment.

The best defense to an enabling transaction claim is to show that the IRA owner could have personally completed the planned investment with personal funds or resources. It is best to show that the IRA owner did not need the IRA to participate to undertake the end investment. If the IRA owner can demonstrate that he or she could have personally accomplished the investment without his or her IRA's funds, then he or she can co-invest with a combination of personal funds and IRA funds without having to be concerned with "enabling transaction" claims from the IRS.

IRA/LLC STRUCTURING, OPTION #4

IRA/LLC structuring option #4, Diagram 14.3, consists of one or more IRAs contributing cash and an individual contributing services. The ownership between the cash IRA member(s) and the individual member (or company) providing services is negotiated by the parties according to the value placed on the individual's services to be performed in the IRA/LLC. The previous structures all involved owners receiving ownership for cash investments where ownership is allocated based on dollars invested. Under Option #4, an IRA/LLC may be structured where an IRA or group of IRAs invests cash into the IRA/LLC, and another member to the IRA/LLC contributes services.

DIAGRAM 14.3, MULTI-MEMBER IRA/LLC STRUCTURE WITH AN IRA AND A SERVICE/WORK PARTNER

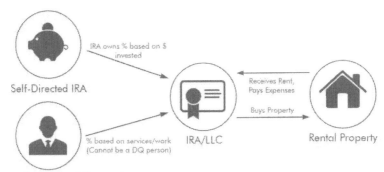

The "service partner" to the IRA/LLC cannot be a disqualified person. The IRA owner or a disqualified person to any IRA invested cannot be the "service partner" as that would amount to ownership being transferred from the IRA to a disqualified person for services rendered and would result in a prohibited transaction under IRC § 4975 (c)(1)(C) and (E) and (F).

ADDITIONAL STRUCTURING OPTIONS & GUIDELINES

There are so many other options and structures that may be accomplished by an IRA that are not outlined above. Whatever the structure, the IRA owner should, at a minimum, pay careful attention to the following three issues:

1. Is the company a newly formed company? If so, disqualified persons may co-invest.
2. Who will be the other owners, and are they disqualified to the IRA? Ensure that the IRA/LLC documents restrict changes of ownership between disqualified persons.
3. If the IRA owner or other disqualified person is a manager, the IRA/LLC documents must appropriately restrict the compensation and level of services of the manager.

Multi-member IRA/LLC structures can be complicated. As a result, IRA owners should seek legal counsel as to the proper structure and documents necessary to properly establish the multi-member IRA/LLC. In general, the checklist and list of documents outlined in Chapter 13 for 100% IRA-owned IRA/LLCs, also applies to multi-member IRA/LLCs.

FREQUENTLY ASKED QUESTIONS

Q. I want to set- up a multi-member IRA/LLC where my IRA owns 1/3, and then a friend of mine who is not a disqualified person to my IRA will own the other 2/3 with his IRA (or personally). Can I be the manager of the multi member IRA/LLC and get a salary or management fee since my IRA owns less than 50% of the IRA/LLC?

A. As a general rule, I would not recommend that you receive a salary or management fee for serving as manager of an IRA/LLC, even when your IRA owns less than 50% of the IRA/LLC. While one could argue that there is no per se prohibited transaction occurring between the IRA/LLC and the IRA owner personally (because the IRA/LLC is not disqualified to the IRA owner), it would likely result in a self-dealing prohibited transaction because the IRA owner is personally benefitting from the IRA/LLCs investment by receiving personal compensation. In certain circumstances, compensation may be permitted, but I would only recommend doing so when proper legal counsel is obtained and when your attorney has considered all of the facts and circumstances in the IRA/LLC company.

Q. Can I form a multi-member IRA/LLC between my Roth IRA and my Traditional IRA?

A. Yes, this is possible. The ownership between the accounts will be set based on dollars invested, and the IRA/LLC will need to file a partnership tax return annually since it will have more than one owner.

Q. Can I form a multi-member IRA/LLC between myself personally and my IRA whereby I obtain personal ownership for providing all of the work?

A. No, a disqualified person cannot obtain ownership in an IRA/LLC for services being rendered as that results in ownership transferring or being given up by an IRA to a disqualified person for services rendered.

Q. I plan to set- up an IRA/LLC with my IRA investing $50,000 and my husband's IRA investing $50,000. Later next year, I will have more money in my IRA as I am retiring and will be rolling over more money from my company retirement plan to my self-directed IRA. Can I then later invest an additional $100,000 that will come from the company rollover when those funds arrive next year in my self-directed IRA?

A. No. Since you and your husband are each putting $50,000 into the IRA/LLC from your IRAs, the IRA/LLC will be owned 50% by your IRA and 50% by your husband's IRA. If you add an additional $100,000 to the IRA/LLC from your IRA, then your husband would also need to add an additional $100,000 from his IRA in order for the ownership of the IRA/LLC to remain unchanged. Any change in ownership between IRAs of disqualified persons would result in a prohibited transaction, so you cannot invest additional capital from your IRA unless your husband matches the same investment amount from his IRA.

Q. I'd like to invest my Roth IRA and my Traditional IRA into a company, but I'm worried about putting more money in pro-rata over time. Also, I don't want to have to file a tax return each year for the IRA/LLC. What other options do I have?

A. Because of the multi-member IRA/LLC restrictions on investing additional money and because of the tax return requirement, many self-directed IRA investors will use multiple 100% IRA-owned IRA/LLCs as opposed to co-investing multiple IRAs into one IRA/LLC. For example, the Roth IRA would have its own 100% Roth IRA owned IRA/LLC, and the Traditional IRA would have its own separate 100% Traditional IRA-owned IRA/LLC. Additionally, some couples choose to do separate IRA/LLCs with their accounts to avoid the additional investment restrictions and the partnership tax return requirement.

Q. I want to create a multi-member IRA/LLC between myself personally and my IRA. The IRA/LLC would own investment real estate. I would like to special allocate the gains and income to the IRA and would allocate the depreciation and losses to myself personally under IRC § 704. Can I do this?

A. No. Special allocation between an IRA and disqualified person would result in a self-dealing prohibited transaction because you are personally benefitting from your IRAs investment by allocating income and loss from the IRA to yourself personally.

CHAPTER 15: Understanding UBIT & UDFI Tax For IRAs

There are two taxes that can apply to income received by a retirement plan. These taxes are unrelated business income tax ("UBIT") and unrelated debt financed income tax ("UDFI").

KEY POINTS
▪ *UBIT tax typically applies when an IRA receives ordinary income, as opposed to passive income, from its investments*
▪ *Passive investments like rental income, interest income, dividend income, capital gain income, and royalty income are exempt and are never subject to UBIT.*
▪ *UDFI tax applies to IRAs when it leverages its investment(s) with debt.*
▪ *If UBIT or UDFI tax is due the IRA owner must file a 990-T tax return for the IRA to the IRS. The IRA is responsible for the tax.*

Most popular self directed IRA investments are not subject to UDFI or UBIT tax, and as a result, most self directed IRAs will not be required to file and pay either of these taxes. However, there a few types of self directed investments that trigger UBIT or UDFI tax; therefore, self directed investors must be familiar with these taxes. The UBIT tax rate is 37% for income over $12,500, and because of this significant rate, it should be carefully considered when making self directed IRA investments. UDFI is also taxed at 37% for income subject to the tax with the capital gains tax rate being available for income subject to UDFI that is from capital gains.

UNRELATED BUSINESS INCOME TAX & IRAS

Unrelated Business Income Tax ("UBIT") applies to ordinary income received by an IRA. IRC § 511, IRS Publication 598, pg. 2 (2017). UBIT was first created as a way of taxing non-profit corporations which engaged in private for-profit activities unrelated to their charitable purpose. The tax was used as a way of separating what income was exempt from tax (e.g., part of a non-profit's charitable purpose) and what was taxable (e.g., unrelated to charitable purposes). When retirement accounts were established, Congress decided that it was important to separate what income would be exempt from taxation in retirement plans and what income would still be subject to tax when earned in a retirement account. IRC § 408 (e).

Since UBIT tax is broadly defined, the best way to understand it is to consider all income subject to UBIT tax unless an exemption applies. The exemptions are vast and will cover most self directed IRA investments, but there are still many investments that will become subject to UBIT tax.

The table below outlines the two most common self directed investments where UBIT tax is due.

TABLE 15.1, COMMON SELF DIRECTED IRA INVESTMENTS SUBJECT TO UBIT TAX

Income Type	Explanation
Ordinary Income Business Not Paying Corporate Tax (e.g., restaurant, tech company, business selling services or goods).	UBIT tax is due from an ordinary income producing business (e.g. selling service or product) when such business is a flow-through company not paying corporate tax. If the company is a C corp paying corporate tax on the profits, as are most publicly traded companies, then UBIT tax is not due as the income then goes to the IRA as dividend income, which is exempt from UBIT tax.
Real Estate Development, Construction, or Short Term Flipping Business.	UBIT tax is due from real estate activities that are not passive in nature. Rental income and capital gain income from the sale of real estate are exempt from UBIT, but there is a special caveat to the capital gain exemption on the sale of real estate which does not allow it to apply when the real property was acquired with intent to immediately sell.

EXEMPTIONS TO UBIT TAX

The exemptions to UBIT tax are found in IRC § 512(b). The exemptions cover most passive investments and are outlined in the table below. If an exemption applies, UBIT tax does not apply. Since the general definition of UBIT covers all sorts of income received by an IRA, I analyze investments and assume UBIT tax will apply and then seek to find an exception. As you can see below, most self directed IRA investments will fit within an exception to UBIT.

TABLE 15.2, UBIT TAX EXCEPTIONS

Income Type	Explanation
Interest Income 512(b)(1)	Interest income, such as interest payments on loans made from the self directed IRA are exempt from UBIT tax.
Dividend Income 512(b)(1)	This is the most common exemption and applies to dividends/profits received by an IRA from a C corporation (e.g., most publicly traded companies). Real Estate Investment Trust (REITs) income may also be considered a qualifying dividend and exempt. IRS Revenue Ruling 66-106.
Royalty Income 512(b)(2)	Royalty income is the income derived from intangible property rights such as intellectual property (e.g., use of name, software licensing, patent license). It also includes royalty income from certain oil and gas, and mineral-leasing activities.

TABLE 15.2, UBIT TAX EXCEPTIONS (CONT'D)

Income Type	Explanation
Rental Income 512(b)(3)	Rental income derived from real property is exempt from UBIT tax. Personal property that is leased in connection with real property is also exempt. Equipment leasing or other personal property leasing can be subject to UBIT tax unless the income can be considered interest income when the leasing is structured as a financing agreement.
Capital Gains 512(b)(5)	Capital gains from the sale, exchange, or other disposition of property, except for "property held primarily for sale to customers in the ordinary course of the trade or business."

CAPITAL GAIN ON REAL ESTATE EXEMPTION TO UBIT TAX

As noted above, the capital gain exemption for the sale of property does not apply when the property was "...held primarily for sale to customers in the ordinary course of the trade or business." IRC § 512(b)(5)(B). The significance for self directed IRAs is that real property purchased and then held immediately for sale can become subject to UBIT tax, as the capital gain exemption to the tax may not apply. Real property acquired with investment intent (e.g., rental or hold for 1 year), on the other hand, will always be exempt from UBIT as the capital gain exemption can be relied on when the property is later sold for a profit.

So the question becomes; how do you know if the real property owned by the IRA is being "held primarily for sale to customers in the ordinary course of the trade or business?" While the question doesn't seem so complicated, the law is very complex in this area.

There are really two different categories of real estate to analyze and determine whether "property is held primarily for sale" as opposed to being held for investment. The first type would be real estate acquired and sold on a short-term basis, such as a real estate investment fix and flip. The second type would be a real estate development project.

SHORT TERM REAL ESTATE FLIPS

As noted above, the capital gain exemption for the sale of property may not apply when an IRA purchases real estate on a short-term basis (less than 1 year) and sells it for a profit. Because of the limitation on the capital gain exemption, self directed IRA investors should avoid engaging in an activity whereby the real estate owned by the IRA is primarily for sale in the ordinary course of the trade or business of the IRA. There are two key components to this rule as applied to short-term real estate. First, is property being purchased and held primarily for sale to customers as opposed to being held for investment (e.g., rent)? And second, are the short-term real estate activities being done in the ordinary course of the IRA's business?

These can be difficult questions to answer and each situation requires careful analysis. In simple terms, one or two short-term real estate sales (aka, flips) conducted by an IRA in one year is likely not going to subject an IRA to UBIT. This is because the IRA will probably not be considered to be in the business of selling real estate in the ordinary course to customers when it only acquires and sells such a small number of properties per year. There are many additional factors to consider in this analysis, but the overriding and primary issue for short-term real estate sales will first be the number of transactions conducted as that determines whether this is something done in the ordinary course of business or whether it is done for investment.

An IRA that buys and sells ten short-term real estate properties per year would likely be subject to UBIT tax, as the capital gain exemption will not apply when so many transactions are conducted in one year. When a significant amount of short-term real estate is bought and sold in a year, the IRA appears to be in the business of acquiring property with intent to sell in its ordinary course of business. This situation is often-times referred to as "dealer" status and disqualifies the IRA income from being passive. As a result, UBIT tax would be due on the profits made by the IRA as no exclusions would apply.

REAL ESTATE DEVELOPMENT PROJECTS

The second type of real estate activity that may be subject to UBIT tax is real estate development projects where real estate is purchased, developed, and sold.

Again, if the property sold is held for investment, then UBIT tax will not apply as the IRA owner can rely on the capital gains exemption. However, if the property is deemed to be held as inventory in the ordinary course of business, then UBIT tax will apply to the profits from the sale of the property. The primary case analyzing whether the capital gain exclusion applies and whether the property is deemed to be held for investment is *Adams v. Commissioner*, 60 T.C.M. 996 (1973). In *Adams*, the U.S. Tax Court adopted a facts-and-circumstances test that is frequently used to analyze whether property is held for investment or held for sale in the ordinary course. The relevant factors are outlined below.

1. Intent. Property bought and held for investment demonstrates that the property is not intended to be held for sale. On the other hand, property bought and immediately held for sale would demonstrate intent to hold for sale in the ordinary course.

2. Holding Time. If the property is held less than a year, it is more likely to be considered property held for sale as opposed to property held for investment. In sum, the longer the property is held the more likely it is to be deemed held for investment.

3. Development, Construction or Improvements. Property which goes from land to fully developed homes or buildings will likely be deemed ordinary business activity and not property held for investment. Development, construction, and improvements make the property and profits from it appear to be conducted in the course of business as opposed to being held for passive investment.

4. Number of Sales or Frequency of Similar Transactions. A large number of sales of property that are short-term in duration will likely cause an IRA to be deemed to be in the ordinary business or selling real estate as opposed to holding and selling for investment.

These factors, when taken together, can help determine whether a property is held for sale and subject to UBIT tax or held for investment and exempt. These factors were analyzed in PLR 8950072 when the IRS was presented with a factual scenario from an exempt organization which owned 260 acres of undeveloped land that it sought to develop and sell. The organization asked the

IRS whether UBIT tax would be due in a number of scenarios but the two relevant for analysis of the capital gain exemption were as follows.:

a. <u>SCENARIO NOT SUBJECT TO UBIT</u>. The exempt organization would complete preliminary development work, which consisted of obtaining permits and city approvals for new uses to the property. The exempt organization would then sell the property in large blocks or parcels to a few developers who would construct the physical improvements to the property. The IRS deemed these actions to not constitute property "held for sale in the ordinary course of business" and would still consider the property to be held for investment and exempt from UBIT.

b. <u>SCENARIO SUBJECT TO UBIT</u>. Contrastingly, the exempt organization asked the IRS whether an alternative plan would result in UBIT tax. Under the alternative set of facts, the exempt organization would develop the property, would manage the improvements, and would market the property for sale. The improvements would include design and construction of streets, curbs, gutters, lighting, and utilities. The exempt organization would then subdivide the property and sell individual lots to the public. The IRS deemed this alternative plan to result in UBIT since there would be physical improvements and since it would involve the selling and marketing of lots to the general public.

The differentiating factor in the two scenarios outlined above, which determined whether UBIT tax would apply, was the physical improvements and construction to the property as well as the marketing and sale to the public.

CALCULATING & REPORTING UBIT TAX

If UBIT tax is due, the IRA must file IRS form 990-T to claim and pay the UBIT tax. Form 990-T is due on April 15th of each year for retirement plans. An IRA may also obtain an automatic three-month extension to file by filing a request for extension, IRS Form 8868. If UBIT tax is not due, then a form 990-T does not need to be filed. The IRS only requires a return to be filed by the IRA when tax is due and payment is being made. Additionally, the IRS only requires the reporting and payment of UBIT tax when annual gross UBIT income is $1,000 or greater. IRS Instructions to Form 990-T (2017). So when there is only incidental UBIT income that is under $1,000, then UBIT tax does not need to be reported or paid.

LEGAL TIP
❖ UBIT Tax only needs to be reported and paid if the IRA has over $1,000 of annual gross UBIT income.

The UBIT tax should be paid from the IRA's funds and should not be paid with personal funds of the IRA owner. The tax rates applicable to UBIT tax are the trust tax rates which cap out at a maximum rate of 37% at $12,500 of annual income subject to UBIT tax. IRS Publication 598 (2017). Additionally, some states also have a state based form of UBIT tax that can apply to an IRA. The state forms of UBIT tax usually only apply if the federal version applies.

TABLE 15.3. UBIT TAX RATE (2018)

ANNUAL INCOME	UBIT TAX RATE
$0–$2,550	10%
$2,551 - $9,150	$255 + 24% of amount over $2,550
$9,151 - $12,500	$1,839 + 35% of the excess over $9,150
Over $12,501	$3,011.50 + 37% of the excess over $12,500

Based on the table above, which is the applicable 2018 tax table, lets analyze what tax a self directed IRA would pay if it invested into a restaurant that is an LLC and receives a K-1 for $100,000 of net taxable income for the LLC for the year. Under this scenario, the IRA would pay UBIT tax of $35,387 and would have after-tax income of $64,613.

This is calculated as follows.

1. $3,011.50 on the first $12,500.

2. 37% on the remaining $87,500, which equals $32,375.

3. The total tax due then is $35,387.

4. The after-tax net amount the IRA would keep is $64,613. ($100,000 minus $35,387 in UBIT tax).

COMPARING UBIT TAX TO CORPORATE TAX

It is important to note that profits from investment into a publicly traded C corporation are also subject to tax on the profits. The difference is that the C corporation pays taxes on the profits at the corporate level. The after-tax profits are then paid to the IRA (or other owners) as dividends. Dividends paid to an IRA are exempt from UBIT tax per IRC § 512(b)(5).

Let's take an example of your IRA investing into McDonalds, Inc., which is a publicly traded C corporation. Let's say that your IRA receives dividends (profits from a C-corp) from the C-corp of $100,000. Because McDonalds must pay corporate-level taxes before distributing profits/dividends to its owners, McDonalds would have paid corporate taxes at a rate of 21%, which is the applicable rate for corporations following 2018 Tax Reform. As a result, after corporate tax is paid you're getting 79% of the income paid to your IRA. Because the corporate rate is now significantly lower than the UBIT rate (max corporate rate of 21% versus max UBIT rate of 37%) IRA investors should utilize C-corp taxation in instances where they would otherwise have to pay UBIT tax.

Remember, dividends/income paid from a C-corp to an IRA are exempt from UBIT tax so the only level of tax in that scenario is the corporate level tax. The major procedural difference is just that the large publicly traded C corporation is paying tax at the company level and after-tax profits are distributed. On the other hand, the flow-through LLC company is not paying any tax on company profits. Instead, it is pushing all income through to the owners for the owners to report and pay tax on.

In the end, either corporate tax is paid at the company level (e.g., publicly traded C-corp), and the corporate tax paid diminishes profits to the IRA. Or, UBIT tax is paid at the IRA level (e.g., flow-through LLC), thereby diminishing total net profits to the IRA at the IRA level.

USE OF "BLOCKER CORPORATIONS" TO AVOID UBIT AND UDFI TAX

Following tax reform in late 2017, Corporate tax rates are now significantly less than UBIT tax rates and blocker corporations should be considered for an IRA incurring UBIT. Because of the lower corporate tax rate, an IRA is well served by establishing a 100% owned C-corporation, which the IRA invests into, and then that C-corporation invests into the ordinary income LLC business and receives the ordinary income. For example, if a self directed IRA invests into an ordinary income business that is an LLC and if that LLC reports $100,000 of net taxable income to the IRA, then the IRA would pay $35,387 in federal taxes based on the UBIT tax table outlined above.

However, if the same ordinary income business paid $100,000 of profits to a C-corporation that was owned 100% by an IRA, then the C-corporation would pay corporate tax of $21,000 based on the new flat corporate tax rate of 21% implemented beginning in 2018. The C-corporation would then distribute its income to the self directed IRA as a dividend which is exempt from UBIT tax, and the IRA in the end would receive $79,000 of the total $100,000 of net income from the ordinary income business.

Use of a C-corporation in a situation like this is often referred to as a "blocker corporation" as it blocks UBIT tax from being due to the IRA in exchange for a less burdensome corporate tax. The table below outlines the tax difference in the example provided.

TABLE 15.4, BLOCKER CORP TAX SAVINGS

Net Income from operational LLC	Tax Paid on $100,000 of net income	Net Receipt By IRA
IRA owns operational LLC directly.	UBIT Tax - $35,387 due	$64,613
IRA owns C Corporation blocker company and blocker company owns LLC.	C-corp Tax- $21,000 in tax paid by C corp. Dividend of $79,000 to the IRA is exempt from UBIT.	$79,000 This is a net tax savings of $14,387.

In the scenario outlined above, use of a C corporation results in a tax difference of approximately $17,000 in favor of the C corporation blocker company tax structure. A short hand method to calculate savings when using a C-corp blocker is to simply take the 17% rate difference between corporate tax rates and UBIT tax rates and to add $17,000 in savings for every $100,000 of income that would be subject to UBIT. The C-corporation blocker strategy can be an excellent tool to be used by self directed IRA investors who are investing into ordinary income producing, flow-through businesses.

In addition to the use of U.S. C-corporations as blocker companies, foreign corporations may also be utilized in certain situations, and such foreign corporations typically have much lower corporate income tax rates than the U.S. corporate tax rates. Use of a foreign corporation blocker company is extremely complex and should only be considered when adequate counsel is obtained and only when significant amounts of money are being invested. If significant amounts are not being invested (e.g., over $250,000), then the cost and hassle of the foreign complexity will not be worth the tax savings. As a result, the U.S. based C-corporation blocker is more commonly used since it is much easier to establish and operate.

UDFI TAX EXPLAINED

Unrelated debt financed income ("UDFI) tax applies to the gains received by an IRA that are attributable to debt. IRC § 514. UDFI tax only applies when debt, such as a nonrecourse loan, is used in connection with an IRA's purchase. UDFI tax is technically a type of UBIT tax, so if UDFI tax is due, it is paid at the UBIT tax rate. Additionally, if UDFI tax and UBIT tax are due, there is no double payment of the tax since it is one income tax and not paid twice on the same income.

UDFI tax will apply to any income that is derived from "debt." This includes rental income and capital gain income, which is otherwise exempt from UBIT tax. UDFI tax is applied to income from "debt financed property" that is subject to "acquisition indebtedness." Debt financed property is defined as property held to produce income that has acquisition indebtedness. IRC § 514(b)(1).

Acquisition indebtedness is defined as debt used to "acquire or improve" property as well as debt incurred before the acquisition if such intent to incur the debt was to allow an acquisition. Additionally, debt incurred after the acquisition of property is acquisition indebtedness if such debt would not have been incurred without the property and if such debt were reasonably foreseen at the time of acquisition. IRC § 514(b)(1). In other words, a purchase loan, improvement loan, or a purchase and then a loan used to strip out the equity would all fall under the definition of acquisition indebtedness and would be subject to UDFI tax.

CALCULATING & REPORTING UDFI TAX

To calculate UDFI tax, you need to know the following three numbers:

1. The income from the property for the year.
2. The average acquisition indebtedness for the year.
3. The adjusted basis for the year (e.g., the cost of the property minus any depreciation).

Once you know these numbers, you can calculate UDFI tax. The first step is to determine the ratio of debt versus the basis (cost) of the property. So, for example, if a property is purchased for $100,000 and if $50,000 of that purchase price is debt, then we take $50,000 (the amount of debt) and divide it against the cost/basis of the property ($100,000), and in this instance we get .5. Therefore, 50% of the income from the property is subject to UDFI tax (ratio of $50,000 debt by $100,000 property cost).

Now that we know the leverage ratio of the property we can next determine the amount of income subject to UDFI tax. So, for example, if there were $10,000 of income on the property for the year, then we take the leverage ratio of 50% and apply it to the income, and we get $5,000 of income that would be subject to UDFI tax. The $5,000 in income is then subject to expenses and deductions, including depreciation expense. IRC § 514(a)(3). Once expenses are taken, the remaining taxable income under UDFI is subject to UBIT tax.

Because of expenses and the ability to take depreciation, many self directed IRAs that own leveraged real estate pay little UDFI tax year to year. However, if debt is still on the property at the time of sale and if the property value has increased, there can be a large amount of tax due at the time of sale. Here is an easy method to approximate UDFI tax:

1. What is the ratio of debt to cost (basis)of the property?
2. Take the debt ratio (e.g. debt to cost of property, $50,000 debt, $100,000 property cost, 50%) and apply that ratio to the amount of income to the property.
3. After you have the income subject to UDFI (this is the income attributable to the debt), you then subtract expenses.
4. After expenses have been taken the remaining net amount is subject to the UDFI tax.

UDFI tax at the time of sale works in a similar fashion to the example above, but the IRA is able to use the capital gain tax rate of 15-20% on profits subject to UDFI as opposed to being subject to the UBIT rate. *Internal Revenue Manual*, Part 2, 7.27.8.4. Unrelated Debt Financed Income, Gain From Sale or Other Disposition of Property, Treasury Regulations 1.514(a)-1(a)(v)(b), IRS Publication 598 (Rev 2017).

For example, let's consider a property held by an IRA and sold for $200,000, with an adjusted basis of $80,000. Let's assume the remaining average debt was $20,000, and that deductions for the year were $5,000. Based on this scenario, UDFI tax would be calculated as follows:

1. $20,000 debt/$80,000 basis = 25% leverage
2. Gain of $120,000 from sale of $200,000
3. 25% of $120,000 = $30,000
4. $5,000 of deductions against $30,000 = $25,000
5. Therefore $25,000 would be subject to the 20% long-term capital gains tax rate.
6. Tax owed would be 20% of $25,000 = $5,000.

UDFI tax of $5,000 would then be reported and paid using IRS form 990-T.

STRATEGIES TO AVOID UDFI TAX

There are a few strategies which self directed IRA investors can use to minimize or avoid UDFI tax.

The first strategy is to avoid having debt involved on the property in the first place. While this is not always available, it is worth considering. For example, if a self directed IRA investor was buying a property for $250,000, was using $100,000 from his IRA, and was getting $150,000 loaned from another real estate investor, the self directed IRA investor would be subject to UDFI tax as there will be debt used to acquire the property. If, however, the self directed IRA and the other investor were to structure the $150,000 investment from the real estate investor as an equity arrangement as opposed to a debt arrangement, then the $150,000 would be outside of UDFI tax. For example, the IRA and real estate investor could enter into a joint venture agreement or form an LLC, whereby a share of the equity is paid to the real estate investor. The deal would be outside of the reach of UDFI as there would be no debt.

The second strategy is to simply pay off the debt before the sale. UDFI tax at the time of sale is calculated by taking the prior 12 month average debt to determine the leverage ratio. However, if there is no debt over the prior 12 month period there would be a zero leverage ratio to apply and therefore no UDFI tax to apply at the time of sale.

The final strategy can be used when an IRA owns an IRA/LLC and the IRA/LLC in turn owns the property or other leveraged asset. Keep in mind that UDFI tax is due and will flow through to an IRA when owned by an IRA/LLC. However, when the self directed IRA sells its LLC ownership to a new buyer as opposed to the real property with debt, the self directed IRA would get gains on the sale of the LLC interest and the LLC interest was not acquired with debt. The applicability of this strategy has been challenged by the IRS in TAM 96-51-001 whereby the IRS essentially stated that debt incurred by a partnership LLC to leverage its assets (e.g. mortgage for real estate holdings) must be considered in the sale of an LLC interest. I'm not aware of any case law on this issue and consequently careful planning and consultation with your attorney or CPA should be taken when selling a partnership interest whereby the underlying company assets are leveraged with debt.

401(k)s & OTHER EMPLOYER PLANS ARE EXEMPT FROM CERTAIN UDFI TAX

401(k) and other employer plans are exempt from UDFI taxes that arise from debt on real property. IRC § 514(9). The tax code specifically exempts plans which are "qualified trusts" under section 401 from the tax code from UDFI tax. IRC § 514I (9)(C)(ii). Section 401 of the code includes pension plans and 401(k)s.

This is a significant benefit to 401(k) and other qualified plans over IRAs and many self directed retirement plan investors who are able to establish a self directed 401(k) plan (e.g., Solo K, Individual K, etc.) will utilize a 401(k) for debt financed retirement plan investments as opposed to an IRA.

Solo 401(k)s and other employer plans exempt from UDFI are still subject to the other aspects of UBIT, including being subject to UBIT tax on real estate development or operational businesses not paying corporate taxes.

FREQUENTLY ASKED QUESTIONS

Q: I've had to pay some UBIT tax on income received in my traditional self directed IRA. Do I again have to pay tax when I take distributions of this income from my IRA at retirement?

A. Yes. Unfortunately, you have to pay tax again at the time of distribution. The fact that UBIT tax was paid does not make distributions of that income from a traditional IRA tax free.

Q. I'm a real estate investor, how many properties can I flip each year with my self directed IRA before having to pay UBIT Tax?

A. This question involves many factors, but in general, 1 or 2 short term real estate deals a year will probably not cause the IRA to be subject to UBIT tax. Consult with your attorney or CPA as to your specific deals and plans. Self directed IRAs are best used in real estate for long-term properties like rentals as that type of income is not subject to UBIT tax.

Q. If my self directed IRA invests into an LLC that sells goods and services, will my IRA have to pay UBIT tax on the profits it receives?

A. Yes, an LLC that sells goods and services is an operational business (as opposed to passive), and as a result, the IRA will have to pay UBIT tax on the net income it receives from the LLC. If the goods and services business is taxed as a C corp and pays corporate tax then the IRA would not be subject to UBIT as dividends/profits from a C corp are exempt from UBIT tax.

Q: What federal Tax Identification Number (aka, "EIN") do I give to businesses/others when my IRA invests? If I have to pay UBIT or UDFI tax, what Tax ID or EIN do I use for my IRA?

A. In most instances, the Tax ID (aka, EIN) for your IRA custodian is the Tax ID that should be given to a company where your IRA is invested, and this Tax ID will be used by the company for purposes of reporting the income to your IRA (e.g., K-1 or 1099-Div). The Tax ID is also used by title companies reporting the proceeds from a property your IRA is selling (e.g. 1099-S). If you have to file and pay UBIT or UDFI tax, you won't use the IRA custodian's Tax ID and will actually need to obtain a new Tax ID from the IRS for your IRA to report and pay the taxes on Form 990-T.

Q: If I invest my IRA into a Real Estate Investment Trust ("REIT') that uses debt to leverage its purchases, will my IRA be subject to UDFI tax or UBIT?

A. In most instances, income from a REIT to an IRA will not be subject to UDFI or UBIT tax. This is because REIT income is typically considered a qualifying dividend and is exempt from UBIT or UDFI tax as dividend income. IRS Revenue Ruling 66-106. REITs are special structures and require, among other things, at least 100 owners, and the company must distribute at least 90% of its profits to its owners each year.

CHAPTER 16: Due Diligence for Self-Directed IRA Investments

KEY POINTS
▪ *self-directed IRA investments can offer exceptional returns but they also require the IRA owner to perform significant due diligence to avoid losses and fraud.*
▪ *Proper due diligence requires adequate documentation as to the investment and verification of backgrounds and claims made by those seeking the investment.*
▪ *Your self-directed IRA custodian acts at your direction and when an investment is made; they are not reviewing the investment to determine whether it is a good investment or not.*

Self-directed IRA investors are the first and sometimes only defense against a bad investment in their IRA. As a result, self-directed IRA investors need to carefully analyze their investments to determine the level of risk involved in the intended transaction and to decide whether they want to bear such risk in their self-directed IRA. Hard asset self-directed IRA investments (e.g., real estate or precious metals) usually do not result in significant risk and will rarely result in total or significant loss scenarios. However, small company offerings and investments where the IRA investment is under the control of a third party are more susceptible to significant loss. For example, a self-directed IRA investment into a blind private real estate offering or into a new start-up business can pose the most risk for a self-directed IRA.

ROLE OF YOUR SELF-DIRECTED IRA CUSTODIAN

When performing due diligence for a self-directed IRA investment, it is important to understand your role in deciding and analyzing investments versus your custodian's role in executing investments on behalf of your IRA. The custodian's role in a self-directed IRA is to process investment requests and transactions as instructed by the self-directed IRA owner. Custodians will process investments so long as those investments do not appear to be in violation of the law and so long as they are deemed to be administratively feasible.

Investments may be rejected by a self-directed IRA custodian because of improper documents or because the custodian does not find it feasible to administer the investment. For example, an investment into a foreign company may be disallowed by the self-directed IRA custodian because the custodian is not familiar with the laws affecting the foreign company; as a result, they may not want to administer that investment.

Additionally, a self-directed IRA investment into a company owned entirely by a disqualified person would, if known to the custodian, likely be rejected by a self-directed IRA custodian as the custodian will not knowingly allow an IRA to engage in a prohibited transaction. And lastly, a company with improper, inconsistent, or incomplete documentation will likely be rejected by a custodian. Keep in mind, however, that self-directed IRA custodians are not reviewing investments to determine whether they are "good" investments for the IRA nor are they investigating the backgrounds of those promoting or selling the investment. This is the responsibility of the self-directed IRA owner.

All major self-directed IRA custodians have account documents and instruction letters which state that the IRA owner is responsible for all investment decisions. Additionally, these documents usually contain release and indemnification clauses, which state that the IRA owner releases the IRA custodian from any claims resulting from their investments. As a result of the common contractual terms in account documents and as a result of the role of the IRA owner in making all investment decisions, the IRA owner and the IRA take on the responsibility and liability for losses on investments.

IRS PUBLICATION 3125

In 2017, the IRS updated and re-issued Publication 3125, *The IRS Does Not Approve IRA Investments* after seeing increased violations by certain IRA investment promoters. In their Publication the IRS clearly states that they do not approve investments and that companies or persons stating that their investment is "Approved by the IRS" or "IRA Approved" is misleading and false advertising as the IRS does not approve investments. The publication provides some addition tips for IRA investors which are noted below.

- Avoid investments touted as "IRA Approved" or endorsed by the IRS.
- Don't buy investments based on T.V. infomercials or radio advertising.
- Beware of no-risk sky high returns.
- Never transfer or rollover your IRA or other retirement funds directly to an investment promoter.

SEC NOTICE 5866

In 2012, the SEC issued Investor Notice 5866, *self-directed IRAs and the Risk of Fraud*. In the notice, the SEC outlined how self-directed IRAs can be susceptible to numerous types of fraud and how self-directed IRA investors can be bilked. The notice outlined some significant cases where investors with self-directed IRAs were involved and where the investors incurred significant losses as a result of fraud and misrepresentations in the companies where the self-directed IRAs invested.

The due diligence issues for self-directed IRAs are not any different from the due diligence issues for individual investors. The concern, however, is that for many self-directed IRA investors, their retirement account is their largest source of funds. Consequently, those accounts can be targeted by crooks. The bottom-line point of the SEC Notice is that self-directed IRA owners should carefully conduct due diligence before investing their self-directed IRA funds.

I have my own thoughts as to appropriate due diligence, which are in accordance with the SEC Notice, and I have outlined those thoughts in the following due diligence "top ten list".

DUE DILLIGENCE TOP TEN LIST

Before you invest your self-directed IRA into a "non-traditional" private business or into a real estate investment, you need to ask some hard questions to the person or business receiving your money. Here are some tips to minimize investment risks with your self-directed IRA.

1. If you don't understand how the business or investment makes the returns being promised, then don't invest.

2. If you aren't given adequate documents outlining what has been explained to you verbally or what has been put into a presentation, then don't invest.

3. If you're told that you can get a commission for bringing others to invest into the same company and if you don't have a license to receive such commissions, then don't invest. If the investment sponsors are willing to violate the law to pay an non-licensed person to raise money from others, then what's stopping them from misappropriating your IRA investment? It is only the law preventing them, which they've proved they will disregard.

4. If your self-directed IRA is loaning money for a real estate venture, then demand a recorded deed of trust or mortgage on title to the property, protecting your investment. Also, make sure that you get a copy of the title report or commitment showing what position your loan is being placed into when the deed of trust or mortgage is recorded. Many savvy investors (and what all banks do) create lending instructions to the title company or attorney closing the real estate transaction that instruct the closing agent to only use the funds being

loaned when the borrower signs the note/loan documents, when the closing agent verifies the priority of the deed of trust or mortgage you are getting (1st position, 2nd, etc.), and when all other defects to title have been cleared.

5. If you're investing into a PPM, a private offering, or a crowdfunding offering, you should receive numerous documents outlining the investment, the use of funds, the background of those managing the company, and also documents regarding your rights as an investor (e.g., offering memorandum and LLC operating agreement or LP limited partnership agreement). Also, check to see if the PPM or private offering was properly filed with the SEC by going to SEC.gov and checking the company name in the SEC database. If no filing record exists for the PPM or private offering with the SEC, then the person raising the funds has possibly disregarded the law. As stated earlier, if someone is willing to disregard the law to get your money, what is stopping them from disregarding the law to not pay you back (it's just the law)?

6. Investigate the background of the person(s) with whom you are entrusting your money. When you are investing with others, you need to think like the bank and do what the bank does. What is this person's credit worthiness? What is their employment or prior business experience? What is their business or investment plan? What are the terms of the investment? Is there a realistic rate of return that fairly recognizes the risk being taken?

7. If you're pressured that this opportunity will pass if your self-directed IRA doesn't invest now, then let the

opportunity pass. Most scams use this technique, and most legitimate investments never have this funding crisis.

8. Make sure a lawyer representing your interests reviews the documents. If a lawyer drafted the documents, it is still important to have a lawyer look at the documents as they relate to your interests and with an eye towards protecting your self-directed IRA. Sometimes, unfortunately, the devil is in the details, and many investments have clauses that can significantly impact your ability to get your money back or that give the company raising the money the ability to pay whatever compensation to themselves that they desire. These are obvious problems that will eat into the bottom line of the profits you may be expecting.

9. Seek the opinion of another investor, business owner, or friend whose opinion you trust. Sometimes, when you explain the investment to someone else, he or she can help you find issues to consider and questions you should be asking.

10. Be comfortable saying no and only invest what you are willing to lose. Non-traditional investments have made many millionaires over the years, but they have also caused lots of financial ruin. Just keep the risk in perspective and don't "bet the farm" in one deal.

I don't want investors to be scared about self-directed IRA investments, but I also don't want investors going into them without having conducted adequate due diligence. It seems that some investors determine whether their IRA can invest based on the prohibited transaction rules but they neglect to determine whether their IRA *should* invest. Keep in mind that you can make great investment decisions that result in large gains in your self-directed IRA, and you can also make terrible decisions that can result in huge losses for your self-directed IRA. It's all up to you.

Keep in mind that you, the self-directed IRA owner, may need to get out of your comfort zone by asking a lot of questions, by demanding additional documentation, or by simply saying no. Remember: you are the best person to protect your self-directed IRA.

CHAPTER 17: Valuations and Distributions

KEY POINTS
▪ *A self-directed IRA accounts fair market value must be updated annually by the account holder. The IRA custodian uses this information in their annual reporting of the IRA with the IRS via Form 5498.*
▪ *Fair market value, in essence, is what a willing buyer would pay to a willing seller after consideration of all relevant facts.*
▪ *In the case of taxable situations (distribution, Roth conversion, RMD), more stringent valuation requirements are imposed on the IRA.*
▪ *An IRA may distribute or convert (Roth) an asset in-kind. The IRA owner will be responsible for the taxes upon distribution or conversion.*

An IRA must report its fair market value to the IRS annually. Fair market value is reported to the IRS by the IRA custodian via IRS Form 5498. For standard IRAs holding stocks or mutual funds, those account values are automatically determined as they simply take the stock or fund price as of the close of the market on December 31st each year and they use these amounts to set the year-end account fair market value.

The regulations regarding IRAs simply state that an IRA custodian should annually report; the amount of contributions, the amount of distributions, the name and address of the trustee, and such other information as the Commission of the IRS may require. 26 CFR § 1.408-5. There is no reference in the regulations as to fair market value but such information has clearly been requested by the Commissioner for the IRS.

For self-directed accounts, fair market values are not readily available and it becomes the IRA account owner's responsibility to obtain their self-directed investment values so that their custodian can properly report their account's fair market value. The value of an account is important for a few reasons. First, the IRS requires it to be updated annually. Second, it is used to set required minimum distributions ("RMDs") for those account holders over age 70 1/2 with traditional IRAs. Lastly, the account value is used when converting an entire account, or a particular investment or portion of the account, from a traditional IRA to a Roth IRA.

WHAT IS FAIR MARKET VALUE

Fair market value of an investment has been broadly defined by the Tax Court as,

> The price at which property would change hands between a hypothetical willing buyer and a hypothetical willing seller, neither being under any compulsion to buy or to sell, and both having reasonable knowledge of relevant facts. *U.S. v. Cartwright*, 411 US 546 (1973).

While all IRA accounts must provide annual fair market valuations, the U.S. Government Accountability Office noted in December 2016 that,

Current IRS guidelines provides **NO** [emphasis added] guidance or advice to custodians or IRA owners regarding how to determine the FMV [fair market value] for unconventional assets held in retirement plans [i.e. IRAs]. United States Government Accountability Office, GAO-17-102, *Retirement Security Improved Guidance Could Help Account Owners Understand the Risks of Investing in Unconventional Assets.* (Dec. 2016).

The absence of guidance, however, has not relieved IRA owners or their custodians from obtaining and reporting this information. While there is no specific fair market valuation guidance for IRAs, there are commonly accepted methods of reporting value used by professionals and companies within the self-directed IRA industry. Most of these methods have been adopted from law and regulations governing employer retirement plans or estates. This Chapter is a summary of those methods and my own professional preferences for reporting values of an IRA.

The level of supporting information and documentation associated with a valuation varies depending on the purpose of the valuation. If the valuation is being used to distribute an asset in-kind or to set the value of a Roth conversion, the level of supporting information increases and the opinion of a third-party professional is usually required since this value has a direct result on the amount of tax due. On the other hand, when the valuation is being used simply to set the annual fair market value for an account that is not subject to RMD and that is otherwise not taxable, then a lesser degree of supporting information is required.

LEGAL TIP

- ❖ If you are making a Roth conversion or an in-kind distribution, then the value of the assets in your IRA will determine the taxes you will owe on the conversion or distribution.

The valuation methods and rules vary based on the type of asset being held by the account. The most popular assets held by self-directed accounts are outlined below.

REAL ESTATE

Most real estate valuations used to determine the fair market value of real estate are conducted using a market data approach. This method of valuing real estate uses comparable sales data from similar properties to determine the value of the property in question. The comparable sales method may be conducted by a real estate appraiser via an appraisal or by a real estate broker via a broker price opinion ("BPO"). It may also be conducted by a real estate professional who prepares a comparative market analysis ("CMA") for the property. In all instances, the report should be completed by a licensed appraiser or real estate professional and it shall also be in writing. If the valuation is being used for a Roth conversion or an in-kind distribution, most IRA custodians will require an appraisal or a BPO as those methods of determining value provide greater detail and analysis.

The two other methods to determine fair market value are the cost approach and the income approach. The cost approach is rarely if ever used to determine fair market value for real estate owned by IRAs and is based on the replacement value of the property. The income approach is commonly used to determine the value of multi-family, retail, or commercial real estate. The income approach takes into account the net operating income and cash flow from the property and is focused on the income generated from the leasing of the property. In many instances, an appraiser will use a combination of the market data and income approach to set the value of the property.

As a general rule, single-family rentals and land are valued using the market data approach. Multi-family, commercial, or retail properties are typically valued using a combination of the market data and income approach.

Most IRA owners annually update the value of their real estate with their custodian using a comparative market analysis report from their real estate professional. Some IRA owners will use Zillow reports, Trulia reports, or their annual property tax assessor's estimate of value to update the property's value to their custodian. These non-professional reports of value are only allowed by some custodians and only in the instance of non-taxable situations.

LEGAL TIP
❖ Most IRA owners annually update the value of their real estate with their custodian using a comparative market analysis report from their real estate professional.

Guidance from the IRS for employer based plans does not specify any particular method for valuation but does state that the "value of real estate or mortgages may be valued incorrectly if based solely on their purchase prices." Internal Revenue Manual 4.72.8.5.2 *Valuation of Assets in Defined Contribution Plans* (Aug. 2016).

NOTES

The value of a promissory note depends on whether the note is secured by an asset (e.g. real estate or equipment) and whether the note is performing and in good standing or whether the note is in default and is non-performing.

For performing notes, secured or unsecured, the value of the note is simply the "unpaid principal, plus interest accrued [and un-paid] to the date [of valuation]." 26 C.F.R. § 20.2031-4 *Valuation of Notes*. This method of note valuation is what is used by the IRS for determining the value of a note for estate tax purposes and is the best guideline to use for determining value for a note held by an IRA. While a note may have a larger face value in the market, depending on the interest rate being charged, the collateral involved, and the credit-worthiness of the borrower, determining such value would be costly and opinions would vary widely. Additionally, future value is hard to make certain as most notes can be pre-paid at any time thereby removing certainty for future value. Consequently, a determination made solely on the amount due as of the date of the valuation is a preferred method for valuing notes.

LEGAL TIP
❖ Promissory notes should be valued using the principal amount due plus accrued and un-paid interest.

For non-performing notes, the value may be reduced by supplying documentation evidencing bankruptcy or insolvency of the borrower. Other supporting evidence can include a letter from a collection attorney engaged to collect on the note who determines the borrower to be uncollectible and not worth suing or otherwise pursuing. Additionally, it may be necessary to hire a valuation professional, note broker, or note expert, who can place a reduced or worthless fair market value on the note.

When a non-performing note is secured by real estate and when the amount due on the note exceeds the fair market value of the property, the note value shall be reduced to reflect the value of the property that secures the note. Internal Revenue Manual 4.72.8.5.2 *Valuation of Assets in Defined Contribution Plans* (Aug. 2016).

For non-performing notes that the IRA owner would like to be determined as worthless, the IRA owner will need to show evidence of bankruptcy and discharge, as may be the case, or they will need a written third-party determination of value from a qualified professional which determines the note to be worthless. If a note is determined worthless, the borrower has been forgiven of debt and consequently should receive a 1099-C for cancellation of debt income from the IRA. In order to issue a 1099-C, the IRA owner should have the SSN or Tax ID of the borrower. Most IRA custodians require this information prior to authorizing a note from an IRA so this information should be readily available. This 1099-C is usually issued by the IRA owner or their accountant. Some custodians will issue the 1099-C to the borrower upon cancellation of the note but may charge a fee for such service.

LLC, LP, or Private Company Interest

Private company investments such as LLCs, LPs, and private corporations should be valued using the guidelines from IRS Revenue Ruling 59-60. Internal Revenue Manual 4.72.8.40 *Valuation of Assets in Defined Contribution Plans, Determining Asset Values* (Aug. 2016). The IRS internal revenue manual outlines seven factors to be considered when valuing interests in a private company. Those seven factors are outlined below and are drawn from IRS Revenue Ruling 59-60.

1. Nature and history of the business
2. General economic outlook
3. Book value of the interest and the financial condition of the business
4. Company's earning capacity
5. Company dividend or profit distribution paying capacity
6. Goodwill value
7. Recent ownership interest sales.

There are two different categories of companies for valuation purposes, operating companies and holding companies. An operating company is one that sells goods or services. A holding company, on the other hand, is one that holds investment assets such as real estate or interests in other companies.

Operating Company Valuation

Let's first address operating companies. For operating companies who sell goods or services, the guidelines in IRS Revenue Ruling 59-60 should be used and greatest weight should be given to company earnings. Internal Revenue Manual 4.72.8.4 (4) *Valuation of Assets in Defined Contribution Plans, Determining Asset Values* (Aug. 2016).

Asset Holding Company Valuation

For asset holding companies (e.g. an LLC that owns rental real estate), the IRS has advised that greatest weight would be given to the underlying assets of the company. Internal Revenue Manual 4.72.8.4(4) *Valuation of Assets in Defined Contribution Plans*, (Aug. 2016). For example, if my IRA owns 20% of an asset holding LLC and if that LLC owns real estate worth $300,000 and has a bank account with $100,000, then the company would be valued at $400,000 and my 20% interest would be $80,000.

Generally speaking, valuations of business interests are performed by a third party professional. In many instances, offering companies from a Private Placement or a Regulation D or A offering will provide an annual valuation of the company to the members, this valuation may used by an IRA member for determining the annual fair market value. For smaller partnership LLCs or private companies, it is unlikely that a third party valuation will be completed each year and as a result it is the IRA owner's responsibility to request this from the company or to have it completed on their own accord and at their own cost. If an investment sponsor frequently works with IRA investors, they would be familiar with this requirement and they should be agreeing to provide this information on an annual basis. Sadly, many investment sponsors fail to provide this valuation information to their IRA investors and as a result the IRA owner ends up having an inaccurate or outdated valuation being used on their account.

Precious Metals

Precious metals bullion is valued and reported to the IRS by most IRA custodians using "spot value". Spot value is the per ounce spot price of the precious metal times the number of ounces. For example, gold closed on December 30, 2016 at a per ounce spot price of $1,115.85. If your IRA held 100 ounces of qualifying gold, the value of the gold would be $111,585. Precious metals that are in coin form are valued differently by most IRA custodians as coins typically sell for a higher per ounce price than bullion. Theoretically, this shouldn't be the case as the metal isn't any different in purity or quality but the actual market has proven this to be true. Therefore, in the case of precious metals in coin form, most IRA custodians will report market price. This can be obtained from daily market pricing summaries known as the Grey Sheets and available and reported on sites such as www.bullionvalues.com.

VALUATION METHOD SUMMARY CHART

Asset	Non-Taxable (Annual FMV)	Taxable (RMD, distribution or conversion)
Real Estate	Comparative Market Analysis (CMA) from a real estate professional is preferred. Some IRA custodians accept property tax assessor values or Zillow reports in non-taxable situations.	Real estate appraisal is preferred. Some IRA custodians accept a broker's price opinion.
Promissory Note	Value of a note can be reported by calculating the principal due plus any accrued and unpaid interest. This is the valuation method used for calculating the value of a note for estate tax purposes.	Same as non-taxable, principal amount due plus accrued and un-paid interest. For notes in default, a third-party opinion of value is typically required in order for the note to be written-down.

Precious Metals	For bullion, use the spot value of the metal in question times the ounces owned. Spot value is widely reported on a daily basis on financial sites. For acceptable coins, use market data for the coin in question via the Grey Sheets available at www.bullionvalues.com.	Same as non-taxable.
LLC, LP, or Private Company Interest	Obtain a third party-opinion of value of the LLC interest. The opinion should rely on IRS Revenue Ruling 59-60. For asset holding companies, the valuation should focus on the value of the assets. For operating companies, the valuation should focus on earnings.	Similar requirement, but the detail of the opinion should be more significant. For example, for an asset holding company where the IRAs interest is determined by the assets of the LLC. A CMA would be acceptable for calculating that assets value in the company in an annual valuation. However, an appraisal of the real estate to calculate in that asset would be required in a taxable situation.

IRS FORM 5498

IRA custodians report the value of an IRAs assets to the IRS via IRS Form 5498. Form 5498 also is an annual report to the IRS on your IRA contributions and distributions. IRS Form 5498 was revised recently to specifically identify IRAs that hold non-publically traded assets and IRA custodians now must indicate in Box 15a of form 5498 whether the assets held by the IRA include non-publically traded assets. Additionally, in box 15b the IRA custodian will report the type of non-publicly traded assets by specifying a certain code that represents common unconventional IRA assets. IRS Form 5498, (2017).

IN-KIND DISTRIBUTIONS AND CONVERSIONS

An IRA may distribute an asset "in-kind" to the IRA owner. For example, say your IRA owns a rental property, which you wish to use personally. In order to have personal use of the property, you must fully distribute it from your IRA. The tax ramifications of this in-kind distribution are the same as if you had taken a distribution of cash and the IRA owner is subject to any early withdrawal penalty and taxes associated with the distribution. In order to determine the value of the distribution, the IRA custodian will typically require an appraisal of the asset. If the appraisal shows a value of $350,000, then you are subject to tax and penalty, as may be applicable, based on a distribution of $350,000. The IRA account owner submits the valuation to the IRA custodian who uses the valuation when issuing a 1099-R to report the distribution to the IRS and the IRA owner.

When the asset is distributed from the IRA to the IRA owner, the asset ownership records will need to be updated. In the case of a distribution of real estate, the IRA custodian will need to sign a deed transferring title out of the IRA to the IRA owner personally.

In the case of private stock or LLC interest, the IRA custodian will transfer the stock via an assignment of interest agreement from the IRA to the IRA owner personally.

A similar process is required when converting assets from your traditional IRA to your Roth IRA. First, an appraisal must be obtained and once the custodian approves the form of the appraisal, they will allow the asset to be transferred to your Roth IRA. Keep in mind that the value of the asset converted to Roth is included into your taxable income in the year you conduct the conversion. Due to the tax burden from the conversion, some IRA owners decide to convert in-kind assets over a series of years so as to avoid the tax ramifications or a large amount of income falling into one year. This may be done by converting some private stock or LLC units over different years or by converting tenants in common interests for real estate over various years.

In-kind Roth conversions were popular for many savvy investors in 2008 and 2009. These account holders decided to take a long-term approach for their asset but realized that while the stock and real estate markets were low, that it was an ideal time to convert at the low valuation to get the asset into a Roth account so that they could later distribute the investment at a higher value when the investment market had recovered.

FREQUENTLY ASKED QUESTIONS

Q. Can I use the K-1 issued to my IRA for its ownership in an LLC or LP?

A. Unfortunately no. A K-1 may report the IRAs capital account value in the LLC but the K-1 does not report the actual fair market value of the LLC interest.

Q. Can I buy approved precious metals coins at a market price and have them valued using spot price for the metal in order to reduce the tax owed on a Roth conversion?

A. No, you should use market value for the coins using the Grey Sheets and reported market values for such coins.

Q. Can discounting be used to discount my IRAs minority partnership interest in an LLC or LP?

A. Yes, this is possible. However, you need to follow proper discounting rules and methodology and the minority discount option is only allowed if the IRAs interest is illiquid and when the IRA (and related parties) own a minority stake in the company.

Q. My custodian has threatened to distribute my IRA if I don't provide an updated valuation, can they do this?

A. Yes, most IRA custodian account agreements require you to provide updated valuations for the assets held by your IRA. If you fail over more than a few years, many custodians will distribute the asset and the last reported value and will send you a 1099-R and you are subject to related tax and penalties on the distribution. It is possible to find a new custodian and you can complete a 60-day rollover but you'll need to act quickly and will need to get an updated value or other supporting information ready for the new

IRA custodian.

Q. My IRA was distributed with in-kind assets that were over-valued? Can I correct the value and contest the taxable amount of the distribution with the IRS?

A. This is possible. You will need to contest this in writing with the IRS and you will need to provide written information or a third-party valuation to the IRS to reduce the value and the taxable amount of the distribution. In many cases, you may need to go to Tax Court to get an IRS Attorney with enough experience or a Tax Court Judge to understand the value issue and to stipulate to the actual value of the asset.

CHAPTER 18: Cryptocurrency and IRAs

KEY POINTS
▪ *A self-directed IRA may own cryptocurrency for investment purposes.*
▪ *The optimal structure to buy and sell cryptocurrency with an IRA is an IRA/LLC, whereby the IRA/LLC bank account is linked to a digital wallet and exchange to buy and sell crypto.*
▪ *The IRS has identified cryptocurrency as property, and the buying and selling of crypto for investment purposes is generally exempt from unrelated business income tax (UBIT).*
▪ *IRA owners should be diligent in how the store their private keys for their cryptocurrency.*

WHAT IS CRYPTOCURRENCY?

Cryptocurrency is a digital currency in which encryption techniques are used to regulate the generation of units and the transfer of funds. Cryptocurrency is privately created and is independent of government-controlled central banks. The most well-known form of cryptocurrency is Bitcoin. Users of Bitcoin pay each other directly without traditional intermediaries such as banks or governments using what is known as blockchain technology to effectuate the transactions. These transactions of cryptocurrency occur on the virtual currencies network and are completed using blockchain technology, which is an open ledger that tracks the cryptocurrency on the blockchain. Cryptography, mathematical proofs that provide high levels of security, is used to strengthen the security of cryptocurrency blockchains. For example, as a Bitcoin user you would authorize a transaction using a secret piece of data called a private key. And lastly, a cryptocurrency transaction isn't finalized until it has been mined, which is a confirmation process by third parties to ensure the integrity of the transaction. In sum, cryptocurrency is a private technological solution to government issued currency.

LEGAL TIP

* ❖ Cryptocurrency is a digital form of money that is considered property and can be transferred between private parties and is not owned or controlled by a bank or government entity.

CAN YOUR IRA OWN CRYPTOCURRENCY?

An IRA can own Bitcoin and other forms of crypto-currencies, such as Ethereum, Ripple, and Litecoin. The only items an IRA cannot invest in is life insurance, S-Corporation stock, and collectibles as mentioned in IRC 408(m), which refers to tangible personal property such as "art, rugs, coins, etc." and "any other tangible personal property the Secretary determines." Cryptocurrency is certainly an intangible item by all accounts and would not be considered tangible. As a result, an IRA can own cryptocurrency since such investments are not restricted.

CURRENT IRS GUIDANCE ON CRYPTOCURRENCY

The IRS issued *IRS NOTICE 2014-21* addressing the taxation of cryptocurrency, and stated that cryptocurrency and other forms of virtual currency are property. The sale of property by an IRA is treated as a capital gain, and as a result the buying and selling of cryptocurrency within an IRA wouldn't cause unrelated business income tax, as the income would be exempt under IRC 512(b)(5).

LEGAL TIP
❖ The IRS has determined that cryptocurrency is property for purposes of taxation and as a result the buying and selling of cryptocurrency is capital gain (short and long-term) and is generally exempt from UBIT tax.
❖ An IRA/LLC is the best structure to buy and sell cryptocurrency with an IRA.

OWNING CRYPTOCURRENCY WITH A SELF-DIRECTED IRA

The most effective way to own cryptocurrency with an IRA is by using an IRA/LLC. Using an IRA/LLC allows the IRA owner to gain control of the purchase and sale process on exchanges and also prevents third parties (e.g., the custodian) from having control or access to the cryptocurrency private keys. Additionally, the funding and settlement of the purchase and sale of cryptocurrency is more easily handled in an IRA/LLC by linking the LLC business checking account to the exchange where the cryptocurrency is being bought or sold. Under the IRA/LLC structure, the IRA owner, as manager of the LLC would control the purchase and sale process on an exchange or through private parties and would be able to avoid the significant fees (10-20% of a transaction at present) currently present with some providers who hold a master account of cryptocurrency whereby an IRA can buy a portion of cryptocurrency from that institution's master account.

There are three steps to owning cryptocurrency with an IRA/LLC and they are as follows.

1. First, you will need a self-directed IRA with a custodian who allows for IRA/LLCs where you can be the manager of the IRA/LLC (subject to certain legal restrictions to avoid prohibited transactions as outlined in Chapter 13, The IRA/LLC Structure).

2. Second, you will invest funds from the IRA into the LLC. Your IRA will own an LLC 100%, and that IRA/LLC will have a business checking account. See Chapter 13 on the IRA/LLC structure for more details.

3. And third, the IRA/LLC will use its LLC business checking account to establish a wallet to invest and own cryptocurrency. The most widely used cryptocurrency wallet and exchange is through a company called Coinbase, and you can use your wallet on Coinbase to buy, sell and digitally store your cryptocurrency. Make certain that your account with Coinbase is set up as a business account (Coinbase sends you to their sister company GDAX for this) under the LLC name and Tax ID so that you personally are not listed and receiving the 1099 for the sales transactions at the end of the year. Another popular exchange option to buy and sell cryptocurrency is Kraken. There are new companies and exchanges opening up each year and investors should be cautious in deciding who to use for exchange purposes and/or for a digital wallet. These companies are presently un-regulated so you should look at

the technology and background of the founders and management when deciding which companies to use.

DIAGRAM 18.1, CRYPTOCURRENCY IRA/LLC

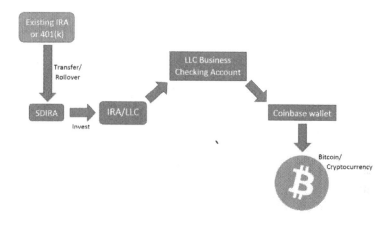

There are already certain publicly traded funds and other avenues (e.g. Bitcoin Investments Trust) where you can own shares of a fund that in turn owns cryptocurrency. There are also certain providers who allow your IRA to buy cryptocurrency whereby your IRA owns a portion of a master institutional account but you are generally subject to significant fees and restrictions in accessing and selling such cryptocurrency in these instances. The best structure to own cryptocurrency from a fee, access, and control standpoint, is to use an IRA/LLC as outlined above.

Keep in mind; Bitcoin and other forms of cryptocurrency have significant potential in the digital age. However, as with any new market investment, make sure you proceed with caution, and don't "bet the farm" or "go all in" on just one investment or deal.

STORAGE OF CRYPTOCURRENCY

Storage of your cryptocurrency keys, what is held by the owner to transmit their cryptocurrency, is made using a wallet. There are various forms of wallets that can hold digital currency and keys and the options are online, desktop, mobile, and hardware. Each has their pros and cons in terms of ease of use (on-line) and security (hardware). A hardware device is usually in the form of a USB thumb drive and is deemed the most secure, as it is removed and "off-line" except when it is being used. However, there are stories of lost hardware devices with keys which is akin to losing the actual currency you owned as such cryptocurrency becomes worthless without the private keys that are necessary to transfer the cryptocurrency to another party.

In all instances, there is typically a cost for such wallet whether it is a fee for the hardware or a fee for the on-line software use and storage. In all instances, the direct fees and costs for the wallet should be paid for by the IRA owned LLC or IRA, as the case may be. Additionally, the wallet should not be used for personal cryptocurrency keys as such actions could cause a self-dealing prohibited transaction. If an IRA owner personally owns cryptocurrency they should use different wallets for their personal cryptocurrency and their IRA owned cryptocurrency.

FREQUENTLY ASKED QUESTIONS

Q: Can my self-directed IRA or IRA owned LLC mine cryptocurrency?

A: Yes, your self-directed IRA may own an LLC or other company that in turn owns servers and other technology and hardware that performs mining of cryptocurrency transactions. However, such income from these mining activities would be deemed "business" or ordinary income and would be subject to unrelated business income tax.

Q: Can I buy cryptocurrency privately from a third-party?

A: Yes, this is possible, again using an LLC where you can have a digital wallet or other device to store the cryptocurrency. Also, the person selling the cryptocurrency cannot be a disqualified person to your IRA (e.g. not you, your spouse, parents, kids, etc.)

Q: If I use a hardware wallet for my IRA/LLCs cryptocurrency, can I hold such hardware wallet in my personal possession?

A: There isn't any restriction on this. If you are using an IRA/LLC and if you, the IRA owner, are the manager of the LLC then presumably, yes, you may personally have the hardware device in your possession. While there are storage requirements on precious metals owned by IRAs, there presently isn't any storage requirement or restriction as to cryptocurrency and IRAs.

Q: Is it okay if I provide my personal information and driver's license to identify myself when establishing a user account with a cryptocurrency exchange or wallet?

A: Yes, this will not cause a prohibited transaction as the provider is typically doing it for identification and fraud prevention purposes. That being said, make sure that the actual account is established as a business account using the LLC name and Tax ID.

CHAPTER 19: Self-Directed Solo 401(k) Plans

KEY POINTS
■ *A Solo 401(k) is an employer adopted retirement plan and is only for business owners who have no other full-time employees other than the owner(s) and their spouse.*
■ *A Solo 401(k) does not require a third-party custodian or administrator like an IRA, though one may be used. The business owner may be the Trustee of the Solo 401(k).*
■ *The Solo 401(k) funds may be deposited and held in a bank checking account for the Solo 401(k), which the 401(k) owner may have control and signing authority over as Trustee of the Solo 401(k).*
■ *Solo 401(k)s are exempt from UDFI on leveraged real estate holdings.*

WHAT IS A SOLO 401(K)

A Solo 401(k) is an employer based retirement plan that is exclusively for business owners that have no employees. The IRS calls it a "one-participant" plan; it is also known as an owners-only plan, a Solo 401(k), or an individual 401(k) plan. Internal Revenue Service, *One Participant 401(k) Plans* (October 25, 2017).

A Solo 401(k) is an ideal plan for those who are self-employed and who want to grow their account with generous contribution limits. The total contribution limit for a Solo 401(k) in 2018 is $55,000 per participant (comprising $18,500 in employee contributions and $36,500 in employer contributions). This annual contribution amount is ten times that of IRAs, which are capped at $5,500 annually. A Solo 401(k) combines the benefits of a typical 401(k) plan without the complex administrative requirements of a 401(k) plan with employees that are subject to employee discrimination rules whereby the generous benefits the business gives to himself or herself also have to be given to employees. But in the Solo 401(k), if you are the only employee and the business owner then you can make the plan as generous as you'd like since all the funds being contributed are going to your own account.

A Solo 401(k) can have a Traditional (tax-deferred) set of funds in a separate account and/or a Roth (tax-free) set of funds in a separate account. You can also convert Traditional Solo 401(k) funds to Roth Solo 401(k) funds.

A Solo 401(k) is established by the employer entity for the benefit of its employee(s). For example, if Sally Smith, Inc. is the owner and sole employee of Sally Smith, Inc., she could establish a Solo 401(k) for her benefit as the only employee. If she had a spouse who worked in the business that spouse could also have an account under the Solo 401(k). To establish a Solo 401(k), Sally would need to do the following.

I.   <u>Adopt an approved Solo 401(k) plan.</u> The employer entity, Sally Smith, Inc., would adopt the plan for the benefit of its employees, Sally, who would have an account in the plan. Solo 401(k) plans must be pre-approved by the IRS and Sally will need to use a plan provider who has a Solo 401(k) prep-approved plan document. Under most Solo 401(k) plans, the business owner is the plan trustee and has the authority to enter into investments and to sign checks and contracts for the plan.

II. Ensure that the plan can be self-directed. Sally needs to make sure that the Solo 401(k) she is adopting can be self-directed into the investments she plans to make. Many brokerage firms offer so called self-directed Solo 401(k) plans, but those Solo 401(k) plans are only self-directed when using the brokerage to buy stocks, bonds and mutual funds. They call it self-directed since you get to pick the stocks or funds. Additionally, it can be difficult to obtain check writing ability with a brokerage Solo 401(k). Find a Solo 401(k) provider who has expertise with non-publically traded self-directed investments.

III. Obtain an EIN for the Solo 401(k). The Solo 401(k) should obtain an EIN. This EIN is used when obtaining the Solo 401(k) bank checking account and for 1099 and K-1 reporting when the plan has income/loss tax reporting from its investments.

IV. Establish a Bank Checking Account for the Solo 401(k) Funds. This bank account will receive rollovers or transfers of other retirement account funds and will receive new contributions. It will also receive investment income and will be used to purchase investments and to pay for investment expenses. The business owner, as trustee of the Solo 401(k) plan, will typically be the signer on the bank account and will have so-called "check-book control" of the Solo 401(k0 funds directly from the Solo 401(k) bank account. If you have multiple business owners or spouses under the plan each will need to have a separate bank account for their own account funds. You also need a separate bank account for participants with Roth or Traditional funds. An LLC is not required to obtain checkbook control in a Solo 401(k) but is used sometimes by Solo 401(k) investors for asset protection or partnership purposes.

WHO QUALIFIES FOR A SOLO 401(k)?

The Solo 401(k) is only or business owners who have no other full-time employees other than the owner(s) and their spouse. The company may have part-time employees (less than 1,000 hours per year), or employees under the age of 21, and these employees will not disqualify the company from adopting a Solo 401(k). However, once any employee 21 or older reaches more than 1,000 hours in a calendar year the Solo 401(k) plan will then be disqualified and will need to be amended to a standard group 401(k) with employee and ERISA protections and then offered to all employees of the company. DOL Publication 4222, *401(k) Plans for Small Business (Rev. 10-2015)*. Or, alternatively, the Solo 401(k) can be made dormant such that no new contributions are made by the business owner but existing plan funds may continue to be invested. It's unclear from the IRS or DOL how long such dormancy may be allowed before the funds should be rolled over to an IRA or other plan of the account owner.

If you are a business owner with employees and you have

multiple businesses, you are only able to establish a Solo 401(k) plan in a company where you have no employees when the following two conditions are met. IRC § 1563 and IRC § 414(c), 26 CFR 1.1563-1(3)(2) *Definition of controlled group of corporations and component members and related concepts.*

1. The company where you have no employees and where you wish to adopt the Solo 401(k) must be a separate business from the business where you do have employees.
2. There must be an ownership difference of 20% or more between the two companies (keep in mind that certain family members do not count in the determination of a 20% ownership difference).

For example, let's say that Steve owns 100% of Steve Real Estate Brokerage, Inc. where he has employees. Steve also owns 50% of a construction business with his friend Todd called ST Construction, LLC, where they have no employees. Steve and Todd would like ST Construction to adopt a Solo 401(k) so they could each have Solo 401(k) accounts. Steve would be permitted to adopt the Solo 401(k) plan, without having to offer the plan to his real estate brokerage since there is a 20% ownership difference in ST Construction, LLC.

If you work for a company where you are not an owner and you participate in that company 401(k) or other employed based plan, you can still establish a separate Solo 401(k) in the event that you have your own separate business or self-employment. Your contribution totals, $55,000 in 2018 for a Solo 401(k), are cumulative though and you must take into account the contributions you and your employer have made to the company 401(k) plan where you work when making contributions to your own Solo 401(k).

WHAT PARTIES ARE INVOLVED IN THE SOLO 401(k)

There are a number of parties involved in a Solo 401(k) and it's important to understand what each does and how each comes together to make rollovers, contributions, and investments for the Solo 401(k).

I.   The Business. A Solo 401(k) is an employer based retirement plan and must be adopted by an employer entity. This can be an s-corporation, a partnership, an LLC, a sole proprietorship, or a c-corporation. The business, however, must have earned ordinary income or self-employment income. This type of income generally arises from the selling of goods and services. The adopting business cannot solely have investment income, such as real estate rental income or interest income. The business is typically referred to in plan documents as the employer entity or the adopting plan entity.

II.   Business Owner/Participant Account Owner. The business owner will have an account within the Solo 401(k) plan. If there are no other owners or a spouse involved then this may be the only account in the Solo 401(k). If there are other owners or a spouse then each participant in the Solo 401(k) must have a separate bank account for their funds and those fund should be invested and accounted for separately.

III.   Solo 401(k) Plan. The plan is adopted by the business for the benefit of its employees who have their own participant accounts under the plan. The Plan is adopted by the business using a pre-approved plan document. The Plan will be on title to assets.

IV. <u>Plan Trustee</u>. The Plan Trustee is typically the business owner and this allows the business owner to have signing control on investments, the bank account, and on contracts that may arise in the Solo 401(k) investments.

V. <u>Plan Administrator</u>. The business owner is usually the plan administrator and has final authority and responsibility for the plan.

VI. <u>Participant Accounts Under Plan</u>. The employees of the business who participate in the plan have participant account(s) under the plan. If the Solo 401(k) Plan participants include the business owner and their spouse then there will be two participant accounts under the Solo 401(k) plan.

The business that adopts a Solo 401(k) can be an s-corp, LLC, sole prop, partnership, or c-corp, however, the adopting business must be one that receives ordinary income (e.g., fees for goods and/or services) rather than investment income. A common example of a business that cannot adopt a Solo 401(k) is an LLC or other company that receives rental income. This type of income is not ordinary income or self- employment income and as a result the company cannot adopt a retirement plan.

In most instances, the business owner is the Solo 401(k) Plan Trustee and Administrator. If you are the Trustee and Administrator you will have control of the plan but you are also responsible for properly administering the Solo 401(k) plan. The only participants of the Solo 401(k) plan are the business owner(s) and their spouse and as a result Solo 401(k) plans are not subject to

ERISA and the typical 401(k) plan requirements that can include, cross-testing, employee notices, highly compensated employee contribution restrictions, and plan investment options. 29 CFR § 2510.3-3.

DIAGRAM 19.1, SOLO 401(k) DIAGRAM

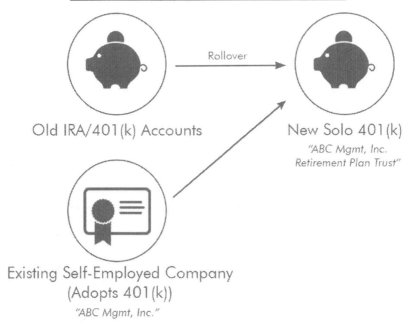

Rollover

Old IRA/401(k) Accounts

New Solo 401(k)
"ABC Mgmt, Inc.
Retirement Plan Trust"

Existing Self-Employed Company
(Adopts 401(k))
"ABC Mgmt, Inc."

ROLLOVER OF EXISTING RETIREMENT ACCOUNTS

Each participant of the Solo 401(k) can rollover most types of qualified retirement account(s) including traditional and SEP IRAs, other 401(k)s, and pensions to their Solo 401(k) account. A couple of instances where you cannot roll funds to a Solo 401(k) occurs with a retirement account of a current employer where the employer restricts existing employees from rolling their funds out of the company plan until the employee reaches retirement age, which for most plans is 55 or 59/12, or until they leave employment from the company. Also, Roth IRA funds cannot be rolled a Solo

401(k), even if the Solo 401(k) has a Roth account. Treasury. Reg. §
1.408A-10, Q&5. Roth IRAs are always Roth IRAs and you cannot
roll those funds to any different type of account. The following
chart from the IRS provides a list of permissible rollovers. IRS.gov,
Rollover Chart (December 2015).

TABLE 19.1, IRS ROLLOVER CHART

<table>
<tr><td></td><td></td><td colspan="2">Roll To</td></tr>
<tr><td rowspan="9">Roll From</td><td></td><td>Traditional 401(k) (Pre-tax)</td><td>Roth 401(k) (After-Tax)</td></tr>
<tr><td>Roth IRA</td><td>NO</td><td>NO</td></tr>
<tr><td>Traditional IRA</td><td>YES</td><td>NO</td></tr>
<tr><td>Simple IRA</td><td>YES, after 2 years</td><td>NO</td></tr>
<tr><td>SEP-IRA</td><td>YES</td><td>NO</td></tr>
<tr><td>Governmental 457(b)</td><td>YES</td><td>NO</td></tr>
<tr><td>403(b) (pre-tax)</td><td>YES</td><td>YES</td></tr>
<tr><td>Traditional 401(k) (pre-tax)</td><td>YES</td><td>YES</td></tr>
<tr><td>Roth 401(k) (after-tax)</td><td>NO</td><td>YES</td></tr>
</table>

When rolling over funds from an existing account (e.g. former employer 401(k) or traditional IRA) to a Solo 401(k) you will generally initiate such rollover using forms requesting the direct rollover or transfer of funds from the current retirement account. This rollover should not be processed as a distribution but instead as a direct rollover to a qualified retirement plan. The check from the previous institution should be made payable to the name of the Solo 401(k) plan, FBO participants name or the participants name can be in the memo line (e.g., Sorensen Consulting Retirement Plan Trust FBO Mat Sorensen).

If you're using an administrator for the Solo 401(k) who receives and processes your funds you would have the funds directed to that administrator for the benefit of your retirement account. A third-party custodian is required for an IRA, however, you can self-trustee your own companies Solo 401(k) and you are not required to use a third-party custodian. That being said, some Solo 401(k) owners use self-directed IRA custodians who are familiar with Solo 401(k)s to hold their funds and process their investments. While a third part administrator is not required, it is a good option for those who want someone to assist in processing and tracking their funds and assets as they go in and out of the Solo 401(k) account.

LEGAL TIP
❖ You cannot rollover or transfer Roth IRA funds to a Traditional or Roth 401(k).
❖ The rollover or transfer of funds should be payable to the name of the 401(k) Plan, FBO Participants name.
❖ Do not take a Rollover in your personal name as that may mean that the funds were processed as a distribution.
❖ 60-day Rollovers should be avoided.

CONTRIBUTIONS TO A SOLO 401(K)

The contribution limits for Solo 401(k)s is significantly higher than IRAs and as a result many self-employed persons who want to make sizable contributions to their retirement account will choose a Solo 401(k) over a SEP IRA or other IRA. The total annual contribution for a Solo 401(k) in 2018 is $55,000. This is per participant in the Solo 401(k) so for a husband and wife owned business you could contribute $110,000 total each year with $55,000 going to each person's Solo 401(k) account. An additional $6,000 is allowed if you're 50 or older.

There are two different types of contributions in a Solo 401(k), employee and employer.

1. <u>Employee Contributions</u>. First, employee contributions are made by the employee based on their W-2 wage or their net self-employment income. Employee contributions can be made in Roth or Traditional dollars up to a total annual employee contribution of $18,500. For persons 50 and older they can contribute an additional $6,000 annually. An employee can contribute employee contributions on every dollar they earn up to $18,500. So, for example, if the employee had a W-2 or net self-employment income of $10,000, they could contribute up to $10,000 as an employee contribution. If they had $30,000, they could contribute only the maximum of $18,500.

2. <u>Employer Contributions</u>. Second, employer contributions are made by the employer entity that adopted the Solo 401(k). The employer contribution is expensed by the employer and can only be made as Traditional dollars. The total maximum contribution amounts for 2018 are $55,000,

and as a result the total employer contribution, after maxing out employee contributions of $18,500, is $36,500. Employer contributions are calculated at 25% of W-2 wage income, in the instance of an s-corp or c-corp, and at 20% of net self-employment income in the instance of a sole proprietorship or general partnership. IRS Publication 560, *Retirement Plans for Small Businesses* (March 2018). Consequently, if you had W-2 income of $100,000 in a given year, then the company would be able to contribute $25,000. If this was $100,000 of net self-employment income in a sole proprietorship then you could contribute $20,000 as an employer contribution. The employer contribution is in addition to any employee contribution.

Employer and employee contributions can be made bi-weekly, monthly, quarterly, or in any incremental time over the year or they can also be made in one-lump-sum. Most Solo 401(k) owners tend to make their annual contributions in one lump sum at year-end. Keep in mind, the contribution limits do not restrict the dollar amount of rollovers or transfers from existing retirement accounts. If you have existing retirement plan funds in a prior employer 401(k) or traditional IRA that you wish to rollover or transfer to the Solo 401(k) there is no limit on the amount of these direct rollovers or transfers of eligible retirement account funds.

<u>DIAGRAM 19.2, SOLO 401(k) CONTRIBUTIONS</u>

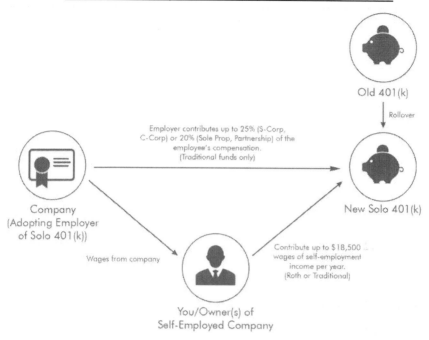

In order to max out contributions annually one would need to have W-2 income of $146,000 for an s-corp or c-corp or $182,500 in net self-employment income from a sole proprietorship. These amounts calculate as follows.

<u>S-Corp Owner Max-Out Contribution</u>

W-2 (Employee Annual Compensation)	$146,000
Employee Contribution	$18,500
Employer Contribution (25% of $146,000)	$36,500
Total Annual Contribution	$55,000

Sole Proprietorship Max-Out Contribution

Net Self-Employment Income	$182,500
Employee Contribution	$18,500
Employer Contribution (20% of $182,500)	$36,500
Total Annual Contribution	$55,000

Keep in mind that these contribution amounts are per employee so if you have an s-corporation with husband and wife as employees (or non-married business partners) with each getting a W-2 for $146,000, then there could be a total of $110,000 in annual contributions between the two participants Solo 401(k) accounts.

CONTRIBUTION DEADLINES EMPLOYEE & EMPLOYER EMPLOYEE CONTRIBUTIONS

The deadline for employee contributions is based on the adopting entity's tax return filing deadline, including extensions. However, if the adopting entity is an s-corporation or a c-corporation, the employee contribution amount needs to be calculated and determined on the W-2, which is due January 31 of the following year. You can wait to make the employee contribution until the tax return deadline but the employee contribution amount must be determined and reported on the W-2 in box 12.

TABLE 19.2, SOLO 401(k) CONTRIBUTION LIMITS AND DEADLINES (EMPLOYEE)

Year	Max. Employee Contribution (if under age 50)	Max. Employee Contribution (if 50 or older)	Employee Contribution Deadline (S-Corp, Partnership)
2018	$18,500	$24,500	March 15th annually, but for s-corps you must determine amount for W-2 by Jan 31. (plus extensions).
Year	Max. Employee Contribution (if under age 50)	Max. Employee Contribution (if 50 or older)	Employee Contribution Deadline (Sole Prop or C-Corp)
2018	$18,500	$24,500	04/15/2018 (plus extensions), but for c-corps you must determine amount for W-2 by Jan 31. (plus extensions).

*Total contributions to a participant's account, not counting catch-up contributions, cannot exceed $55,000 for 2018. Additional $6,000 if 50 or older.

EMPLOYER CONTRIBUTIONS

Employer contributions can be made at any time before the company files its tax return for that year. IRS Publication 560, *Retirement Plans for Small Business* (March 2017). When the adopting entity is an s-corporation or partnership the company tax return is due on March 15, unless an extension is filed. If an extension is filed then the new deadline for contributions is the extension deadline. For sole proprietorships and c-corporations the deadline is April 15, again, unless an extension is filed. Employer contributions should be made before the company return deadline and are made by making a deposit into the participant's 401(k) bank account from the company account. Employer contributions must be traditional funds and are expensed by the company on the company's tax return.

LEGAL TIP
❖ The business owner's accountant and/or payroll company should track employee contributions and in the event a W-2 is created they must be reported on the W-2.
❖ Employer contributions should be reported on the company books and tax returns and are an expense of the company.
❖ Employee contributions can be either Traditional or Roth.
❖ Employer contributions can ONLY be Traditional.
❖ Separate bank accounts need to be established for Traditional dollars and Roth dollars. They cannot be comingled in one account due to their different tax status.
❖ Each participant, even husband and wife need to have separate bank accounts for their account funds.

Employer contributions can be made monthly or quarterly but the total amount should be evaluated at year-end once the gross annual compensation is calculated to make sure the employer contribution amount does not exceed 25% (when using a W-2) or 20% (when using net self-employment) of the employee gross annual wage compensation or net self-employment.

TABLE 19.3, SOLO 401(k) CONTRIBUTION DEADLINES (EMPLOYER)

Year	Employer Contribution Deadline (S-Corp or Partnership)
2018	March 15th, unless extension filed then Sept. 15th.
Year	Employer Contribution Deadline (Sole Prop or C-Corporation)
2018	April 15th, unless extension is filed then Oct. 15th.
*Total contributions to a participant's account, not counting catch-up contributions, cannot exceed $55,000 for 2018. Additional $6,000 if 50 or older.	

IN-PLAN ROTH CONVERSION

Beginning in 2010, 401(k)s plan funds could be converted from Traditional dollars to Roth 401(k) dollars. The amount that you convert to Roth will be deemed as taxable income for the year in which you make the conversion. For example, if I convert $100K from my Traditional 401(k) to Roth 401(k) in 2017, the plan should issue me a 1099-R and I will include that $100K as income on my 2017 tax return and will then pay any federal and state taxes due on that income.

There are three common situations when you should consider converting your Traditional 401(k) or other retirement account to Roth:

1. Up-Side Investment Opportunity – I've had numerous clients over the years convert their traditional funds to Roth before investing their account into a certain profitable investment. They've done this because they've had a tremendous investment opportunity arise where they expect significant returns. They'd rather pay the tax on the smaller conversion investment amount now, so that the returns will go back into their Roth 401(k) or Roth IRA, where it can grow and come out tax-free. When deciding whether to convert, many people say, I'd rather pay tax on the small seed than on the large harvest." These clients have invested in real estate deals, start-ups, pre-IPOs, and other potentially lucrative investments. If you have an investment that you really believe in and that will likely result in significant returns, then you're far better off converting to Roth now and paying a little tax on the amount being invested before the account grows and returns a large profit. That way, the large profit goes back into the Roth

and will continue to grow and will come out entirely tax-free at retirement.

2. <u>Low-Income Year</u> – Another situation where you should consider converting Traditional funds to Roth is when you have a low-income year. Since the only downside of the conversion is that you have to pay tax on the amount that you convert, you should convert when you are in a lower tax bracket to lessen the tax burden. For example, if you are married and have $100K of taxable income for the year and you decide to convert $50K to Roth, you will pay federal tax on that converted amount at a rate of 22%, which would result in $11,000 in federal taxes. Keep in mind that you also pay state tax on the amount that you convert (if your state has state income tax), and most states have stepped brackets where you pay tax at a lower rate when you have lower income. If you instead converted when you were in a high-income year, let's say $300K of income, then you'd pay federal tax on a $50K conversion at a rate of 32% which would result in federal taxes of $16,000. That's more than twice the taxes due when you are in a lower-income year. You may not have taxable income fluctuations where this opportunity will arise but for those who are self-employed, change jobs and have a loss of income, or have investment loses where taxable income is lower than normal for a year, you should think about converting your retirement funds to Roth. You may not have a more affordable time to get to Roth.

3. <u>Potential Need for a Distribution After Five-Years</u> – Once of the perks of Roth accounts is that you can take out the funds that are contributed or converted after five

years without paying tax on the early withdrawal penalty (even if you aren't 59 ½). For Roth conversions, the amount you convert can be distributed from the Roth account five years after the tax year in which you converted. The five-year clock starts to tick on January 1st of the tax year in which you convert, regardless of when you convert within the year. Therefore, if you converted your Traditional 401(k) to a Roth 401(k) in November 2017, then you can take a distribution of the amounts converted without paying tax or penalty on January 2nd, 2022. If you try to access funds in your Traditional 401(k) before you are 59 ½ , then you will pay tax and a 10% early withdrawal penalty even if the amounts you distribute are only the contributions you put in. Clearly, the Roth account is much more accessible in the event you need personal funds. Keep in mind, you don't get this perk immediately: you have to wait 5 years from the tax year in which you converted before you can take out the converted amount tax and penalty free.

COMPLETING A ROTH SOLO 401(K) CONVERSION

To complete a Roth conversion of Traditional Solo 401(k) funds to Roth Solo 401(k) funds, you must complete the following.

1. Written Election. The decision to convert funds to Roth must be requested in writing by the account owner. This can be a simple form that includes the plan name, participant account owner name, the date of the conversion, and the amount being converted. This election is not filed anywhere but should be maintained with the plan records.

2. Separate Account. The funds being converted to Roth should be kept in a separate Roth account that is distinct

from Traditional funds of the participant (if there are any left).

3. <u>1099-R</u>. The Solo 401(k) plan should issue a form 1099-R to the account participant for the amount converted. The account owner adds that amount to their taxable income for the year converted on line 15.a of their personal 1040 tax return.

PARTICIPANT LOAN

Rather than taking a taxable distribution from a 401(k), a Solo 401(k) account owner can access a portion of the funds in their Solo 401(k) pursuant to a participant loan from the Solo 401(k). The loan must be paid back to the Solo 401(k) and can be used for any purpose by the participant. The loan must be documented and contain certain required terms. The participant loan is considered an investment asset of the plan.

The maximum participant loan amount is $50,000 or 50% of the participant's account balance, whichever is less. So, if the Solo 401(k) has $200,000 in assets the maximum $50,000 loan may be taken. If the Solo 401(k) has $40,000 in assets, then the maximum loan amount is $20,000. The loan must be properly documented with a promissory note and an amortization schedule. The following loan terms are required in all participant loans.

- The loan must be paid back within 5 years, with limited exception. If the funds are used to purchase a primary residence, the loan term may be up to 30 years.
- Payments of principal and interest must be made at least quarterly. The loan repayment cannot be a lump-sum balloon amount.

- The interest rate must be the prime rate plus 2% per annum. Some professionals recommend prime plus 1%, but the industry accepted rate, which has been suggested by the IRS, is prime plus 2%.

Any amount not repaid under the participant loan will be considered a distribution and any applicable taxes and penalties will be due by the account owner. For example, if you take a loan out for $50,000, and you repay $40,000 but don't pay the remaining $10,000 balance, the $10,000 balance will be considered a distribution and you will pay applicable taxes and penalties on the $10,000. Loan that are in default more than two consecutive quarters should be distributed. Treasury Reg. 1.72(p)-1, Q&A-10(a).

LEGAL TIP
❖ Participant loans can be taken and used for any purpose.
❖ A participant can take a loan of up to $50,000 or 50% of the FMV of the account, whichever is less.
❖ The interest rate for participant loans is prime plus 2% per annum.
❖ Participant loans must be documented with a promissory note and amortization schedule.
❖ Participant loans must be paid back within 5 years, with payments being at least quarterly. If the loan is used to purchase a personal residence then a 30 year term may apply.

INVESTING WITH A SOLO 401(K)

The Plan Trustee has authority to make investments from the Solo 401(k) and signs any documents as part of the investment. The plan Trustee also has authority to manage the Solo 401(k) bank account and to sign checks and send wires from the plan bank account(s).

A deed for real property should be vested in the name of the 401(k) plan, for the benefit of (FBO), participant's name, type of account.

Sorensen Consulting Retirement Plan Trust FBO Mat Sorensen Trad 401(k), Grantee

A Corporation, LLC or LP interest would be vested as follows:

<u>Member or Limited Partner</u> *Sorensen Consulting Retirement Plan Trust FBO Mat Sorensen Trad 401(k).*

In some instances, a county recorder or institution may require the asset to be titled in the name of the trustee, in these instances title may be vested as follows.

Mathew Sorensen, Trustee, Sorensen Consulting Retirement Plan Trust FBO Mat Sorensen Trad 401(k), Grantee

Ownership of an asset in the name of the trustee when it is clearly in their capacity as trustee of the Plan and participant account is not a prohibited transaction.

Generally, speaking the same assets available to IRAs are available to Solo 401(k)s and the same restrictions apply. For example, a Solo 401(k) cannot own S-Corporation stock but it may own C-Corporation stock, LLC interests, LP interests, real property, secured and un-secured notes, qualifying precious metals, and other common self-directed assets. IRC § 1361(b)(1)(B).

SOLO 401(k) PROHIBITED TRANSACTIONS

The prohibited transaction rules are the most important rules to understand when you self-direct your retirement accounts. These rules restrict not what investments your retirement plan may acquire, but whom your plan may transact with.

A prohibited transaction occurs when a retirement plan (e.g. self-directed IRA or Solo 401(k)) transacts with a disqualified person. IRC § 4975, ERISA § 3(14). For Solo 401(k)s, the prohibited transaction rules found in IRC § 4975, which also apply to IRAs, apply to Solo 401(k)s as do the prohibited transaction rules found in ERISA. Under ERISA, a "disqualified person", who is someone your Solo 401(k) cannot transact with, is called a "party in interest." The rules for prohibited transaction under ERISA are nearly identical to the rules found in IRC § 4975 and as a result there is no difference involved in determining whether something is a prohibited transaction for an IRA versus a Solo 401(k) since the rules are the same. *Refer to Chapters 4 through 7 as to Prohibited Transactions for IRAs and Solo 401(k)s.* The only distinction as to the prohibited transaction rules between IRAs and Solo 401(k)s is the consequence to the prohibited transaction.

The consequence of a prohibited transaction for an IRA is distribution of the entire IRA while the consequence to a Solo 401(k) or other employer based plan is a 15% excise tax on the amount involved and an additional 100% penalty if the transaction is not corrected. IRC § 4975 (a), IRC § 4975 (b). In order to correct a prohibited transaction with a Solo 401(k), or any employer plan, you must return the account back to the position it was in before the prohibited transaction occurred. In many instances, this is simply a return of the funds involved in the prohibited transaction to the Solo 401(k).

The prohibited transaction consequence for a Solo 401(k) is certainly more forgiving since only the "amount involved" is penalized. In an IRA, the entire IRA is distributed. For example, let's say that a $250,000 Solo 401(k) account lends $30,000 to the Solo 401(k) owner's daughter so that the daughter can start a business. The loan is certainly a prohibited transaction as the loan is a transaction with the Solo 401(k) account owner's daughter who is a "party in interest" and a disqualified person. The consequence to the Solo 401(k) would be as follows.

1. <u>15% Penalty on Amount Involved per IRC § 4975 (a)</u>. The amount involved is $30,000 so the 15% penalty is $4,500.

2. <u>100% Penalty on Amount Involved if Not Corrected per IRC § 4975(b)</u>. The 100% penalty would be $30,000 since the prohibited transaction was $30,000. However, this prohibited transaction may be corrected by returning the $30,000 loan proceeds to the Solo 401(k).

In sum, the prohibited transaction consequence on the $30,000 prohibited transaction would be the excise penalty of $4,500. This assumes that the $30,000 amount involved was returned to the Solo 401(k) to correct the prohibited transaction.

If this prohibited transaction occurred in an IRA, the consequence would be distribution of the entire $250,000 account. IRC § 408 (e)(2)(A). As discussed in Chapter 7, there is no 15% or 100% penalty but instead entire IRA account involved ceases to be an IRA and the entire amount is subject to the normal rules and taxes due on an IRA distribution.

The parties who are a disqualified person or a "party in interest" to a Solo 401(k) are more detailed in Chapter 4.

SOLO 401(k)/LLC

Similar to an IRA/LLC, a Solo 401(k) can own 100% of an LLC and the account can be the manager of the LLC. The 401(k)/LLC can then invest in the same type of investments as the 401(k) and the LLC provides the added benefit of asset protection. The LLC protects the 401(k) owner and the 401(k) from liabilities that can arise from the assets of the LLC. It also allows the 401(k) owner to more easily manage his or her 401(k) by being able to accomplish investments as the manager of the LLC (e.g., can sign contracts and checks, and receive income and pay expenses as the manager of the LLC).

Rental real estate, real estate rehab projects, and other investments which can create potential liability benefit from the asset protection characteristics of a 401(k)/LLC. Other assets such as raw land, private stock, or promissory notes and trust deed investments do not typically create liability (other than the investment risk) and as a result do not benefit as significantly from the asset protection characteristics of a 401(k)/LLC. Refer to Chapter 13, The IRA/LLC Structure, for additional information on structuring and restrictions.

DIAGRAM 19.4, SOLO 401(K)/LLC

New Solo 401(k)
"ABC Mgmt, Inc.
Retirement Plan Trust"

New 401(k)/LLC
"XYZ Investments, LLC"

Rental Property

401(k) Owns
100% of LLC

Receives Rent,
Pays Expenses

Buys Property

MULIT-MEMBER 401(k)/LLC

A multi-member 401(k)/LLC structure consists of a Solo 401(k) as a member and at least one other member. The additional member may be another Solo 401(k) or an IRA, your spouse's Solo 401(k) participant account, or it may be an individual. There are unique issues that arise in multi-member 401(k)/LLCs and these are more fully detailed in Chapter 14, The Multi-Member IRA/LLC. The structuring issues and rules for IRAs and 401(k)s in LLCs are the same but Solo 401(k) accounts have a unique partnership and ownership vesting issue. This typically arises in two situations. First, when spouses who have accounts under the same Solo 401(k) plan invest into the same LLC. And second, when investing a participant's Traditional funds into an LLC along with the same participant's Roth funds in the Solo 401(k). The issue is whether to list the Solo 401(k) plan as the 100% member of the LLC or whether to list each separate participant account under the plan as an owner for its specific allocated ownership percentage.

If both you and your spouse participate in the Solo 401(k) and/or if you are investing your Traditional funds and your Roth funds from the Solo 401(k), then you have two options when forming a 401(k)/LLC with these set of funds. First, the Solo 401(k) plan as a whole can own the LLC 100% and investment percentages between each of the participant accounts must be tracked and accounted for at the Solo 401(k) plan level and the proper distribution and allocation of funds, profits and losses must be accounted for based on the dollars invested from the respective accounts. For example, if you want to invest $70,000 of your Solo 401(k) account funds into the LLC and your spouse will invest $30,000 of their Solo 401(k) account funds into the LLC, then the investment gains/returns back to each account will be allocated as 70/30 back into each of the separate participant 401(k) accounts, as the ownership and profit/loss should be set based on the dollars invested.

In this instance, where the Solo 401(k) plan owns the LLC 100%, the LLC is a disregarded entity for tax purposes and a federal tax return does not need to be filed for the LLC. However, proper accounting and distribution of investment amounts and profits must be properly allocated to each participant account.

The second option is that each spouses Solo 401(k) participant account will be members of the LLC at the specified percent of ownership and this will be detailed in the operating agreement of the LLC. This creates a partnership LLC and a partnership tax return will be required.

The ownership tables below outline the two different options.

LLC Owned 100% By the Plan Itself

	Membership	Profit	Loss
ABC Management Retirement Plan Trust 1234 Green Street Anywhere, USA, 98765	100%	100%	100%

LLC Owned By Each Participants 401(k) Account

	Membership	Profit	Loss
ABC Management Retirement Plan Trust FBO John Smith 1234 Green Street Anywhere, USA, 98765	70%	70%	70%
ABC Management Retirement Plan Trust FBO Sally Smith 1234 Green Street Anywhere, USA, 98765	30%	30%	30%

SOLO 401(k) PLAN TAX REPORTING

A Solo 401(k) plan must file a form 5500-EZ when plan assets exceed $250,000. IRS, *Instructions for Form 5500-EZ* (Dec 2017). The valuation of plan assets includes all accounts under the Solo 401(k) plan (e.g. all owners and their spouse) as of December 31 of each year.

For plans with $250,000 or less, there is no plan tax return required unless the plan is terminated. In other words, Solo 401(k)s must file a Form 5500-EZ when,

1. Plan assets exceed $250,000.
2. The Plan is terminated, regardless of plan asset values.

Form 5500-EZ returns are due July 31 each year for the prior year. There is no tax due on the return but the annual reporting is critical as failure to file can result in failure to file penalties up to $15,000. There has been a significant amount of confusion on Solo 401(k) filing requirements for self-directed Solo 401(k)s and standard brokerage Solo 401(k)s. As a result, the IRS began a penalty relief program for those who have failed to file. This program was made permanent in 2015 and allows delinquent Solo 401(k) owners to file old 5500-EZ filings and avoid penalties. In order to qualify for the penalty relief program, your Solo 401(k) plan must have not received a CP 283 delinquent notice for any past due 5500-EZ filings. There is a filing fee of $500 for each delinquent return up to a total of $1,500. In order to qualify and receive a waiver of penalties under the program, you must complete the following pursuant to IRS Rev. Proc. 2015-32.

1. File all delinquent returns using IRS Form 5500-EZ. These must be paper filings using the form for the appropriate year.
2. Mark on the top margin of the first page, "Delinquent Return Submitted Under Rev. Proc. 2015-32."
3. Complete and include IRS Form 14704.
4. Mail the Form 5500-EZ to the IRS Ogden, UT office.

Although there is no tax due or paid via a form 5500-EZ, the IRS has significant penalties for failure to file. Consequently, it is critical to ensure that form 5500-EZ is filed for any Solo 401(k) with assets over $250,000 or for a Solo 401(k) that has been terminated.

SOLO 401(k)s & OTHER EMPLOYER PLANS ARE EXEMPT FROM CERTAIN UDFI TAX

Solo 401(k) and other employer plans are exempt from UDFI taxes that arise from debt on real property. IRC § 514(9). The tax code specifically exempts plans which are "qualified trusts" under section 401 from the tax code from UDFI tax. IRC § 514I (9)(C)(ii). Section 401 of the code includes pension plans and 401(k)s.

This is a significant benefit to Solo 401(k) and other qualified plans over IRAs and many self-directed retirement plan investors who are able to establish a self-directed 401(k) plan (e.g., Solo K, Individual K, etc.) will utilize a 401(k) for debt financed retirement plan investments as opposed to an IRA.

Solo 401(k)s and other employer plans exempt from UDFI are still subject to the other aspects of UBIT, including being subject to UBIT tax on real estate development or operational businesses not paying corporate taxes.

TABLE 19.4, GENERAL DO'S AND DON'TS FOR MAINTAINING AND OPERATING YOUR SOLO 401(k) PLAN

DO's	DON'TS
• Perform rigorous due diligence on the investments in which your Plan intends to participate • Set up a bank account for each participant of the Plan and between roth and traditional funds and maintain separate bookkeeping and records of contributions, distributions and investments • Report any Unrelated Business Income Tax (UBIT) that arises from the operations of your Plan (reported on Form 990-T and form 5500-EZ) • File a Form 5500-EZ annually for the Plan when the FMV of assets exceeds $250,000 or if the plan is terminated	• Allow the Plan to lend cash or to otherwise transact with a disqualified person or party in interest (other than a qualifying participant loan) • Pay yourself or other disqualified persons or parties in interest for performing management or services to the Plan • Enter into a Contract in your personal name or party in interest's name when the Contract should be with your Plan or your 401(k)/LLC • Sign a personal guarantee or give personal credit for a Plan investment • Take funds from your Plan other than as a proper distribution or documented loan

DO's	DON'TS
• Update your Beneficiary Designation forms	• Rent, Live In, or otherwise use or benefit from any property or assets owned by the Plan
• Consult with your CPA or Attorney for your specific situation in order to avoid prohibited transactions or unintended tax consequences related to your Plan's investments	• Transfer ownership in the Plan to or from a party in interest or related party
• Amend or freeze the Plan if you end up having qualifying full-time employees who are not owners or spouses and who qualify to participate in the Plan	• Co-mingle personal or other non-retirement assets or expenses within the Plan
• Become educated regarding the laws and your obligations as Trustee of the Plan	• Use Plan funds to pay for personal expenses, even if those expenses are somewhat related to the Plan

USING A SOLO 401(k) OR A SELF-DIRECTED IRA

The table below summarizes the differences between a self-directed IRA and a self-directed Solo 401(k).

TABLE 19.5, DIFFERENCES BETWEEN AN IRA AND SOLO 401(K)

	IRA	Solo 401(k)
Qualification	Must be an individual with earned income or funds in a retirement account to rollover.	Must be a self-employed with no other employees besides the business owner and spouse/partners
Contribution Max	$5,500 max annual contribution. Additional $1,000 if 50 or older.	$55,000 max annual contribution (it takes $140k of wage income to max out). Contributions are by employee and employer.
Traditional & Roth	You can have a Roth IRA and/or a Traditional IRA. The amount you contribute to each is added together in determining total contributions.	A Solo 401(k) can have a traditional account and a Roth account within the same plan. You can convert traditional sums over to Roth as well.

	IRA	**Solo 401(k)**
Cost and Set-Up	You will work with a self-directed IRA custodian who will receive the IRA contributions in a SDIRA account. Most of the custodians we work with have an annual fee of $300-$350 a year.	You must use an IRS pre-approved document when establishing a Solo 401(k). This adds additional cost over an IRA. Our fee for a self-directed and self-trusteed Solo 401(k) is $1,200.
Custodian Requirement	An IRA must have a third party custodian involved on the account (e.g. bank, credit union, trust company) who is the trustee of the IRA.	A 401(k) can be self trustee'd, meaning the business owner can be the trustee of the 401(k). This provides for greater control but also greater responsibility.
Investment Details	A self-directed IRA is invested through the self-directed IRA custodian. A self-directed IRA can be subject to a tax called UDFI/UBIT on income from debt-leveraged real estate.	A Solo 401(k) is invested by the trustee of the 401(k), which could be the business owner. A Solo 401(k) is exempt from UDFI/UBIT on income from debt-leveraged real estate.

Keep in mind that the Solo 401(k) is only available to self-employed persons while the self-directed IRA is available to everyone who has earned income or who has funds in an existing retirement account that can be rolled over to an IRA.

Based on the differences outlined above, a Solo 401(k) is generally a better option for someone who is self-employed and still trying to maximize contributions as the Solo 401(k) has much higher contribution amounts. On the other hand, a self-directed IRA is a better option for someone who has already saved for retirement and who has enough funds in their retirement accounts that can be rolled over and invested via a self-directed IRA, as the self-directed IRA is easier and cheaper to establish.

Another major consideration in deciding between a Solo 401(k) and a self-directed IRA is whether there will be debt on real estate investments. If there is debt and if the account owner is self-employed, they are much better off choosing a Solo 401(k) over an IRA as a Solo 401(k) are exempt from UDFI tax on leveraged real estate.

FREQUENTLY ASKED QUESTIONS

Q: I currently have my own business that has a few employees; can I use this business to set up a Solo 401(k)?

A: If your employees do not work more than 19.25 hours per week or 1,200 hours annually, your company may adopt a Solo 401(k). If your employees work more than 19.25 hours per week or 1,200 hours annually, your company may adopt a standard 401(k) plan option. One used by some business owners is a simple safe harbor 401(k) with a company who provides self-directed non-publically traded investment options to everyone but usually on the business owner utilizes. This is a complex plan option but is an option for a business owner who wants to self-direct out of a 401(k) or other employer plan and has employees. .

Q: My business is a sole proprietorship and I am the only employee; can I use this business to adopt my Solo 401(k)?

A: Yes. For purposes of setting up a Solo 401(k), this is fine. However, for tax and legal liability purposes, you may want to consider another type of entity for your business, such as an S-Corporation or at least and LLC. Also, the sole proprietorship will need a separate EIN in order to adopt a plan.

Q: Can I start a new business and then adopt a Solo 401(k)?

A: Yes. A new company can adopt a Solo 401(k). One caveat is that your new business must be legitimate, in other words, the intent of setting up your business must be to earn profits and pay yourself wages or other self-employment income. Additionally, if there is no legitimate business activity or if there are consecutive years of losses the business may be disallowed under the IRS hobby loss rules and the 401(k) would then need to be shut down and rolled out to an IRA.

Q: Can I set up a Solo 401(k) if I have a 401(k) with my current employer?

A: Yes. You can have a 401(k) with your employer AND a Solo 401(k) for your own business.

Q: I have an LLC that invests in rental properties; can I use this company to adopt my Solo 401(k)?

A: Possibly. Ideally, a Solo 401(k) should be adopted by a company that is receiving ordinary/operational income rather than passive income such as rental income. You will need to create an operational business or a management company that can receive income for managing your rentals and that company could possibly adopt a Solo 401(k). You could not adopt the Solo 401(k) directly in the rental property LLC.

Q: Are there required minimum distributions for Traditional and Roth Solo 401(k) funds?

A: Yes, Solo 401(k) accounts are subject to the required minimum distribution ("RMD") rules beginning at age 70 ½. RMD is required of Traditional and Roth accounts in all 401(k)s. This is different from the IRA rules as Roth IRAs are not subject to RMD. However, Roth 401(k) plan funds are subject to RMD. One solution is to simply rollover Roth 401(k) funds to a Roth IRA to avoid RMD. Another quirk in the rules is that owners of 401(k)s cannot use the exemption that allows a working person to avoid RMD in their 401(k). As a result, even if you are still working you will be required to take RMD from your Solo 401(k) at 70 ½.

Q: Are there minimum contribution requirements into my Solo 401(k)?

A: It is possible for your Solo 401(k) account balance to consist of only your rollover amount. However, you should have a legitimate intent to contribute to your Solo 401(k) as the employee and the employer.

Q: How Do I Make a Participant Loan From My Solo 401(k)?

A: A participant loan needs to be documented with a Promissory Note and Amortization schedule with the proper interest rate (prime plus 2%) and terms (5 years at least quarterly payments).

Q: Who Is The Custodian?

A: There is no Third Party Administrator or Custodian required for a Solo 401(k). The Solo 401(k) owner can act as the Administrator/Trustee of the Solo 401(k). Some Solo 401(k) owners use a custodian or third party administrator to hold their funds and process transactions but that is not required.

Q: I have heard that Solo 401(k)s are better protected from creditors than IRAs, is this true?

A: No, this is false. The general federal law effecting employer based plans is called ERISA and it provides significant creditor protection for employer based plans that fall under it. IRAs, on the other hand, have creditor protection laws based on state law and some states (e.g. California) have weak protections for IRAs. As a result, many people have mistakenly presumed that a Solo 401(k) should be treated like a plan under ERISA and that it would get ERISA creditor protection. However, the Courts have already ruled that Solo 401(k)s are not subject to ERISA and as a result would not get ERISA creditor protection. *Yates V. Heldon,* 541 U.S. 20-21. As a result, they would have similar treatment to IRAs based on state law.

Conclusion

Self-directed IRAs have proven to be a powerful investment tool for many investors. While they aren't for everyone, they are an excellent tool for individuals who have profitable investment opportunities in non-publicly investments. self-directed IRAs allow for greater control and enable an individual to invest into assets they know.

Consider the following high-profile figures who have built significant IRA holdings by making self-directed IRA investments.

- Mitt Romney, former CEO of Bain Capital, and Presidential Candidate, who invested his IRA into early stage or turn-around private businesses that were not publically traded. His IRA value was reported at $20M to $100M. *Bain Gave Staff Way to Swell IRAs by Investing in Deals*, Mark Maremont, The Wall Street Journal (March 22, 2012).
- Paypal founder and CEO, Peter Thiel, who reportedly bought shares in his Roth IRA for $510,000 and received $31.5M for them when the company sold to eBay. *Why— And—How Congress Should Curb Roth IRAs*, Deborah L. Jacobs, Forbes (March 26, 2012).
- Yelp founder and Chairman, Max Levchin, whose Roth acquired shares in the early stages of Yelp (at excellent

value) and was worth $95M in 2012, when numbers were reported. *Id.*

But it's not just persons in the public eye who have built significant retirement accounts through self-directed investments. In my law practice, I routinely encounter investors with $1M plus self-directed IRAs (some Traditional, some Roth) who invest in real estate, private companies, and other investment assets that aren't available in standard brokerage IRAs.

Most U.S. retirement accounts are used to build wealth solely with publically traded stocks, bonds, and mutual funds. However, you are only limited to those options if you choose to be. If your experience and investment opportunities are in non-traditional IRA investments (e.g., real estate, private companies), you should consider using a self-directed IRA as part of your investment strategy. Remember though, as you begin investing with a self-directed IRA, it is critical that you learn the issues that can arise in self-directed IRA investments. You should also seek out licensed professionals with expertise in the field of self-directed IRAs, who can help you navigate and understand issues specific to your investments.

In conclusion, I hope that this book gives you the knowledge, framework, and concepts to make profitable decisions when self directing your IRA. Best wishes.

INDEX

ABOUT THE AUTHOR

Mat has been at the forefront of the self-directed IRA industry since 2006. He is the CEO of Directed IRA & Directed Trust Company where they handle all types of self-directed accounts (IRAs, Roth IRAs, HSAs, Coverdell ESA, solo Ks, and custodial accounts) which are typically invested into real estate, private company/private equity, IRA/LLCs, notes, precious metals, private REITS, and cryptocurrency.

For self-directed accounts, go to www.directedira.com.

Mat is also a partner at KKOS Lawyers, and serves clients nationwide from its Phoenix, AZ office. KKOS Lawyers assists clients nationwide from its offices in Arizona, Utah, Idaho, and California. His law firm's website is www.kkoslawyers.com.

Mat's law practice has a particular emphasis on self-directed retirement plan law. Most of Mat's clients are self-directed retirement account owners who are structuring their investments. Mat's clients have included trust companies, financial institutions, insurance companies, hedge funds, and third-party administrators. In addition to his legal practice, Mat also serves as an instructor for the Retirement Industry Trust Association's ("RITA") self-directed IRA Professional certification program.

Visit Mat's website www.sdirahandbook.com for testimonials, case updates, and for additional resources for self-directed IRA investors.

Made in the USA
Columbia, SC
25 February 2023

12948755R00185